MATERIAL ACTS IN EVERYDAY HINDU WORLDS

SUNY series in Hindu Studies
———
Wendy Doniger, editor

MATERIAL ACTS IN EVERYDAY HINDU WORLDS

Joyce Burkhalter Flueckiger

Cover image: Bangle seller breaking a woman's old bangles and replacing with new ones, Chhattisgarh. Photo by the author.

Published by State University of New York Press, Albany

© 2020 State University of New York

All rights reserved

No part of this book may be used or reproduced in any manner whatsoever without written permission. No part of this book may be stored in a retrieval system or transmitted in any form or by any means including electronic, electrostatic, magnetic tape, mechanical, photocopying, recording, or otherwise without the prior permission in writing of the publisher.

For information, contact State University of New York Press, Albany, NY
www.sunypress.edu

Library of Congress Cataloging-in-Publication Data

Names: Flueckiger, Joyce Burkhalter, author.
Title: Material acts in everyday Hindu worlds / Joyce Burkhalter Flueckiger.
Description: Albany : State University of New York Press, 2020. | Series: SUNY series in Hindu studies | Includes bibliographical references and index.
Identifiers: LCCN 2019048693 | ISBN 9781438480114 (hardcover) | ISBN 9781438480121 (pbk.) | ISBN 9781438480138 (ebook)
Subjects: LCSH: Hinduism and culture—India. | Material culture—Religious aspects—Hinduism.
Classification: LCC BL1215.C76 F48 2020 | DDC 294.5/37—dc23
LC record available at https://lccn.loc.gov/2019048693

10 9 8 7 6 5 4 3 2 1

Contents

List of Illustrations		vii
Note on Transliteration		xi
Acknowledgments		xiii
Introduction		1
Chapter 1	Agency of Ornaments: Identity, Protection, and Auspiciousness	19
Chapter 2	Saris and Turmeric: Performativity of the Material Guise	45
Chapter 3	Material Abundance and Material Excess: Creating and Serving Two Goddesses	73
Chapter 4	Expanding Shrines, Changing Architecture: From Protector to Protected Goddesses	99
Chapter 5	Standing in Cement: Ravana on the Chhattisgarhi Plains	133
Afterword: Returning to Material Acts		161
Glossary of Key Terms		167
References		173
Index		183

Illustrations

Figure I.1	Maladasari, base of footpath up to Tirumala, site of temple of Shri Venkateshvara.	2
Figure I.2	Pilgrim prostrating next to the Maladasari.	3
Figure 1.1	Bangle seller breaking a woman's old bangles and replacing with new ones, Chhattisgarh.	20
Figure 1.2	Ornamented elder, Hyderabad.	25
Figure 1.3	*Tali*, black beads and coral, and amulet metal canister on turmeric thread, Hyderabad.	28
Figure 1.4	Odiya *lakshmi nara*, upper right arm, eastern Chhattisgarh.	35
Figure 1.5	Arm tattoos, Chhattisgarh.	37
Figure 1.6	Odiya foot tattoos, eastern Chhattisgarh.	38
Figure 1.7	Odiya Lakshmi-footprint tattoos, eastern Chhattisgarh.	41
Figure 2.1	Gangamma Jatara *stri vesham*.	46
Figure 2.2	Kaikala *dora* (prince) *vesham* with Chakali minister *vesham*.	50
Figure 2.3	*Sunnapukundalu* (lime pot) *vesham*.	52
Figure 2.4	*Matangi vesham*.	54
Figure 2.5	*Matangi* at rest.	55
Figure 2.6	Lay *stri vesham* with mother.	57

Figure 2.7	Photograph of Srinivasan *stri vesham*.	62
Figure 2.8	Gangamma's turmeric *vesham*.	67
Figure 3.1	Women cooking for Varalakshmi Puja, Jupally village, Telangana.	77
Figure 3.2	Beginning of Varalakshmi Puja (ritual ingredients contained), Jupally village, Telangana.	80
Figure 3.3	Varalakshmi silver mask, Hyderabad.	83
Figure 3.4	Transformation of cement pillar to goddess.	89
Figure 3.5	Wrapping saris on *kodistambham*.	89
Figure 3.6	Gangamma's *ugra mukhi* on final day of *jatara*, Tatayyagunta temple.	94
Figure 4.1	*Gramadevata* shrine in middle of major Hyderabad thoroughfare.	101
Figure 4.2	Potu Raju and female Bonalu festival celebrant flanking doorway of Nalla Pochamma shrine.	103
Figure 4.3	Kumhar matriarch, 2014.	106
Figure 4.4	The goddess in Nalla Pochamma shrine, 2014.	106
Figure 4.5	Nalla Pochamma new temple, 2016.	111
Figure 4.6	Sandhya standing in front of original Maisamma shrine.	122
Figure 4.7	Bhagya Laxmi shrine at base of Charminar, with flags flying, 2011.	124
Figure 4.8	Bhagya Laxmi marble image behind silver *kavacham*, 2014.	126
Figure 5.1	Ravana, Tumgaon village, 2014.	134
Figure 5.2	Ravana, Tari village, 2014.	136
Figure 5.3	Ravana with visible donkey atop his middle head, Ghirola village, 2014.	140
Figure 5.4	Ravana cement image and burning effigy, Ravan Bhatha, Raipur, 2014.	143

Figure 5.5   Ravana, Dhamtari, 2015.   145

Figure 5.6   Shitala greets Ravana, Pirhapal village, 2014.   150

Figure 5.7   Ravana, Mandodari (*right*), and Kumbhakarna (*left*),
             Chilhati village, 2014.   153

Note on Transliteration

I have chosen not to use diacritics in this book so that the prose will be accessible to non-specialists, on the assumption that specialists in South Asia will already know the correct pronunciation of Indian-language terms. A glossary of key terms and diacritics indicating their correct pronunciation appears at the end of the book. Proper, caste, and place names are capitalized and also appear without diacritics. For ease in pronunciation, I have rendered both *ś* and *ṣ* as "sh" and *c* as "ch" in Indian language words; thus *shakti* rather than *śakti*, and Chhattisgarh rather than Chattisgarh. I have rendered plurals with the addition of an "s" at the end of Indian-language transliterated words rather than giving their plural forms in each language (*veshams* rather than *veshallu* in Telugu).

The chapters of this book draw on ethnographic research in several languages: Chhattisgarhi, Odiya, Hindi, and Telugu. I have generally followed the transliteration system of Sanskrit for words and names that are common across these languages. So while Hindi and Chhattisgarhi would pronounce Ram, Ramayan, Ravan, and *math*, I have transliterated these as Rama, Ramayana, Ravana, and *matha*. Exceptions are made in direct quotations or proper names that do not include the final "a," such as Ravan Bhatha. An exception to the choice of Sanskrit transliteration is in words such as *darshan* (rather than Sanskrit *darshanam*) that have become common in English publications of South Asian materials.

Acknowledgments

The fieldwork for this book spans many years across three geographic fieldwork sites (Chhattisgarh, Hyderabad, and Tirupati). Thus, my gratitude has compounded many layers that I can never fully excavate.

In Chhattisgarh, I have found a welcoming home with the royal family of the erstwhile princely state of Kanker. The present Rajmata's quiet strength and grace inspires all of us who have found a place in the family. Surya Pratap Deo (Jolly) and Ashwini Pratap Deo (Jay) provided logistics for many field trip outings, in particular to attend Dussehra village celebrations in fall 2014; I have learned from them many subtleties of Chhattisgarhi culture. Aditya Pratap Deo has been an important intellectual conversation partner and friend about all things Chhattisgarhi.

Akhilesh Nand, whom I've known since he was a baby when I lived with his family in a Chhattisgarhi village during my PhD fieldwork, is now a teacher at Salem English School in Raipur. I thank him for taking me on the back of his motorcycle to the Dussehra celebrations in Raipur in 2014 and helping me navigate crowds of thousands. Folklorist and Raipur resident Mahendra Mishra served as a guide to many Ravana images sprinkled across Chhattisgarhi landscapes, which I would have never found on my own.

In Hyderabad, the Thangavelu family has welcomed me to their home—over and over again, almost yearly, since 1989. I have learned so much from each of them over cups and cups of tea during morning newspaper reading and sitting on the verandah late afternoons. In Tirupati, the Kaikala family—in particular, Venkateshvarlu and his mother, Kamalamma—was more patient than anyone should have to be with my unending questions about Gangamma traditions over multiple return trips. Kamalamma periodically reminded me, "I already told you that last year!" but she would always try again.

I am grateful for generous support from several funding agencies at different steps along the way of this project. Emory University's University Research Committee provided funding for a semester free from teaching that gave invaluable time to read theoretical scholarship on materiality in order to prepare me to write subsequent fellowship applications. In 2014–2015 the John Simon Guggenheim Memorial Foundation Fellowship and National Endowment for the Humanities Summer Stipend Award supported new research conducted for this project and time to begin writing this book. The American Institute of Indian Studies supported my fieldwork on Gangamma goddess traditions in Tirupati in 1999–2000. The Center for Faculty Development and Excellence at Emory University provided support to hire an external editor for the manuscript of this book before it was submitted to press. I have never worked before with an editor at this stage and am so thankful for the keen eye and imagination of Katie Van Heest of Tweed Academic Editing. At SUNY Press, series editor Wendy Doniger, James Peltz, and Jenn Bennett-Genthner shepherded the book to publication with grace, when there were significant shifts at the press.

Ann Grodzins Gold and Tulasi Srinivas were readers of the manuscript for SUNY Press, and they pushed me to refine my arguments; however, their friendship and intellectual companionship have been the real gift. Over so many years, Kirin Narayan, Leela Prasad, Susan Wadley, and David Shulman have been invaluable friends in fieldwork and writing. Velcheru Narayana Rao has remained my guide long after he was my dissertation guide/advisor. To each of them, I offer gratitude.

At Emory University, Marko Geslani (now at the University of South Carolina), Ellen Gough, Jim Hoesterey, Harshita Mruthinti Kamath, Sara McClintock, Devaka Premawardhana, and Brajesh Samarth have been important conversation partners. The chair of the Department of Religion at Emory over the period I was researching and writing this book, Gary Laderman, has provided invaluable friendship—and departmental travel funds. One of the greatest joys of my years at Emory has been working with creative graduate students from whom I have learned new intricacies of everyday Hindu worlds; each one has gifted unique perspectives and data from their fieldwork research and responses to my own research and writing.

My children and their partners, Peter and Rebecca Flueckiger and Rachel and Matt Angrisani, and now precious grandson, Benny Flueckiger, have helped me keep my center amid the swirls of fieldwork, writing, and teaching. A heart full of thanks, which words cannot fully hold, to my husband, Michael Flueckiger, for his continual support of my frequent trips to India, when he has kept home fires burning, and of my passions for everyday Indian worlds about which I write.

The section of chapter 1 about the *tali* in Gangamma traditions and an earlier version of chapter 2 first appeared in Joyce Burkhalter Flueckiger, *When the World Becomes Female: Guises of a South Indian Goddess* (2013) and are reprinted with permission from Indiana University Press. © 2013 Joyce Burkhalter Flueckiger.

Some ethnographic descriptions in chapter 3 first appeared in Joyce Burkhalter Flueckiger, *Everyday Hinduism* (2015) and are reprinted with permission from Wiley Blackwell. © 2015 Joyce Burkhalter Flueckiger.

A version of chapter 5 first appeared in Joyce Burkhalter Flueckiger, "Standing in Cement: Ravana on the Chhattisgarhi Plains," *South Asian History and Culture* 8, no. 4: 461–77. It is reprinted with permission from Taylor and Francis.

Introduction

> To be accounted for, objects have to enter into accounts.
>
> —Bruno Latour, *Reassembling the Social*

At the base of the footpath up to the great pilgrimage temple of Venkateshvara, the god on the mountain in Tirumala-Tirupati, Andhra Pradesh, a four-foot cement image of a devotee lies prostrate, with arms stretched out in *pranam* (greeting) above his head toward the mountain. His body is covered with turmeric and vermilion powders (*pasupu-kumkum*) and encircled with a garland of yellow marigolds. To his right side are three much smaller images similarly covered with pasupu-kumkum, whose features are not as distinguishable as those of the larger image (Figures I.1 and I.2). I met this figure when I first walked up the mountain on the 3,350-step cement footpath several years after having regularly taken a bus uphill. This early morning I was accompanied by Peta Srinivasulu Reddy, an anthropologist from a local university, who seemed intent on running up the mountain and who didn't stop with me when I paused to photograph the image. My first impulse was to lie down next to the pasupu-kumkum-covered image. For those few minutes there were no other pilgrims in the vicinity, but when I returned later in the week, I saw that male pilgrims did just this—prostrated themselves next to the image with its same body pose, arms extended above their heads. Women, on the other hand, touched the feet of the image and placed some flower petals on it or sprinkled it with a little pasupu-kumkum.

As we continued walking up the footpath after my encounter with the image, Srinivasulu identified it as a Maladasari, a cobbler from a formerly untouchable community of the same name. It is said that in

2 / Material Acts in Everyday Hindu Worlds

Figure I.1. Maladasari, base of footpath up to Tirumala, site of temple of Shri Venkateshvara. Photo by the author.

earlier days he had provided the god on the mountain a new pair of *chappals* (sandals) every day. But he had not been permitted into the temple due to his low caste status, so he used to prostrate himself at the foot of the mountain where he now lies, as close to the god as he

Figure I.2. Pilgrim prostrating next to the Maladasari. Photo by the author.

could physically get. However, Srinivasulu continued, Venkateshvara was so impressed with the Maladasari's devotion that he came downhill to meet him. As I sat on the steps next to the image several days later and observed pilgrims' interactions with the figure, I asked several pilgrims who he was. None of them knew, only that he was a devotee like themselves. Several suggested I ask the priest in the nearby Pada Mandapam (lit., foot pavilion) temple that enshrines Venkateshvara's footprints as a pair of cement feet.[1] The priest affirmed that the image was a cobbler devotee who had turned to stone when he wasn't allowed uphill to visit the god. The priest did not know the history of the image but described numerous disputes about whether the image of the Maladasari should be allowed to be there at all, in such a prominent position. However, he recounted, each time someone tried to remove the image, a catastrophe would strike that person or his family.

---

1. Devotees at this temple circumambulate the god's feet with a pair of oversized brass chappals (provided by the temple) atop their heads.

Meeting this Maladasari was one encounter that started my thinking about the agency of objects in India—materials that have an effect,[2] that cause something to happen that may be beyond what a human creator of that material intended. I had felt compelled to respond to the figure, to want to lie down next to it, before I had seen anyone else do so. Other pilgrims too were drawn to the figure—whom they could only generically identify as a devotee—in a similar way. Either they were imitating other pilgrims prostrating themselves or touching its feet, or they knew the appropriate bodily response from other temple sites where similar, but much smaller, figures are engraved in courtyard stone flooring. Alternatively, like me, they may have been compelled by the figure itself—whose ritual significance was created through the application of pasupu-kumkum, themselves agentive materials (as we will see in subsequent chapters). Several elements of encounters with the Maladasari are noteworthy: the history of human intention of the person(s) who created the image is lost, the identity of the figure himself is not widely known (and contested by some of those who do "know"), and the material figure has been left to create its own effect without intervention of any ritual specialist. The agency of the Maladasari is created in part by an "assemblage" of materials (Deleuze and Guattari 1987; Bennett 2010, 4–5, 23–24):[3] its physical location at the base of a pilgrimage footpath, pasupu-kumkum applied to the gray cement—causing it to glow—the marigold garland encircling the image, and other human bodies responding to it.

---

2. I have chosen to use the words" "material" or "materiality" rather than "things," even though many materiality scholars use the latter when they mean to refer to materiality that exceeds human agency. (See, for example, Morgan 2020; Brown 2003; Houtman and Meyer 2012.) Houtman and Meyer write, "We invoke the term *things* . . . because it signals indeterminancy—something that cannot be clearly circumscribed and that creates some degree of nervousness or anxiety" (2012, 16). However, for many English speakers "things" carries resonances of materials that are and can be manipulated by humans, in which contexts humans are the primary agents rather than the materiality; thus I prefer "material" and "materiality."

3. Drawing on Gilles Deleuze and Félix Guattari (1987), Jane Bennett characterizes an assemblage as an "an ad hoc grouping, a collectivity whose origins are historical and circumstantial, though its contingent status says nothing about its efficacy, which can be quite strong, . . . [whose] power is not equally distributed across the assemblage, . . . [and which is] made up of many types of actants: humans and nonhumans" (2005, 445n2).

Indian cultures are replete with examples of materials that are assumed to cause things to happen or to prevent them from happening, which both create and reflect an indigenous theory of the agency of materiality.[4] Specified gemstones, set in rings, deflect the negative forces of particular planets (*grahas*, those planetary bodies that, literally, grab) (Shukla 2008, 140–43) or may grant their wearers prosperity and auspiciousness or bring healing (Cerulli and Guenzi 2016). Black kohl markings on the soles of babies' feet or on the sides of their foreheads deflect the evil eye; similarly, amulets may deflect the evil eye but also transform relationships and physical environments (Flueckiger 2006). Rice-flour designs (Tamil, *kolams*; Telugu, *muggus*) drawn every morning by South Indian female householders (or a woman working in their houses) in front of entryways protect the home from the evil eye and invite the goddess Lakshmi to come in (Nagarajan 2019). Many Chhattisgarhi female householders light clay oil lamps (*diyas*) and set them outside doorways at dusk to invite Lakshmi to enter and protect their homes. This daily ritual is not usually accompanied by a discursive act such as prayer or a setting of intention; rather, the lighted diyas themselves are assumed to "do the work." Glass bangles, quite literally in the Telugu expression, "make a bride" (*pelli kuturuni cheyyadam*) and are broken to "make a widow." The very earth one lives on, landscapes, and the water one drinks affect the personhood of those dwelling in those places (Daniel 1987; Ramanujan 1999).

Material traditions in India emphasize the agency (ability to act, to have an effect) of material itself—material acts—without dependence on human intervention in causing the assumed effects (although, of course, human bodies may be needed to produce or carry the materials). While materialities shape the daily lives and ritual performances of Hindu practitioners—and they may agree that these materialities have agency—not all of them may agree on what materials are worthy of serious study. For example, while many South Indian Hindu women consider the creation of kolams every morning in front of the entrances of their homes to be an activity as significant to the well-being of their homes as their daily worship of deities in their domestic shrines, some male Sanskrit scholars may not think kolams (or ornaments, or food selection for particular

---

4. Several of these material agents, such as amulets and coconuts, cross religious boundaries. Their very materiality enables boundary crossing in ways that theological discourse does not (Flueckiger 2006, chapter 5; Raj and Dempsey 2015).

festivals) to be as worthy of scholarly consideration as the textual traditions in which they are experts. Until relatively recently, religious studies scholars in the Western academy have followed suit in marginalizing many everyday materialities that shape Hindu worlds (Narayanan 2000).

Over the last two decades, there has been a renewed intellectual energy in religious studies (including South Asian religions) around visual and material culture to counter the historically dominant textual/discursive focus in the discipline.[5] Some religious studies scholars have explicitly situated their studies of materiality as a pushback against post-Enlightenment, Protestant devaluation of materiality that asserts the primacy of the nonmaterial and belief over body, material, and ritual (Vasquez 2011; Houtman and Meyer 2012; Pintchman and Dempsey 2015). However, in their turn to materiality, many of these same scholars have focused on human agency in relationship to materiality: what humans do with materials and the ways human actions give objects their significance (Feld and Basso 1996; Houben 2007). Or they emphasize what materiality and visual culture reflect about humans, their identities, and/or their theologies (Elias 2012; McDannel 1998; Morgan 2005 and 2010a; Shukla 2008; Tarlo 1996; Vasquez 2011). Janet Hoskins calls objects "a metaphor for the self" (1998, 3). S. Brent Plate narrates human engagement, over centuries, with five everyday classes of material objects—stones, incense, drums, crosses, and bread—and how they are "put to use in highly *symbolic*, sacred ways" (2014, 4; my emphasis). In line with Arjun Appadurai's *The Social Life of Things* (1986), Richard Davis's *Lives of Indian Images* (1997) constructs historical biographies of select images of deities as they are acted upon by human communities. While these person-centered and historical approaches do not preclude the possibilities of material agency, the emphases remain on what humans have done with and how they have experienced objects.

One subset of materiality studies focuses specifically on visual culture—materials that are seen and meant to be seen by humans. David Morgan argues that visual images are agentive, or act, when "they touch or move us [and] *when we have reason to care about them*. . . . In other words, images move us because of our interest in what we take them to portray" (2018, 56; my emphasis). While Morgan identifies human and

---

5. One indication of the increasing focus in religious studies on materiality was the establishment in 2005 of the journal *Material Religion: The Journal of Objects, Art and Belief.*

nonhuman networks behind an image (which he calls a "focal point" that obscures these networks), his focus remains on the impact on humans of visual images about which humans "care."

In the study of Indian religions, the visual gaze is often identified as *darshan*, specifically darshan of consecrated images of deities (*murtis, vigrahams*), in which the gaze has been assumed to be mutual, between deity and devotee: "to see and be seen" (Eck 1998).[6] Readers familiar with Hindu traditions may wonder at the absence in this book of discussion of darshan and the example of agentive materiality of murtis.[7] I have not included analyses of material deities because they are a particular kind of materiality, invested with a theology, about which much has been written both within and outside of the study of Hinduism (Babb 1981; Waghorne et al. 1996; Eck 1998; Cort 2012; Pintchman and Dempsey 2015; Flueckiger 2015). Nevertheless, the agency of murtis contributes to an indigenous theory of materiality and helps us to recognize the potential agency of other forms of materiality in India. In Indian cultures, a stone is often not just an inert stone but may have had a past life or may have the potential to become "something else," including an enlivened deity (Gold 2008; Shulman and K. Vimala 2008).[8] Other scholarship on visual culture in India includes, among others, foci on print culture, such as religious comic books (McClain 2009) and religious calendar art (Jain 2007; Pinney 2004), photography (Pinney 2008), and recently proliferating oversized, non-consecrated (that is, not actively worshiped) cement images of deities such as Hanuman and Shiva (Jain 2016; Lutgendorf 1994).

While the materials analyzed in this book are, of course, capable of being seen, my analyses focus less on the visual nature of the materials than on their presence. The cement Ravanas discussed in chapter 5 are seen but often not noticed outside of the festival of Dussehra; even during

---

6. Based on an ethnographic study of Caitanya Vaishnava communities, Anandi Silva Knuppel's 2019 dissertation argues that darshan between deity (image) and devotee encompasses more than the visual gaze. It can include a wide range of devotional practices involving the body and multiple simultaneously engaged senses.

7. Similarly, I am not directly addressing the human body as a distinct material in the range of materialities analyzed in this book, although bodies carry ornaments, physical guising, and turmeric, and may be part of the assemblage of other materials.

8. See, for example, the story of Ahalya (found in several *puranas* and the Ramayana), who was cursed by her husband, the seer Gautama, to become a stone when he suspected her of infidelity. She was brought back to her human form only when Rama's divine feet stepped on that same stone.

the festival, they are not objects of ritual darshan per se. South Indian wedding pendants (*talis*; chapter 1) explicitly should not be seen and are tucked underneath a woman's clothing, pulled out only at certain ritual moments.[9] While the application of turmeric and vermilion powder on a human body or material may cause their features to stand out visually, these powders or pastes work primarily through their material presence rather than visually. (See chapter 3.)

New materialists such as Jane Bennett (2010) and Bruno Latour (2005) critique the human-centric focus so common in materiality studies, including approaches of visual culture studies in which objects are subordinated to humans who may interact with them. Christopher Pinney aims a critique directly at the "social life of things" approach: "The fate of objects in the Appadurai . . . accounts is always to live out the social life of men, or to become entangled in the webs of culture whose ability to refigure the object simultaneously inscribes culture's ability to translate things into signs and the object's powerlessness as an artififactual [*sic*] trace. . . . Narratives of the social lives of things . . . reaffirm the agency of those humans they pass between" (2005, 259). What materials can tell us about human history and the humans who interact with them is, of course, important. However, these approaches often do not account for the agency of materiality itself and what materiality does that may go beyond human intention, agency, and discourse. While I assume a "distributed agency" (Bennett 2010) between humans and materials, this book shifts focus from human agents of materiality to the agency of materiality that affects humans and deities. I am looking less for the human-attributed meaning of materials than what they do, perform, create.

Consider the architectural system of *vastu* (lit., dwelling)—itself a theory of material agency—which is a lively topic of conversation among many middle- and upper-class Hindus in contemporary India and to which numerous popular periodicals dedicate advice columns and articles. According to the system of vastu (much like the Chinese system of

---

9. See Sarah Horton's analysis of hidden *hibutsu* Buddha images in Japan (2007, chapter 6). James Robson describes similarly hidden but agentive and enlivening "consecration certificates" that are sealed into the torso cavities of Chinese domestic statues (2016). Horton and Robson participated with me in the 2017 Association of Asian Studies presidential roundtable, organized by then-president Laurel Kendall, titled "The Magic of Things: A Conversation across Regions and Disciplines about Agentive Statues and Masks."

feng shui), the orientation of a building, the directional orientation of its entry, and the placement of its contents—a bed or desk, or the placement of a kitchen or bathroom in relationship to the rest of the house—can affect the social and physical lives of those who live in that commercial or domestic building. When I was conducting fieldwork in the city of Hyderabad in 1994 and 1995, I lived for nine months in the student hostel on the grounds of the American Studies Research Center (ASRC) on the campus of Osmania University and in the following years returned for many shorter visits. Although the center's library was world-renowned and visited by scholars from across Asia and Africa, it was in a precarious financial situation when it lost American government PL 480 funding in 1998.[10] Rumors of funding cuts led the center's director and governing board to try numerous schemes to bring in additional income (such as offering the space for academic conferences). At the same time, one immediate material response was to move and rebuild at a different place (opening in a different direction) the entrance to the library. Following the shifting prescriptions of specialists in vastu, the entrance was rebuilt at least three times in the late 1990s—prescriptions that ultimately failed, at least to keep the institution of the ASRC in its original configuration as an independent center housed on the grounds of Osmania University.

The ASRC's entry reorientation is only one of many examples of public buildings renovated according to vastu prescriptions for "preventative health" or for healing of "troubles" in the activities conducted inside those buildings. In 2014, when the governments of the newly formed states of Telangana and Andhra Pradesh divided the secretariat building to be (temporarily) shared by both governments, new entryways on both sides were built according to vastu prescriptions in order to ensure the success of the respective governments—a matter of sufficient significance so as to appear in local newspapers. A vastu specialist told anthropologist Tulasi Srinivas that the flow of space in a home is equivalent to the flow of blood in a body and must be adjusted when the flow is blocked (Srinivas 2018, 53). Traditions of vastu assert the agency of architectural materiality, but the agency of specific architectural features is often not noticed (beyond

---

10. PL480 was a US government aid program that sold surplus American food commodities to countries needing the food, including India, who were able to pay in local currencies rather than the dollar. The American rupee funds in India supported a range of collaborations and exchanges between American and Indian institutions and libraries.

their aesthetics or utility) until the human lives encompassed by that materiality begin to go awry. Humans can manipulate materiality (walls, beds, desks), but in an Indian way of thinking it is the materiality that is the primary agent of vastu.

All the materialities analyzed in this book require human action at some point in their life cycles (humans creating or wearing the objects). However, I want to bring materiality to the center of our understanding of everyday Hindu worlds. I call on readers to *notice* materials and their capacity to become agents independent of human intention or activity. The human intention and identity behind the creation of the Maladasari has been lost, but the cement image glowing with turmeric continues to compel pilgrims to prostrate next to it. A woman's tattoo or wedding pendant continues to materially work—and make her auspicious—long after she is first tattooed or first puts on the tali.

Material Agency

I began this project with Indian ways of thinking about the agency of materiality, observing cues of indigenous discourse about and performance of material agency in my ethnographic research. I then turned to scholarship of Euro-American new materialisms, much of which has not yet entered into religious studies as a central analytic paradigm. This scholarship helped to give me more precise language for, and to identify the complexities of, what I have come to mean by the word "agency."

The title of this book, *Material Acts*, plays off J. L. Austin's term "speech acts"—utterances that *do* something rather than simply convey information (1975), such as the pronouncement at many Christian weddings "I now pronounce you man and wife." My assumption, shared with performance studies scholars (for example, Bauman 1984; Bell 1998; Taylor 2016) regarding ritual and narrative performance, is that material objects do not simply reflect preexisting ideologies and identities but that their performativity also *creates* identity, theology, transformation; they *do* something—material *acts*. I have found this linguistics-derived phrase to be generative of analytic frameworks for materiality, although I agree with many of the critiques of the "linguistic turn" of the 1960s–1980s in analyzing nonlinguistic phenomena. These semiotic foci assumed, quoting Christopher Pinney, that "the visual was essentially 'translatable,' capable of an unravelling or decoding as a result of which 'meaning' would appear" (2006, 132). Christopher Tilley has warned, "Clearly linguistic analogies may serve to obscure as much as they may illuminate the nature and meanings of things as material forms" (2006, 23). "Artefacts perform active metaphorical work in the world that words cannot. They have their own form of communicative agency" (25). With the important caveat that material is not language, the assumption of the creativity of performance is shared between analyses of language and materiality.

Three scholars have been particularly influential in raising questions and providing language for the analyses of material agency in this book: Alfred Gell, Bruno Latour, and Jane Bennett. While each addresses a different scholarly literature and questions, they share an assertion of the agency of materiality as more than signs or reflections of social relations or cultural practices, as well as the importance of accounting for relationships and networks between different material and human agents.

In his discussion about the relationship between art objects and social agency, Gell defines agency as being "attributable to those persons (and things [as secondary agents] . . .) who/which are seen as initiating causal sequences of a particular type, that is, events caused *by acts of mind or will or intention*" (1998, 16; my emphasis). He asserts that nonhuman things "cannot, by definition have intentions" (17); they have effect only due to "physical laws." Gell continues to build his argument: while material objects may have effect, they are only media of human agency and are therefore only "secondary agents . . . through which primary agents distribute their agency in the causal milieu, and thus render their agency effective" (20). These parameters of primary and secondary agency are not as solidified as they may first appear. Gell insists that by identifying objects to be secondary, he does not mean to imply they are less important. After all, primary (intentional) agents are dependent on secondary agents: "Objectification in artefact form is how social agency manifests and realizes itself, via the proliferation of fragments of 'primary' intentional agents in their 'secondary' artefactual forms" (20). Gell leaves open the possibility that while creation of many material forms depends on primary agents who may have specific intentions in relationship to these same materials, secondary agents may also create something beyond these intentions.

Bruno Latour, in *Reassembling the Social: An Introduction to Actor-Network Theory* (2005), pushes back against Gell's assumption that agency requires intention:

> The main reason why objects had no chance to play any role before was not only due to the definition of the social used by sociologists, but also to the very definition of actors and agencies most often chosen. If action is limited a priori to what "intentional," "meaningful" humans do, it is hard to see how a hammer, a basket, [etc.] . . . could act. . . . By contrast if we stick to our decision to start from the controversies about actors and agencies, then *any thing* that does modify a state of affairs by making a difference is an actor. . . . Thus, the questions to ask about any agent are simply the following: Does it make a difference in the course of some other agent's action or not? (71)

Here, Latour critiques a binary distinction between things and people, arguing that they are always implicated one with the other.

Political theorist Jane Bennett, in *Vibrant Matter* (2010), employs the term "distributed agency" to analyze a range of possible interactions between "vibrant things," human and nonhuman—those things "with a certain effectivity of their own" (xvi). Her aspiration, she writes, "is to articulate a vibrant materiality that runs alongside and inside humans to see how analyses of political events might change if we gave the force of things more due" (viii). As I observed with the Maladasari, Bennett points out that material actants never act alone but rather in "assemblages." She explains that an actant's "efficacy or agency always depends on the collaboration, cooperation, or interactive interference of many bodies and forces.[11] A lot happens to the concept of agency once nonhuman things are figured less as social constructions and more as actors, and once humans themselves are assessed not as autonoms but as vital materialities" (21).

My working definition of "agency" is *the capacity of a subject to act, to cause an effect*. To assert that materials (often in "assemblages") can be agents does not imply consciousness or will on the part of that material object; the very presence of a material object or structure, without will or intention, may have an effect on both other materialities and human subjects. Agency may be distributed between human and nonhuman

---

11. David Morgan calls these networks an "ecology of things" (2018, chapter 4). See also Latour 2005.

subjects, but human will or intention regarding the creation or use of a material does not limit or control what that material may create.

Ethnographic-Performative Methodologies

One purpose of this book is to extend the range of materialities brought into the account of religious studies, and, as Bennett writes, "to linger in those moments during which [we find ourselves] . . . fascinated by objects, taking them as clues to the material vitality that they share with them [vital materialists]" (2010, 17). Lingering among these materialities, Latour urges us to "make things talk": "Once built, the wall of bricks does not utter a word—even though the group of workmen goes on talking and graffiti may proliferate on its surface. . . . This is why specific tricks have to be invented to *make them talk*, that is, to offer descriptions of themselves, to produce *scripts* of what they are making others—humans or nonhumans—do" (2005, 79).

But how to make them "talk"?

Methodologically, this project presented a challenge to me as an ethnographer used to depending primarily on verbal conversations and performed songs, narratives, and commentaries as primary evidence for analyses. I have not dropped altogether these discursive commentaries; rather, I have used them as cues for further material observation and performative analyses.[12] One goal of this book is to identify indigenous theories of material agency—my interlocutors do not need Gell, Latour, or Bennett to tell them that materials act. And so, I include (perhaps more than many materiality studies do) indigenous discursive commentaries about the materialities under consideration, as well as my own experiences of materiality in some ethnographic contexts. For example, I learned about the agency of ornaments by being admonished or praised by my friends for something I was doing with my own ornaments. However, the ways in which people spoke about different kinds of materials differed significantly—for example providing fragmental comments about ornaments

---

12. In his introduction, the editor of *Material Vernaculars*, Jason Baird Jackson, identifies a similar methodology shared by contributors to that volume: observing the relationships between materiality and indigenous personal and sacred narratives (2016, 4).

and longer commentary or narrative performances about Ravana but not his cement images. About turmeric-vermilion my interlocutors had little to say at all, but they were confident in their own actions incorporating them into rituals and their material effect.

The challenge was both to take into account human agency, intentions, and commentary about specific materials and to let the materials "speak" performatively to their own agency, beyond human intention.[13] Christopher Pinney warns us, citing Carlo Ginzburg (1989, 35), not to read into the image what we have determined "by other means" (2005, 260). In this case he is critiquing interpretations of materiality (the object) as necessarily reflective or growing out of a particular historical moment, thus precluding possibilities for multiplicity and difference in their creative potential (264).[14] I take Pinney's warning a little differently: not to attribute to materiality what I may have learned *only* through other means such as narratives and indigenous commentary but also to analyze what materials create performatively, perhaps outside of human intention. The most significant material effect of the cement Ravanas of Chhattisgarh, for example, is their creation of his literal, material presence in Chhattisgarhi landscapes in which the Ramayana protagonist Rama is (relatively) absent. The agency of these material Ravanas exceeds discursive commentary and histories and cannot be tied down to particular Ramayana narratives and human intentions.

One strategy for observing how materials act is to place the materials in a performance studies analytic frame, which assumes that performance is emergent in each of its iterations, "always and only a living practice in the moment of its activation" (Taylor 2016, 7). Each material performance has the potential to create differently than the iteration before it. Material

---

13. Hillary Kaell has a similar goal, to account for human intention and independent material agency, in analyzing large roadside Christian crosses in rural Quebec: "In Quebec, *humans* act by enhancing a cross's visibility so that *it* can act on other humans.... Yet human action and nonhuman prescription sometimes align imperfectly and despite caretakers' efforts, things go awry. Wood breaks down, foliage grows erratically, and people still routinely fail to see the crosses or recognize them for what they are" (2017, 145).

14. Pinney quotes Siegfried Kracauer's *History: The Last Things before the Last* (1969): "We tacitly assume that our knowledge of the moment at which an event emerges from the flow of time will help us account for its occurrence" (Pinney 2005, 263).

acts do not simply reflect preexisting ideologies, theologies, norms, or human intention; rather, the reiteration of their performances helps to both create ideologies and norms and potentially disrupt them (Butler 1990, 1997; Hollywood 2002). While performances may fail or contradict human intentions behind them, through a performance studies lens that looks for what *is* created, there is no failure (Flueckiger 2013b). Material acts may have unpredictable effects but not failed ones.[15]

Repertoire is another important facet of performance analyses. In the case of material acts, to place individual materialities in repertoires of similar and performatively related materials provides material commentary about the agency of their individual members. To identify different forms of male, female, and goddess guising in a South Indian goddess tradition as elements of a single performative repertoire, for example, helps us to recognize the creative potential of such material acts that may not be as easily discerned were only a single form of guising to be analyzed. This book also places several different material repertoires (ornaments, guising, turmeric-vermilion and other ritual materials, goddess-shrine architecture, and cement Ravanas) in relationship to one another. This inter-materiality is another mode of commentary about the ways in which material agency is performed in everyday Hindu worlds. The broad repertoire of different forms of materiality also highlights that while each form is agentive, it is agentive in a unique way. That is, not all materialities work in the same way. The deeply ethnographic approach of this book is, in part, to acknowledge and perform how specific materials are deeply embedded in human and other material worlds. The ethnographic details are also intended to provide bases for questions by the book's readers that may go beyond my analyses.

Five Sites of Material Acts

Material Acts analyzes five forms or sites of materiality from three field sites where I have conducted extensive fieldwork: the central Indian state

---

15. This assertion stands in contrast to J. L. Austin's identification of failed performatives (what he calls "misfirings")—failed speech acts that do not accomplish what their speakers intend—when the statement is not made by the "correct"/right person, to the right audience, under the right circumstances (Austin 1975, 14–19; Hollywood 2002).

of Chhattisgarh, the city of Hyderabad in the Deccan Plateau, and the South Indian pilgrimage town of Tirupati. I begin with two forms of materiality that are indigenously and explicitly articulated to be agentive: ornaments and material guising. I accept these articulations and performances to reflect an Indian theory of materiality, which I use as an analytic framework within which to identify the agency of other materials that human participants/observers may not discursively acknowledge—abundant and excessive ritual items, village-deity temple architecture, and cement images of Ravana, the antagonist of the Ramayana epic.

Indigenous articulation and assumptions about the agency of materiality is clearest in the case of ornaments, the focus of chapter 1. One Indian-language term for ornamentation, *alankara*, literally means "to make adequate," privileging what the ornaments themselves do rather than the agency of persons who may give or wear them. Ornaments are protective; they make women auspicious; they create relationships; and in the case of tattoos they have agency beyond the demise of the human body that they ornament.

Chapter 2 analyzes the transformative potential of material guising (*vesham*) of both humans and the goddess in the context of a South Indian village goddess festival, Gangamma Jatara. Here, we see the importance of identifying a repertoire of different kinds of guising as a form of indigenous commentary on some of its elements about which there is little discourse. While the festival is best known for men taking female guise (*stri vesham*: saris, ornaments, breasts, and braids), women also identify the turmeric powder applied to the dark stone goddess's face as vesham, and those with whom I spoke were explicit about its transformative power—that is, turmeric vesham makes a demanding (*ugra*) goddess satisfied (*shanta*). Taking this as a performative cue, I argue that stri vesham too has transformative possibilities, changing the nature of masculinity of those men donning the vesham.

In chapters 3, 4, and 5, we shift to materials about which human participants had less to say, directly, about material agency. Chapter 3 analyzes the proliferation of materiality in two ritual sites: a South Indian women's vow ritual (Telugu, *mokku*) called Varalakshmi Puja and the festival of Gangamma Jatara. The explicit purpose of Varalakshmi Puja is to invite Lakshmi, the goddess of wealth, prosperity, and abundance, into the home. I argue that she is created, quite literally, through an abundance of material substances: turmeric-vermilion powders/pastes, an abundance of varieties and amounts of food items, and an abundance of women's (auspicious) bodies. In Gangamma Jatara a proliferation of materiality similarly both calls and creates the goddess (Gangamma), but the material proliferation and the goddess herself are excessive rather than abundant. The distinction between abundant and excessive materiality is created in part through spatial boundaries in which their respective rituals are performed, the specific kinds of materials offered, and the wide range (caste and gender) of participating human bodies.

The expanding and shifting architecture of village goddess shrines in Hyderabad is changing the very nature of the goddesses so enshrined. These *gramadevata* goddesses traditionally lived in open spaces, at village boundaries, or on the banks of bodies of water. However, the rapidly expanding city of Hyderabad has encompassed the shrines, and sites that were once on village outskirts are now in the middle of bustling urban traffic. While human intention in altering and expanding these shrines was often articulated to be literal protection of the goddess, I argue that these architectural changes have the potential to change (and in some cases have already changed) the very nature and sometimes identities of the goddesses sheltered within. Chapter 4 ends with a counterexample, of sorts, of an expanding shrine for which (highly politicized) human agency is ultimately erasing what the materiality of the shrine itself may have initially created.

Finally, chapter 5 analyzes the creative potential of the unique Chhattisgarhi cement images of Ravana that stand throughout the year seemingly unnoticed by passersby until the annual Dussehra festival, when they are incorporated into the festivities. While narratively Ravana is killed by the god-hero Rama, materially he remains standing. The agency of these Ravanas goes beyond what their human creators explicitly intend. To quote Webb Keane, "Only by positing the existence of objects independent of human experiences, interpretations and actions can we allow, analytically, the possibility of unforeseen consequences" (2006, 201)—in this case, consequences that are creating nonverbalized alternative theologies and politics.

Not all forms of materiality are indigenously recognized as agentive in India. However, that some *are* leaves open the possibility that other materialities, unrecognized discursively as agentive, may be; I have followed that possibility in the chapters that follow. I conclude with a return to the question of where agency lies: in the materials or humans who may interact with them—or distributed between them—and the significance of context in answering this question. By foregrounding material agency, I hope to expand our understanding of Hindu worlds and the parameters of what we might call "religion."

Chapter 1

Agency of Ornaments

Identity, Protection, and Auspiciousness

When I return to India, I normally replace the Chhattisgarhi silver bangles that I wear in the US with glass bangles. But several years ago, on a trip to Chhattisgarh that was to last only a few days, I hadn't taken off the silver bangles. Although I knew that among my lower-caste and lower-class friends in Chhattisgarh, to wear silver only was not appropriate for a married woman, I thought that for this short trip when I wasn't going to be conducting formal fieldwork, my silver would pass. However, I learned otherwise. I met a long-time Gond (*adivasi*, tribal) friend, Rupi Bai, in the town of Dhamtari for a very quick visit. After serving me tea and some preliminary conversation about how my children were, she began to finger my silver bangles, up and down my forearm, and then said in a resigned tone, "This isn't good [*yeh to accha nahin hai*]." I knew immediately what she was referring to and stumbled around for a response. But she had a plan: "Let's go to the temple and buy you some glass bangles [*churis*]." And soon my arm was graced with twelve auspicious red glass bangles, with bits of gold-color paint daubed in the cut indentations on each bangle (figure 1.1).

My bangle advisor, Rupi Bai, had been widowed for about fifteen years, at which time, according to custom, a female relative had broken Rupi Bai's glass bangles. While, according to Gond custom, she would have been permitted to still wear silver ornaments, she had not owned silver before becoming a widow, so for many years her arms had remained empty

20 / Material Acts in Everyday Hindu Worlds

Figure 1.1. Bangle seller breaking a woman's old bangles and replacing with new ones, Chhattisgarh. Note ornamentation of Gond tattoos on the woman's forearm. Photo by the author.

except a single bent-aluminum bangle. In most Indian communities, glass bangles are appropriate only for unmarried girls (optional) or married women (traditionally required). In lower-caste Chhattisgarhi communities, glass bangles, rather than a wedding pendant (*tali* or *mangalsutra*), are the primary ornament of marriage. Among castes that permit divorced women or widows to get married again, the second wedding ritual is called "putting on churis" (*churi pahinana*, lit., to cause churis to be put on). As one of my elder friends asserted when showing me and naming her various ornaments, "Only a *churi-walli* [one who wears glass bangles] can wear all the other ornaments; the bangles are first."

Rupi Bai's intervention to replace my silver bangles with glass suggested that wearing silver only, without interspersed glass bangles—a sign of widowhood—may bring misfortune to my own married state.[1] The

---

1. I learned another example of materiality affecting a woman's marital state when I gifted saris to the flower sellers in one of Tirupati's Gangamma temples at the end of

silver bangles had their own agency, despite my human intentions. On this visit Rupi Bai was wearing white plastic bangles (the first time I had seen these), which suggested that it is not only ornamentation that helps to create a woman's auspiciousness: the physical substance of the glass of those bangles has its own agency. Glass is both fragile (much as marriage itself) and tinkles, alerting the presence of an auspicious woman,[2] whereas plastic is relatively permanent (like widowhood in this community, in which remarriage is rare) and gives no sound. However, Rupi Bai continued to wear other auspicious ornaments: tattoos. She is part of a Gond community among which there is a common saying, referring to tattoos: "A Gond woman will never die without her ornaments." The saying became particularly poignant to me after Rupi Bai became a widow; even though her glass bangles had been broken, her tattoos remained.

While the materials and designs of ornaments vary widely in different regions in India, there is a shared assumption across regions that ornaments are not just decorative; they *do* something: they protect; they make whole; they create auspiciousness; they signal and help to create regional, caste, and class identities; they reflect and create relationships.[3]

---

a year of fieldwork, during which I had met them almost every day. Although I had taken my (unmarried) fieldwork associate with me to purchase the saris and told the sales clerk why I was buying so many saris of the same style, neither of them suggested that I needed to buy a piece of blouse cloth to give with each sari. I learned from my flower seller friends differently. They were somewhat aghast that I had not included blouse pieces. They explained that only widows didn't wear blouses and suggested that my flawed gifts had the potential to threaten their auspicious married states.

2. In many South Indian communities, a woman's fifth or seventh month of pregnancy is marked by a ritual called *simantam*, during which married women gift the pregnant mother glass bangles (and other auspicious gifts). Several women told me that the bangles are "a must" and that their tinkling sound brings joy to both the baby in utero and their mother. The tinkling of a mother's bangles is an early, embodied memory for many Indian babies.

3. I thank Elizabeth Hornor, the director of Education Programs at the Michael C. Carlos Museum, Emory University, for her invitation to give a public lecture about talis in conjunction with the 2010 exhibition on Indian jewelry, "Blossoms of Gold: Indian Jewelry from the Susan Beningson Collection." I first began photographing talis in India to prepare for this lecture, which initiated my interest in the agency of ornaments.

Examples of the agency of ornaments abound, and this chapter gives only a small sampling; many Indian readers will have examples from their own families that both support and may contradict some of my descriptions.

To be ornamented is to be complete, fully human.[4] "A person or thing apart from its appropriate ornaments," art historian Ananda Coomaraswamy asserts, "is valid as an idea, but not a species" (1938, 252; cited in Waghorne 1994, 258).[5] The term *alankara* literally means to make adequate, to make present, to strengthen.[6] In India bare arms and necks, without some form of ornamentation, be it a simple thread or silver, gold, or glass ornaments—for babies, girls, and women, in particular—are inauspicious, incomplete, vulnerable, and invite the evil eye. As art historian Vidya Dehejia observes, "To be without ornament is to provoke the forces of inauspiciousness, to expose oneself to danger, even to court danger" (2009, 24).[7]

While all ornaments are on some level protective, some are more consciously thought of as such than others, and some bodies need more protection in certain contexts than do others. Ornamental protection begins at birth. Babies are particularly vulnerable to the evil eye (*nazar*; *drishti*) of relatives, neighbors, and strangers who may look upon the baby wishing for one of their own, of others who may be envious of the good health and beauty of a baby, or even of the inadvertent evil eye drawn by well-wishers' positive comments about a baby. (To avoid the latter, traditionally it is culturally inappropriate in India to comment on a baby's beauty or cuteness.[8]) And so many babies are protected with dots of kohl on the side of their forehead and at the bottom of their little feet and a simple protective string (which may hold an amulet) around their necks or waists. Some babies wear plain black glass bangles or little black bangles studded with pieces of reflective glass that are believed to literally deflect the evil eye.

---

4. Images of deities are also ornamented in worship; these ornaments are similarly agentive, performing relationships (between devotees and god) (Packert 2010) and sometimes transforming the nature of the deity itself. (See chapter 2 of this book.)

5. Art historians have paid more attention to ornamentation (jewelry) than have scholars of religion.

6. The term "alankara" is used not only in reference to jewelry but also refers to ornamentation in poetry, music, and architecture.

7. The high ornamentation of kings suggests anxiety about the physical harm that may threaten those bodies (Geslani 2018); and in premodern India, Molly Aitken reminds us, "a defiant warrior who was brought to heel expressed his submission by removing his weapons *and jewelry*" (2004, 9; my emphasis).

8. Some families go so far as giving their babies unflattering nicknames (pet names, as they're called in Indian English) as another means to deflect the attention of the evil eye.

Ornaments of Marriage

Ornaments become particularly important for women upon marriage. As girls they may wear threads around their necks, glass bangles, and perhaps small earrings (or often in villages, a small bamboo stick in their pierced ears), but when they get married, glass bangles and silver or gold ornaments of particular (regional and caste-associated) designs mark and help to make their new status as married women. We get a clue about the agency of ornaments through a Telugu ritual called *pelli kuturuni cheyyadam* (lit., making a bride). The bride is "made" in a ritual gifting of glass bangles by other married women, who individually put the bangles on the bride's wrist. "Modern," educated women often do not keep wearing these glass bangles on a daily basis, preferring one or two gold bangles, but for this Telugu ritual glass bangles are still essential.[9] In some Chhattisgarhi communities, a similar ritual makes a bride when married women (most of whom attend this ritual highly adorned) take a small bit of *sindur* (vermilion) powder from the parts of their hair (only married women wear this sindur) and apply it to the part of the bride.[10] When all the married women have done so, the groom appears briefly in the women-only ritual to apply the final pinch of sindur to his bride's part; now she is fully "made." In both rituals, the assumption is that the materiality of glass bangles and sindur is not only reflective of an intended marital status but also that such ornamentation has agency to both transform and thereafter maintain the marital status of a woman. Similarly, at a very different life stage, the poignant removal of auspicious ornaments (sindur, bangles, wedding pendant, and toe rings) make a woman a widow. Significantly, this ritual, as described to me by a Telugu Brahmin friend whose sister had just become a widow, does not occur in their families until the tenth day after the husband's death. The woman without a living husband is not fully a widow until she takes off the ornaments that have earlier made her a bride.

---

9. For a woman of my educational and class level to wear an armful of red glass bangles every day is an anomaly. My Indian university professor friends are often amused by my glass-bangled arms and comment with something like "How quaint."

10. I was struck when attending a Tamil wedding in Hyderabad a few years ago that most of the female guests were wearing red or gold/yellow saris, the auspicious colors of the bride herself. Similarly, in this ritual many of the women were adorned as a bride may be, materially performing their auspiciousness as married women.

A common term for ornamentation, *shringar*, means adornment and can also have connotations of erotic love (being one of the nine *rasas*, or aesthetic emotions.) This would be one reason it is not appropriate for widows to wear auspicious ornaments such as glass bangles, since traditionally widows would be exempt from participating in (or suggesting) eroticism. For brides and queens, the traditional number of ornaments is sixteen (Hindi, *solah shringar*)—from hair ornaments, earrings, armbands, necklaces, waist belt, ankle bracelets, to toe rings. (The specific ornaments may vary from region to region.) Shringar ornamentation is not limited to jewelry; it can also include (in the listing of sixteen) clothing, fragrance, hair styling, and henna (Dehejia 2009, 34–36). Many Sanskrit and vernacular-language literary texts, as well as folk songs, describe human or divine bodies as adorned from head to toe (*sikha nakha*) or toe to head (*nakha sikha*) (figure 1.2). Ideally, every part of an auspicious woman's body is adorned—thereby protected—although, of course, many (even most) brides' families cannot afford to adorn their daughters in full solah shringar.

In most regions of India, married women wear some form of wedding chain or string around their necks. In many parts of North and Central India, the chain—*mangalsutra* (lit., thread of auspiciousness)—is composed of gold and black beads that may or may not hold a gold pendant; in Chhattisgarh, the mangalsutra of mid-level and upper castes is a row of gold leaf-shaped pendants hanging on a black thread. In South India, married women wear a gold tali either on a turmeric-rubbed string, or, if affordable, the thread may be replaced by a more durable gold chain after the wedding rituals. In the South, women say they should never take off their talis, even while bathing and sleeping, suggesting that even a few hours without the tali may threaten a woman's marital status and auspiciousness;[11] whereas in the North, many women either come from castes that do not wear mangalsutras or do not wear them on a daily basis. (Folklorist Pravina Shukla suggests that the equivalent "must-wear" sign of marriage in Benaras is sindur [2008, 372–75].[12]) While many women may buy and sell their gold ornaments for needed cash flow, or may have them remade in new designs

---

11. While I wear a Telugu tali, I do take it off to sleep and periodically forget to put it back on in the morning. One of my South Indian friends always notices if I have forgotten to put it on, simply from the absence of its chain on the back of my neck. I obviously have not yet fully internalized the tali's agency or I would not forget.

12. Like glass bangles, many educated women no longer apply the long line of sindur in their hair parts. They may drop it altogether or apply only a small dab at their front hairline; after all, many women have short hair these days and no hair part at all.

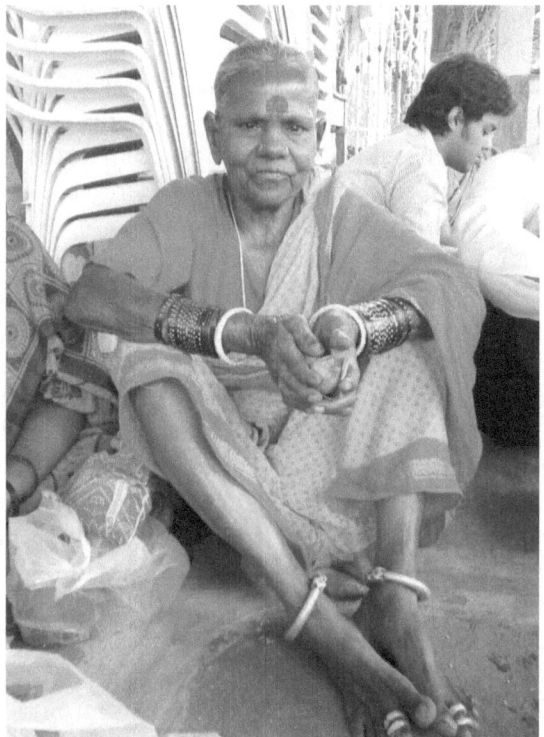

Figure 1.2. Ornamented elder, Hyderabad. Photo by the author.

to keep up with fashion, a living woman's tali is never sold or exchanged. Shukla observes that jewelers know this fact about talis and mangalsutras, so, ironically, the chance that the gold of these ornaments may be tainted is better than that of other ornaments, since the wedding pendant/chain "will never be sold and therefore never tested" (2008, 179).

The mangalsutra or tali is not worn for show or evaluation, in contrast to many other ornaments that are worn to be seen and may be evaluated for aesthetics, taste, style, monetary value, and so on.[13] Traditionally, the South Indian tali should not be visible but should remain tucked inside

---

13. In her book on North Indian dress and adornment, Pravina Shukla emphasizes the choices women make regarding dress and ornamentation: "All express an awareness of the fact that women are seen and visually judged. . . . Women are not only the subjects of viewing, they are viewers themselves, making assessments based on visual cues" (2008, 53–54).

a woman's clothing, hanging between her breasts. (On occasion when my own tali has fallen outside my sari blouse or kurta, South Indian friends have often discreetly tucked it back in beneath my clothing.) The "work" of a tali is not visual. The pendant itself is not primarily a display of wealth, although one may deduce the economic class of its wearer, depending on whether a woman is wearing her tali on a turmeric thread or gold chain and by the thickness of such chain, which can be seen around the back of the neck. Nor are the designs of talis personal or aesthetic choices; a woman wears the traditional tali design of her husband's family, caste (*jati*, *kulam*), and region.

With arranged marriages, of course, the bride's and husband's castes are traditionally the same. However, in cross-caste marriages (which remain a very small minority), the tali design is generally that of the husband's family. When one of my Indian American Tamil graduate students married a Gujarati American man, the tali design was a topic of negotiation—although that there would *be* a tali was assumed. The compromise was that her husband tied a Gujarati-designed mangalsutra around her neck during the wedding ritual, and she chooses to wear daily a small version of the Tamil tali design of her own family. This tali had originally been made to offer to a small image of a goddess, hence its tiny size; it was more convenient, my student said, to wear with non-Indian clothes on a daily basis. While the design and materials of talis, mangalsutras, and other ornaments perform regional and caste identities and, as such, are of particular interest to the anthropologist, most women are not reflexive about this aspect of the agency of their ornaments.

I saw many of my friends' talis for the first time only when I asked them to pull them out from beneath their saris so that I could photograph them. In the courtyard of a goddess temple in Tirupati, I learned that talis are either too powerful or too vulnerable (it wasn't clear which) for two women to show me theirs at the same time; taking turns, the flower sellers pulled out (from under their saris) their talis, one by one. While the women couldn't further explain the prohibition of two talis not being visible at the same time, they thought I might be right about my conjecture that the reason for the prohibition was the power (*shakti*) of the talis. Through their talis, I also learned the castes and regional identities of women, which was sometimes a surprise. For example, seeing the shape of her tali, I found out that the husband of one of my Tirupati friends was Tamil rather than Telugu, which I had always assumed. She explained that although her husband had been born in and had lived in Tirupati all of his life, his family still identified as Tamil and gave Tamil-designed talis to their daughters-in-law. The sectarian affiliation of some Brahmin women became apparent when I saw their tali designs—whether they were from a Shri Vaishnava Iyengar family (the tali designed with Vishnu's *namam*) or a Shaiva Iyer family (the tali marked with a Shiva *linga).*

On the occasion of the wedding of a Kannada Brahmin graduate student from Emory University, I learned that in many families, a bride is given two talis: one from her mother and one from her husband. I observed a pre-wedding ritual during which the student's mother tied a tali, hanging on a turmeric thread, around the neck of a ritual pot (a form of the goddess Lakshmi). At the end of the ritual, she tied the same tali around her daughter's neck—before the wedding. In this family it was the custom for the bride to wear this maternal tali for fourteen or twenty-one days after the wedding, on a separate string from that of the tali tied by the husband during the wedding ritual itself. Many women thereafter wear the two talis together on a single string or chain. The maternal tali helps to create a woman's auspiciousness as a bride and performs her continuing link to her maternal family; the tali tied by the husband marks her auspiciousness as a wife. A Telugu woman who was surprised that I was wearing only one tali, not two (a matter about which I have been frequently questioned and even chastised), explained why she wore two: "One is given by my mother and one by my mother-in-law." Significantly, she identified her mother-in-law, not husband, as the person who "gave" the tali; it was a "women's matter."

In some South Indian castes, a girl is given a small tali on the occasion of her first-menstruation ritual.[14] Traditionally, this ritual has been a very public affair—much like a wedding—during which relatives shower the girl with gifts and extended family members and friends are feasted. The tali on this occasion celebrates the auspiciousness of the girl's potential fertility rather than marriage per se. Of course, the two used to be more closely associated in time than they are today; girls used to get married soon after reaching puberty, whereas today the rituals are separated by several years.[15] Girls in these families also wear a sari for the first time at

---

14. In Tamil the ritual is called *mancal nir* (lit., yellow water, referencing the turmeric bath the girl is given before the ritual); in Telugu the ritual is called *peddamanishi avadam* (lit., becoming a big person).

15. With the Prohibition of Child Marriage Act (2006), the legal age of marriage for girls is eighteen and for boys twenty-one. (The 2006 act is a repeal and replace of the Child Marriage Restraint Act of 1929 and amended relevant portions of the Hindu Marriage Act of 1955.)

this ritual, and turmeric is applied to her face, both materials identifying and creating the auspiciousness of her new womanhood.

After it has been tied by the husband, the tali hangs outside the bride's sari for the duration of the wedding ritual, visible for all to see; thereafter it will remain tucked inside her clothing. As mentioned earlier, the tali is not a showpiece of a family's class status; rather, it is the center of a woman's power, its string or chain often holding an amulet, house key, and several safety pins (figure 1.3). Women who can afford to do so exchange the tali turmeric string with a gold chain after the wedding; in this case the women traditionally tie the tali to the ends of the gold chain with a few inches of turmeric-rubbed string. This string, like the protective ritual threads described below, must be periodically replaced and renewed. Religion scholar Amy Allocco described to me an annual Tamil ritual held on the banks of the Cauvery River during which married women exchange turmeric-rubbed cords/threads and replace their old tali threads with these new ones. Sometimes women who are having difficulty

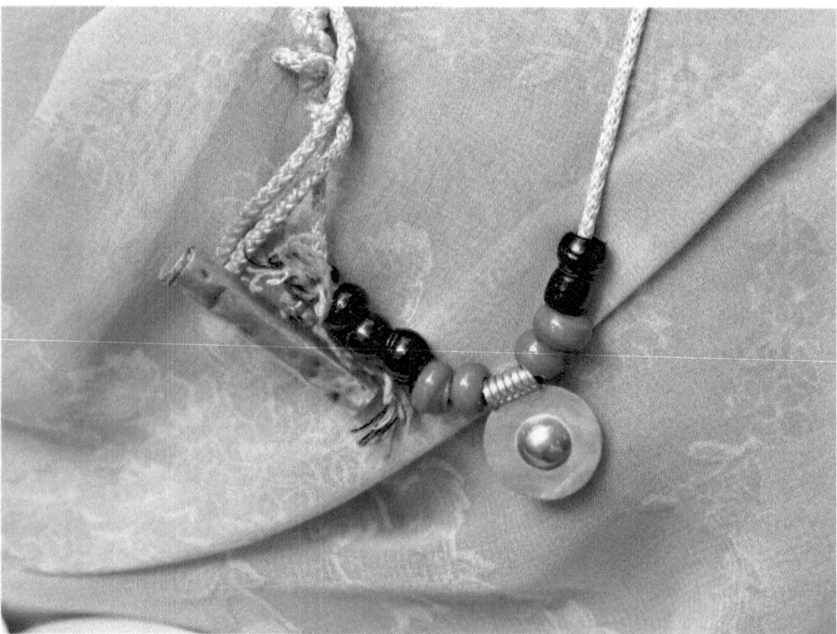

Figure 1.3. *Tali*, black beads and coral, and amulet metal canister on turmeric thread, Hyderabad. Photo by the author.

conceiving tie the new tali threads first around a *naga* (snake) stone, before their husbands (re)tie it around the women's necks. The ritual keeps the tali strong, the marriage strong (implying the long lives of the husband), and may confer fertility. Tali turmeric strings are also often part of ritual gifts (*tambulam*) exchanged between South Indian women, along with an uncut piece of material for a sari blouse, a betel leaf and nut, small packets of turmeric and vermilion, and a few glass bangles. These same "women's things" are frequently offered to temple goddesses and are given back to female worshipers as goddess-empowered ornaments.

Following the ritual grammar of renewing the tali thread described above, an elder Tamil female householder living in Hyderabad explained and demonstrated a daily turmeric ritual that she had been taught, as a new bride, by her oldest sister-in-law but that she no longer practices regularly. The full length of her tali string is knotted many times in order to shorten it enough to tie between the two ends of her long gold chain. She explained that women used to apply turmeric to the thread every day during their baths, renewing and sustaining the power of the tali. The material of turmeric is itself efficacious in maintaining the agency of another material, the tali.

The tali is an agent of auspiciousness for the woman wearing it, but rituals around talis also create and strengthen relationships between women and transfer their auspiciousness from one to another. After living in Tirupati for several months while conducting research on the goddess Gangamma (Flueckiger 2013), during which I wore only a thin silver chain with a pendant, I bought myself a gold tali—this after more than twenty years of marriage, contrary to all tradition in which it is tied during the wedding ritual itself. Only then did I realize the significance of the tali in creating and strengthening relationships between women. On my first visit to a friend's home after I began wearing my tali, as I was leaving, she asked me to pull it out from beneath my sari, and she ritually applied a dab of vermilion powder to it—a ritual, she explained, through which women share their auspiciousness and shakti (female power) with one another.

The very physical properties of gold are also agentive; gold is inherently pure (*shuddha*) as a substance—" 'purified by the movement of air,' say the Kashmiri Brahmans—and it purifies whatever/whoever comes in contact with it" (Madan 1985, 17). Several years ago, when I went to visit an elderly Punjabi Indian woman in Atlanta to say good-bye before I left for India, she admonished me, "Now, Joyce, don't be stingy with your gold."

It took me a minute to register what this might mean. I asked if she was afraid I wouldn't wear my tali to India for fear of chain snatching in big crowds (not an infrequent occurrence in crowded buses or bazaars; for this reason, some women wear costume jewelry on a daily basis instead of their real gold ornaments, which they pull out of safes for weddings and other special occasions). Yes, she replied, "Too many women take off their gold. But you *need* to wear it, *especially* in India; letting water run over the gold onto your body when you're taking your bath will protect you; and it's good for your health." Imitation costume jewelry raises a question about whether it is the ornament or its physical properties that protect its wearer and create auspiciousness.[16] Whereas some women who wear costume jewelry may be convinced that wearing the ornament is sufficient, this elder friend felt strongly that the protective quality of ornaments depended on its materiality (gold) and that wearing a gold tali outweighed the risk of having it snatched off in a crowd.

The Tali in a South Indian Goddess Tradition

I began to rethink the agency of the tali while conducting research on the village goddess Gangamma in Tirupati (Flueckiger 2013). I noticed that the unmarried goddess and her unmarried sisters each wore a tali, which up until that time I had associated exclusively with marriage. When I first asked Gangamma's temple attendants and flower sellers who Gangamma's husband was, since she was wearing a tali, they looked puzzled, as if the question had never occurred to them, and then answered that she had no husband. But when I returned several years later, the female caretakers of Gangamma's largest Tirupati temple answered the same question with the name of the male god Shiva; however, he is nowhere present in Gangamma narrative, ritual, or iconographic traditions. In that same conversation, one of my friends continued to insist there was no husband, saying, "She's Adi Shakti [primordial Shakti or goddess]. Who would be able to bear her [power] by getting married to her?" (Flueckiger 2013, 219–20). Religion scholar Anne Feldhaus similarly describes unmarried river goddesses in Maharashtra who wear the auspicious ornaments of a married woman. She observes that a husband may be implied but that

---

16. See the discussion at the beginning of the chapter about Rupi Bai's plastic bangles being acceptable for a widow, whereas glass ones would not be, suggesting that the material of at least some ornaments matters.

none of the goddesses' worshipers seemed concerned about who he might be; Feldhaus calls these river goddesses "husbandless wives" (1995, 53–55).

Several months into my yearlong Gangamma fieldwork in Tirupati, I learned about a class of women of unmarried women called *matammas*, who, like Gangamma and her sisters, are unmarried and wear talis. Matammas enter a ritual relationship with the goddess by exchanging talis with her; thereafter, these women are under obligation to ritually serve the goddess and she is under obligation to protect them. Although matammas do not traditionally marry human males, they may enter sexual relationships with them and have children (one of the unmarried Tirupati Gangamma sisters herself has children). That a goddess or woman with no husband wears a tali led me to question my assumptions about the relationship between talis and marriage, as well as scholarly interpretations that characterize talis as, quite literally, "binding" a married woman to the control of her husband. (See Reynolds 1991, quoted below.) Like married women, matammas are considered to be auspicious, a status that is created, in part, and marked by their talis. However, these talis are not tied by husbands; furthermore, unlike women married to men, matammas are always auspicious (*nityasumangali*), because they never lose their talis as widows do upon the deaths of their husbands; the goddess with whom they have exchanged talis never dies.[17]

One of the matammas I came to know in Tirupati, Pujaramma, was unusual in that she had married a human after entering a tali relationship with Gangamma. However, she was equally unusual in that as a married woman she did not take off this tali when her husband died. When I initially didn't recognize her to be a widow because she was wearing a tali and *bottu* (vermilion forehead marking), Pujaramma noticed my confusion and explained, "One hundred and one Gangammas gave me my bottus; why should I take them off when my husband dies?"[18] Bottus and

---

17. For discussion of similarly ever auspicious (*nityasumangali*) *devadasis* (ritual specialists and dancers married to temple male deities), see Kersenboom 1997.

18. Pujaramma's comment reminds me of the decision of the mother of a Brahmin friend living here in Atlanta made regarding continuing to wear a small bottu upon becoming a widow. When soon after she became a widow and visited her daughter in the US, the daughter asked why she wasn't wearing a bottu anymore, suggesting to her that it wasn't her husband who had first given it to her. The mother had worn a bottu before marriage, and the daughter thought there was no reason to take it off now. With some reluctance, but also relief, the mother agreed to begin wearing a small, black bottu again.

pasupu-kumkum are equated here with the tali as signs of the goddess and auspicious womanhood, not marriage.

The matamma tradition belies Holly Reynolds's generalizations about and interpretation of, in *The Powers of Tamil Women* (1991), the tali in Tamil culture:

> When a man ties a *tali* around the neck of a woman, he binds her to him with a symbol of all his culturally and socially derived identities, *makes* [my emphasis] that woman a cumankali [*sumangali*; auspicious woman], and entrusts to her the well-being of himself and his lineage, an act that paradoxically makes the wife the protector of the husband. . . . In owning the *tali*, the husband controls the auspiciousness of his wife; he confers cumankali status upon her at marriage and deprives her of it at his death. (45–46)

She continues: "The *tali* delimits boundaries, sets up barriers, confines woman to a specified domain, that of her husband. . . . It declares that sexual relations are permissible only with the owner of the *tali*, for at issue here is control over and possession of female generative power" (46).

In her oral narratives, Pujaramma expressed a very different experience of the tali; the tali relationship was not one of restriction, but of both compulsion and freedom to move. She reported that the goddess had ordered her to keep wandering, from village to village, hill to waterfall; then, "I keep going around every *uru* (village). I don't know when she'll stop me and where she'll allow me to build [a permanent place]" (Flueckiger 2013, 219). An exchange of talis between matammas and the goddess creates a relationship in which the women are obligated to serve and obey the goddess but through which they also have the freedom to move more than most middle-class, middle-caste women—and the goddess is obligated to protect them as they do so.

In my book on the goddess Gangamma, *When the World Becomes Female*, I questioned Reynolds's conclusions, asking, "Is the auspiciousness traditionally attributed to a married woman, concretized through her *tali*, *given* by marriage (i.e., a husband), or is marriage a socially sanctioned context in which pre-existing auspiciousness (fertility) may be performed?" (2013, 215)—a subtle but important distinction.[19] I found that most mar-

---

19. See Gentes 1992 for a description of tali rituals in pre-twentieth-century Kerala that were performed for pubescent, unmarried girls. Gentes writes that when a girl

ried women do not associate the tali with binding or restriction; nor was there any suggestion that, by virtue of the talis tied around their necks by husbands during the wedding ritual, they were "owned" by their husbands. Rather, the women I spoke with associated the tali with their own auspiciousness and female power (shakti). It is not an ornament of display; its agency works on a different level, by strengthening a woman's inherent auspiciousness. For married women, the tali protects and strengthens her marriage; for matammas, the tali creates and sustains a ritual relationship with the goddess—both frameworks within which tali women can openly perform their female auspiciousness.

Fragile Threads and Permanent Tattoos

The simplest of ornaments are (relatively) fragile threads or strings tied around necks, wrists, upper arms, or waists. Threads (often red or yellow; sometimes threads of both colors twisted together) are often tied on the wrists of both male and female participants, under bangles or beside a wristwatch, in particular rituals; the threads should be worn until they naturally break or fall off. These threads both protect the participants during the ritual and, thereafter, physically carry the blessings or benefits of the ritual on the body of the participant. The significant materiality is the thin twisted cotton strands of the thread—a material available to anyone, of any class. The individual strands are fragile, as is protection itself. Hence, such threads need to be periodically replaced, often at an annual ritual.[20]

The festival of Raksha Bandhan (lit., to tie or bind protection) explicitly names the protective nature of threads. Celebrated on full-moon day of the lunar month of Shravan, the central act of this festival is for sisters to tie *rakhi* threads on the wrists of their brothers. A week before the festival, bazaars are lined with street carts selling rakhis, ritual

---

was married, it was not as a "wife" but as "one who has the power to create and withhold life" (318).

20. Threads may also have agency *off* the human body when they are tied on tree branches or through metal or marble screen cutouts at temples and *dargahs* (Muslim grave shrines to saints). These are often tied by devotees as part of a vow to the deity or saint, for healing of the physical or social body. During some vow rituals, female participants wrap tree trunks with threads each time they round the tree for a vowed number of times (such as 108 times); the tree itself is thereby visually ornamented.

threads cut to a length appropriate for the wrist. While only a thread is ritually required, these days rakhis are usually decorated with beads, tinsel medallions, or (at their most elaborate) even semiprecious stones or bits of silver or gold. The protection implied in the thread tying is two-way: sisters protect their brothers ritually, while brothers are then obligated to protect their sisters both materially and emotionally. The rakhis not only reflect sister-brother relationships, but they also create and strengthen them. Many girls and women tie rakhis on the wrists of boys or men who are not their "blood kin" (including across caste and religious boundaries); the thread tying creates a fictive kinship, which in India is taken no less seriously than blood relationships. That rakhis are accepted as being agentive can be observed when (several female students told me), on college campuses, some young men stay home on the day of Raksha Bandhan in order to preclude one of their female classmates from tying a rakhi on them, which would also preclude them from having romantic interests in that young woman.

In Odiya (eastern India) communities, many married women of higher castes wear a thread called a *lakshmi nara* (lit., Lakshmi thread or string) (figure 1.4). The turmeric-soaked golden thread is made of ten strands of thin thread twisted together and knotted, at regular intervals, ten times. Participating women wind the threads around their upper arm during the ritual of Sudasa Vrat, a vow ritual performed by married women for the well-being of their families (performed once or twice a year, whenever there is a confluence of a Thursday on the tenth day of the waxing phase of the moon). The ten knots represent ten forms of Lakshmi;[21] during the ritual, the goddess of wealth and prosperity is offered ten kinds of grains, ten ritual grasses, ten leaves, ten sweetened rice balls, and ten coconuts.[22] Wearing the lakshmi nara, women carry with them at all times—and, at some level, *are*—the goddess who both is

---

21. One Odiya woman wearing a Lakshmi nara recited the ten names of Lakshmi as Lakshmi, Kamala, Padma, Haripriya, Daridra Bhanjani (remover of poverty), Bimolaya, Jagatmohini, Chanchala (wealth that moves, doesn't stay still), Janaki, and Uma.

22. The numbers are significant; their abundance helps to create the very abundance that the ritual is invoking from Lakshmi. This ritual is a regional variant of the Varalakshmi Puja *vratam* (vow ritual) discussed in chapter 3, where I analyze further how ritual abundance creates Lakshmi. During Varalakshmi Puja, a cotton ball is tied to the tali of all participants, similar to both the Lakshmi nara and the Dasa Mata thread tied in the Rajasthani ritual described below.

Figure 1.4. Odiya *lakshmi nara*, upper right arm, eastern Chhattisgarh. Photo by the author.

and creates auspiciousness, wealth, and well-being. They keep the thread wound around their upper arms until it is replaced the next Sudasa Vrat.

Threads as ritual ornaments are common across Hindu cultures.[23] Anthropologist Ann Gold recounts a narrative told at a Rajasthani women's vow ritual of the dire consequences of such ritual threads being purposefully broken (2010). The story (*vrat katha*) is performed on the last day of the ten-day *vrat* of Dasa Mata (lit., Tenth Mother; a goddess identified

---

23. The "sacred thread" (*janeu*) worn by "twice-born"-caste men (particularly Brahmins) is another example of threads worn on the human body. During the ritual of *upanayana* (lit., the act of drawing near), a boy's father or another senior male transmits to him the sacred Gayatri Mantra, thereby initiating him into some of the rights and responsibilities of adulthood. The twisted cotton thread is tied over the left shoulder of the initiate, crossing his torso to the right. Traditionally the upanayana was performed between the ages of eight and eleven, but today it is often performed as a pre-ritual to a man's wedding. I have not discussed the janeu in this chapter because of its unique ideological implications and the fact that it is not identified indigenously as an ornament.

with Lakshmi). Gold reports that on the tenth day, a skein of yarn "is twisted into necklaces called Dasa Mata's strings which all participating women wear throughout the year that follows" (113). Like the Odiya Sudasa Vrat strings, these too have ten knots; they too are the goddess herself. The strings should be removed only when there is a birth or death in the family, polluting events that are incommensurate with auspicious threads. The strings are untied only at the end of the next year's Dasa Mata Vrat, when the old strings are carefully placed in a body of water or other auspicious place, such as under a basil bush (in much the same way images of deities are disposed of when they are damaged, etc.) and new strings have been tied.

The Dasa Mata vrat katha tells of King Nala, who was offended when he saw the simple white Dasa Mata string on the neck of his queen, Damayanti. Thinking she should wear only gold and jeweled ornaments befitting her status, the king yanked off his wife's Dasa Mata string and burned it. Damayanti was aghast and told her husband he would soon learn of the powers of the string, if not in that night's dreams, then surely by the next day. And so it was: things immediately began to go awry—the king gambled away his kingdom, the couple lost their children, and they were banished from their former kingdom to wander the jungle in rags. The queen blamed their misfortune on her broken Dasa Mata thread (indirectly blaming her husband). The next year, when Dasa Mata Vrat came around again, Damayanti prayed to the goddess and asked forgiveness, insisting that her husband too worship the goddess. When she tied on the new Dasa Mata threads of that year's ritual, prosperity returned to the royal couple. The vrat katha performs not only the efficacy and importance of women's rituals (things that men seem to have little knowledge of and disregard for) but also the agency of the threads themselves. To perform the ritual with intention and to worship the goddess is not enough; a female participant must also wear and carefully guard Dasa Mata's threads, as they create and sustain auspiciousness and wealth only if they remain unbroken.

In contrast to the fragility of ritual threads, the ornamentation of tattoos is permanent, even following a woman into the next world after death. While threads require periodic replacement, and thus human action, once tattoos are created, they take on an agency of their own, without human intention, and are hardly noticed—until a widow takes off her other ornaments or until young "educated" girls refuse to be tattooed. "No one wears gold [ornaments] all the time," one Odiya woman explained to me, "but tattoos, always" (figures 1.5 and 1.6). Remember the Gond saying, referring to tattoos, "A Gond woman will never die without her ornaments." More specifically, according to the explanation given by my Gond friend Rupi Bai, a woman may traditionally have to take off her glass bangles and other ornaments when she becomes a widow, but no one can take away her tattoos. They are the only ornaments that go with her to the afterlife. In a Gond worldview, tattoos are not dependent on the bodies on which they have been inscribed, which are cremated or

Figure 1.5. Arm tattoos, Chhattisgarh. Photo by the author.

38 / Material Acts in Everyday Hindu Worlds

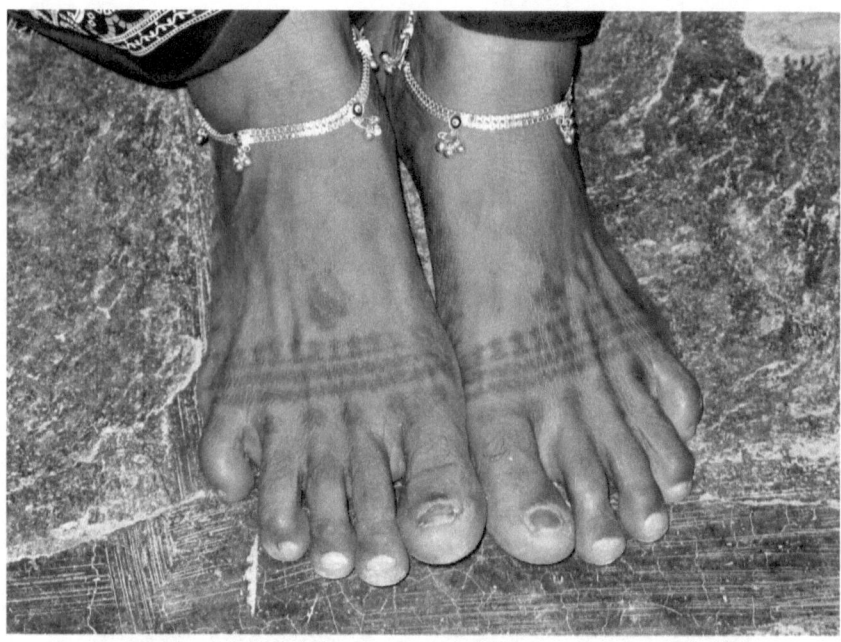

Figure 1.6. Odiya foot tattoos, eastern Chhattisgarh. Photo by the author.

buried.[24] Their materiality is not constrained to this world but crosses the boundaries between human worlds and that of the afterlife.

Rupi Bai explained, matter-of-factly, that after one dies, god (*bhagvan*) takes the tattoos, "one by one by one"—reflecting the Gond tattoo style of a series of dots or small triangles rather than a continuous line—and "sells them, sells them, sells them" so that he has money to buy you food. She elaborated: "Bhagvan patiently collects the tattoos; if you don't have them, your soul flies around like a chicken with its head cut off." I asked what happens, then, to girls or women who are no longer getting tattoos because they feel that this practice is not "modern," an old-fashioned practice of their grandmothers and great grandmothers. She paused and

---

24. Alfred Gell describes a Polynesian tattoo subculture (1993) in which tattooing performs just the opposite from the Gond culture regarding their relationship to the dead body. In Marquesan mortuary practices, tattoos are, quite literally, stripped from the corpse: "Marquesans were not just tattooed, they were also detattooed. . . . Tattooing provided a means of controlling and mediating sacredness; in death participation in the sacred became unmediated and total, and for this reason, I think, tattooing had to be removed before the soul could enter paradise" (216–17).

then suggested, "I guess they will be hungry." A few years later, when she repeated the same reason for tattoos—to enable bhagvan to feed you after death—I asked about men, who in her community do not traditionally get tattoos; she speculated that they would "eat only air" after death.[25]

The idea that tattoos survive death of the human body was confirmed by many of my female Chhattisgarhi interlocutors in conversations about tattoos, including a middle-age Lohri-caste (ironworker) woman, Dilip Bai. When I asked if I could photograph her unusual silver ornaments, she immediately held out her bangled arms and pulled out her silver-coin wedding necklace from underneath her sari and asked, "Do you want me to sing about them?" Her first song named each piece of jewelry, one by one, followed by the phrase "And I wear this in the name of Krishna." I wondered what it meant to wear an ornament for god (Krishna); but Dilip Bai clarified that Krishna didn't refer to god but to a husband, whose name a wife should not say out loud and who is, after all, bhagvan (god). And then I noticed her tattoos on her forearm, under her bangles. She had a song about those too. Again naming each ornament, she sang that one's mother gives one this or that ornament but that each of these eventually breaks; only tattoos last forever, even after death.

A Gujarati woman living in Hyderabad confirmed the importance of tattoos after death but for a very different reason: "I got my tattoos so that something will remain of me after I die, after all my skin and bones go away," adding, "This way people will also be able to identify me, after death, as Hindu." (This statement was made by a Hindu woman living in a Muslim-majority neighborhood of Hyderabad; Muslims in India traditionally do not get tattoos.) Her husband also has tattoos: his full name (so that, he explained, he too could be identified should he get lost and not know who he is, and after death), a small flying Hanuman, and a sun representing the sun god Surya. The designs of his tattoos are not ornamental, as are those of his wife's, and they are also more individualized in design choice than are women's.

---

25. Gell observes that the belief of the agency of tattoos beyond death is widespread in India, although he heard different accounts than I have of what they actually do after death: "Especially among lower castes and tribes, it was considered necessary for women, and sometimes men, to be tattooed, in order to avoid punishment in the land of the dead. . . . These same people believe that Yama, the God of death, and his demons will devour the untattooed, but will not harm the tattooed women because they cannot solve the 'puzzle' that her tattoos present" (1998, 90; citing his own unpublished essay of 1994).

One of Rupi Bai's Chhattisgarhi neighbors, listening to our conversation about tattoos, confirmed, "Our elders say that when you die, you take nothing with you except for tattoos [*godai*]. . . . The one above [*uparwalla*; god] will ask, 'What did you bring with you?'" This woman did not get her tattoos until she was an adult and had already had four children, rather than being tattooed upon marriage, as was the custom of her Raut (cow herding) caste. She remembered, "My elders scolded me: 'You're the mother of four children and you look just like that?'" That is, they were aghast that she was unornamented with tattoos at such a late stage in her life, after giving birth to her children. Her now-married daughters, however, have resisted the traditional tattoo designs of their mother and grandmothers—asserting that "modern" women do not get these kinds of tattoos—and have only their names in English letters tattooed on their forearms.

When a twenty-seven-year-old unmarried rural community development worker from the Kurmi jati (cultivating, mid-level caste) showed me her forearm tattoo, she asserted, "It is a *must* to get tattooed before marriage." She had received her tattoos when she was about five years old, although it is more common to get them at puberty, after the body has stopped growing, so that, I was told, the designs don't stretch and change shape. Another Chhattisgarhi woman reported that tattoos showed what kind of family a woman was from—if you're from a "good" family, then surely you'll be tattooed. One of her neighbors, emphasizing the gendered nature of tattoos, asserted, "Without tattoos, a woman's hands and feet are like a man's."

Like mangalsutras or talis and other caste- and regional-associated ornaments, most women's tattoo designs are not individual creative choices (the kind of designs Alfred Gell calls "unanchored" [cited in Schildkrout 2004, 330]) or an expression of counterculture or defiance, as they were until quite recently in American cultures (Barron 2017). I estimate that at least 80 percent of women above the age of forty—mothers, grandmothers, great-grandmothers—in the Chhattisgarhi villages in which I have lived and worked are tattooed. The designs of traditional Indian tattoos are relatively limited and shared by a woman's regional and caste community. Vince Hemingson observes that tattoos in America invariably elicit the question to the tattooed person, "What does it *mean*?" (2009, 19; cited in Barron 2017, x; my emphasis). In Odiya and Chhattisgarhi cultures, tattoos are inscribed not because they *mean* something but because they *do* something.

I met two Chhattisgarhi male tattooers in the summer of 2017; it was not an easy task to find tattooers, since they are itinerant, traveling

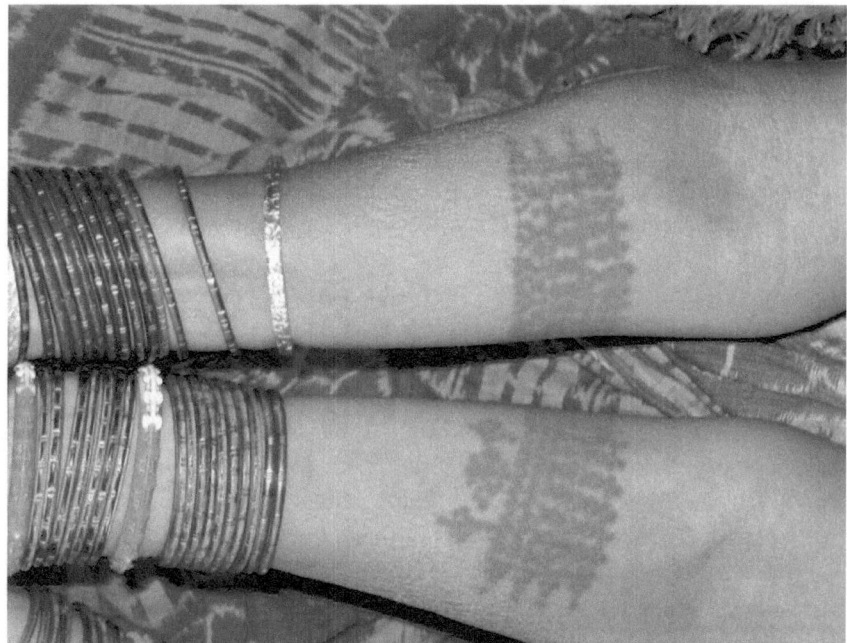

Figure 1.7. Odiya Lakshmi-footprint tattoos, eastern Chhattisgarh. Photo by the author.

between temples, fairs, and villages to which they are called. Both men showed me sheets of "anchored," or traditional, tattoo patterns from which women choose, a limited number of the same basic style, mostly geometric or floral designs.[26] One tattooer, however, showed me a separate sheet of "unanchored," what he identified as "modern," designs that he takes with him when he's not busy and sits outside one of Raipur's modern shopping malls. He asserted that many "modern" young people choose to get tattooed by him because his prices are much cheaper than those of the tattoo parlor inside the mall.

In Odiya communities of eastern Chhattisgarh, one common design tattooed on the inner forearm is identified as the footprint of the goddess Lakshmi (although visually I could not decipher footprints in the design) (figure 1.7). Chhattisgarhi Gond women often have single dots

---

26. Gell writes that many traditional tattoo designs he observed in India were the same designs used in *kolams*. These tattoos, he argues, defend "not the threshold of the house [as do kolams], but the skin, the threshold of the body" (1998, 86).

on their chins or foreheads. Their inner forearms may be tattooed with geometric designs made of dots or small triangles, and they may have an ankle-bracelet form tattooed around the edges of their feet. More rarely these days they may have necklaces tattooed on their upper chests. Some women, more recently, have the names of their husbands or their own name and that of a *saheli* (female ritual friend) tattooed on their inner forearms. Several times when I have asked a Gond woman the name of her husband, she has shown me his name tattooed on her forearm (although she may not be literate and thus unable to read the name herself). Telugu designs are often floral, whereas Odiya women's foot designs are a series of triangles edging the foot. Some younger women are taking more liberties in tattoo designs, such as one ninth-grade-educated woman I met working on house construction, who proudly showed me her inner-arm tattoos: a heart surrounding the Hindi word "Papa" and an arrow going through it and the phrase praising the goddess, "Jai Ma Durga [victory to the goddess Durga]."

Elders with whom I discussed some of these new-fashioned, self-choice designs did not approve; one commented, "How will anyone know who she is [if a girl simply chooses any design she wants]?" Here, "who she is" refers both to her virtue as a woman and her caste identity. While an ethnographer may identify certain communities by particular tattoo designs, my female interlocutors rarely spoke of tattoos as creating ethnic identity or as being exclusionary. They spoke inclusively: we Odiya [or Gond, etc.] women tattoo in such-and-such a way. More important than marking ethnic identity, tattooing was important for creating proper womanhood. Like other ornaments, tattoos make a woman auspicious and protect her. Tattoos traditionally appear on arms, feet, face, and lower calves—all exposed parts of the body that need protection from dangerous gaze—and, uniquely, they give her identity upon death. As one Chhattisgarhi woman remarked, "Only with our tattoos will god [bhagvan] know who we are." When I asked her how bhagvan will know who the un-tattooed men are, she was puzzled and simply responded, "Good question." Among Gonds and Odiya castes practicing tattooing, it would seem that male identity is assumed; male souls are anchored and after death do not need tattoos to keep them from "flying around like a chicken with its head cut off"; male bodies are less vulnerable and do not need the protection of tattoos. Through tattooing, women are, quite literally, the marked category of human.

Resisting Ornaments

Most women in contemporary India are ornamented, however minimally. Married women wear wedding pendants of some kind, bangles (gold or glass), and toe rings that signal their marital status. Some professional women simply wear one or two thin gold bangles on one arm, a thin chain or small pendant around their necks, and earrings; many college professors I have met wear "ethnic" silver jewelry associated with a region or caste not their own. Lower-class women still wear glass bangles and may buy lacquer, glass-studded, heavier bangles for festivals; and they too usually wear some kind of chain or thread around their necks. While outsiders may interpret these ornaments primarily as reflections of economic status and regional and caste identities, in traditional Indian worldviews, they create much more than these identities. Through their verbal commentary and actions around ornaments, women articulate their own theories of materiality: ornaments protect, make wearers auspicious, and create relationships.

However, Indians' relationships with ornaments are changing in some contexts. With increasing consumerism of the growing middle class in India, there is a tremendous burden on many families throughout India to provide gold ornaments, in particular, as part of a bride's dowry.[27] (India is the largest consumer of gold ornaments among world economies [D'Souza 2016].) In the context of a wedding, a family's economic and social status is visibly displayed on women's bodies through ornamentation. The lightweight tali itself is not usually a big-ticket item in this cost; its agentive significance may be fulfilled by even a tiny bit of gold that hangs on a turmeric thread. However, because of the cost of other ornaments, often causing a family to go deeply into debt, there is, among a small minority of women in contemporary India, resistance to this ornamentation.

P. V. Sreebitha, an English professor at Central University of Karnataka, reports some upper-caste feminists who are refusing to wear any gold at all on their wedding day as resistance to both the dowry system and a woman's worth being "weighed" in gold (2013). She argues, however, that

---

27. To demand a dowry of a bride's family is illegal in India according to the Dowry Prohibition Act of 1961; however, the practice is still common.

it is easy for upper-caste and upper-class women to decide not to wear gold, since they already have the social status gold creates. In contrast, the prohibition (writing specifically about the South Indian state of Kerala), until the twentieth century, of wearing gold and precious stones for castes identified in the Indian constitution as "Other Backward Classes" and Dalit castes lingers in family and community memory; for some women of these families, now that they can afford it, simply wearing gold can be an act of resistance.

Similarly, some educated women from communities that traditionally tattoo are resisting this form of ornamentation, which they perceive to be a form of branding, indicating that they are owned by someone else. In a 2017 online BBC article, Geeta Pandey describes the tradition of tattoos in her North Indian (Uttar Pradesh) family:

> For me, a decision to not get a tattoo was my version of rebellion, an assertion of my hard-fought independence. It was my way of saying: "I will not toe the line." I grew up thinking of tattoos, along with nose and ear piercings, as symbols of the subjugation of women. . . . My family told me that if I didn't have a tattoo, no one in my matrimonial home would drink water or take food offered by me. I'd be considered impure, an untouchable. . . . My father, of course, didn't need to get one because, as mum says, "he was a boy." (Pandey 2017)

However, a more common reason for the younger generations to resist getting tattooed—a resistance often supported by their tattooed mothers and grandmothers—is that this form of everyday ornamentation is considered to be "backward," not modern, and a sign of their wearer's being uneducated.[28] Given that the designs of so many gold and silver ornaments and tattoos are closely associated with caste, for some women, to resist wearing them is also an act of resisting visual caste identity. The agency of ornaments may thus be performed by their absence.

---

28. This view of tattooing is very different from those cultures in which tattoos, rather than non-tattooing, have been signs of resistance to or subversion of dominant cultures (Mifflin 2013; Schildkrout, 330–31).

Chapter 2

Saris and Turmeric

Performativity of the Material Guise

On the last days of the village goddess Gangamma's annual festival (*jatara*), celebrated in May at the height of summer heat in the South Indian pilgrimage town of Tirupati, the streets leading toward Gangamma's largest temple become filled with *stri veshams* (lit., female guises)—men who have taken the guise of women through wearing saris, breasts, braids, and ornaments (figure 2.1). While for onlookers outside the tradition, particularly as reported in the press, these stri veshams are the most notorious feature of the jatara, there are also other forms of guising connected with Gangamma traditions. Over the weeklong festival, men of a particular weaving-caste family take on a series of ten guises of Gangamma, embodying her primary narrative (in which she herself takes disguises). These *veshams* transform the men into the goddess herself, who then walks through the streets of old Tirupati, where she is worshiped by female householders at the doorways of their homes. Women who participate in the jatara also identified the turmeric powder or paste applied to the dark stone face of the goddess and the faces of some of her female worshipers as vesham. Placing stri vesham within this wider repertoire of practices surfaces the material agency of all vesham forms, which transform those who take these guises.

Scholars of dress and fashion such as Joanne Eicher often distinguish everyday clothing from specialized, periodic dress (such as stri vesham) that

Figure 2.1. Gangamma Jatara *stri vesham*. Photo by the author.

one might call costume or masquerade (2010, 151–52). Folklorist Pravina Shukla accepts this general distinction but argues that the performance identity created by costume is an intensification of the everyday, not distinct from it: "In wearing costume we do not become someone else; rather, we become in some context a deeper or heightened version of ourselves. Costume provides an outlet for expression of certain identity markers that do not have an outlet in ordinary life" (2015, 15). Here Shukla suggests that both costume and everyday clothing reflect preexisting social and existential identities rather than transform them. However, other studies focusing specifically on guising and masquerade raise the possibilities of transformation, arguing that masquerade creates a moment of reflexivity that raises questions of the ultimate nature of reality—of the construction, deconstruction, and/or transformation of self through concealment and revelation (Handelman 1990; Napier 1986; Tseelon 2001).

The Telugu term "vesham" makes no distinction between everyday clothing, disguise, masquerade, or costume, suggesting that all clothing and material guising has the potential to be transformative. Gangamma Jatara veshams may reflect identities of the persons or deities who wear them, but they also have the potential to transform identities and selves. This possibility is one supported by the performative approach to materiality taken in this book—the materiality of the guise *does* something.

Kaikala Gangamma Veshams

The Gangamma veshams taken by male ritual specialists from an extended family of a weavers caste, the Kaikalas, give us an indigenous cue regarding the transformative and creative power of the material vesham. Here, it is the physical clothing and ornaments of the goddess that literally transform human males into the goddess. Venkateshvarlu—a Kaikala man who regularly participates in these goddess veshams—told us that when he takes the vesham of a prince (itself a disguise that Gangamma takes in her narrative), "as soon as I hold the sword and put on the crown, full *ugram* (power) comes to me. While roaming the streets, I feel like the goddess going to war" (figure 2.2). Each day of the weeklong jatara, the Kaikala guises perambulate the streets and gullies of the oldest neighborhoods of Tirupati, their rounds becoming longer and longer as the goddess becomes more powerful with each vesham. The goddess (Kaikala men in vesham) is met at domestic doorways by female householders who anoint her feet with turmeric and vermillion powders; make offerings of coconut, flowers, camphor, and new pieces of cloth; and perform *harati* (flame offering).

A week or so before each jatara, the Kaikala matriarch pulls out an old tin trunk in which are stored the jumbled material pieces of the veshams that will create the goddess. She lays out each day's vesham, checking the condition of the ornaments, ankle bells, saris, headpieces, earrings, and other accoutrements unique to that day's vesham. The oversized papier-mâché ornaments may need a new application of gold foil, necklace clasps may need repair, saris may need to be laundered. Presentation of new handwoven saris for the most powerful veshams who appear at the end of the festival is a ritual right and responsibility (*mirasi*) of families from particular castes, and these saris are given to the Kaikalas the week before the jatara. The Kaikala women have very clear ideas about what dress and ornaments the goddess both desires and require; they are meticulous in their preparations.[1]

Adolescent boys take the initial Kaikala-worn veshams; as the goddess becomes more powerful (*ugra*) in the vesham sequence throughout the week, later veshams are taken by married men. The first year I attended the jatara (1992), a sixteen-year-old boy took the Chetti (merchant) vesham. His mother carefully applied a smooth covering of turmeric paste on his face; his grandmother adorned him with oversized, gold foil–covered earrings and headpiece, around which white jasmine flowers were circled, before she wrapped around him a white, red-bordered sari. His transformation complete, the boy goddess walked quickly (nearly running) alongside his father, with his head covered with a white cloth, to the temple of Veshalamma (lit., goddess of veshams; one of the Seven Sister village goddesses, of whom Gangamma is one). The vesham-ed goddess was not revealed to the public until she had worshiped Veshalamma and her head was uncovered; only then did she begin her perambulations of old Tirupati that gave opportunity for female householders to greet and worship the goddess, in her Chetti vesham, at their doorways.

---

1. These desires of the goddess are also widely known in communities that worship her. When I attended the jatara in 1992 and wanted to buy the goddess a sari, the shopkeeper, when he learned of the intended recipient, immediately pulled out an array of appropriate cotton saris in maroon, green, and turmeric-color hues, with gold threads decorating the borders. Another year, when I asked the Kaikala matriarch what kind of sari I should buy the goddess, she made very clear that for this particular occasion I should gift a green silk sari with a gold border.

This sixteen-year-old boy's father, Venkateshvarlu, called the Kaikala veshams Gangamma's "festival forms" (*utsava murtis*), similar to the small brass forms of deities taken out in temple festival processions—an assertion that the veshams are indeed the goddess. Like utsava murtis, the Kaikala Gangamma veshams make the goddess present and accessible outside of her shrines and temples. Significantly, the transformed Kaikala males are not imitatively female; their ornaments are oversized and not "real" gold, and their gait and gestures remain culturally "male" as they stride purposefully down Tirupati's gullies. This is in stark contrast to stri vesham taken by male dancers in Kuchipudi classical dance, where male dancers try to approximate, but sometimes exaggerate, female gait, gesture, and voice while performing female roles (Kamath 2019).

The Kaikala veshams not only become the goddess, but those of the first four days also materially reenact her primary narrative.[2] Oral traditions tell the story of a pubescent human girl who reveals herself as the goddess. Gangamma was found as a baby in a dry rice field by her adoptive Reddy-caste family, who had no idea that she was the goddess. As a pubescent girl, Gangamma is spotted drying her hair on her rooftop by a local chieftain (*palegadu*), known for sexually exploiting beautiful young women in his domain. He demands Gangamma's hand in marriage. Knowing the reputation of the palegadu, her father is, of course, reluctant to agree and becomes (quite literally) sick with worry. But the young Gangamma urges him to agree to the palegadu's demand, saying she will take care of herself. As the couple—Gangamma and the palegadu—is rounding the sacred fire to solemnize the marriage, Gangamma turns around to show her true form (*vishvarupam*; the goddess now without the guise of the human body) to the palegadu, as a goddess who "stretches from earth to sky." Fearful for his very life, the palegadu jumps off the wedding stage and runs to hide from the excessively powerful (ugra) goddess. Gangamma chases him, taking a series of disguises (veshams), so that he will not see her before she sees him. Ultimately, in the disguise of a prince, she beheads him.

In the narrative, the human body itself serves as a material vesham for the goddess, disguising her true divine identity; in her search for the palegadu, she also takes a series of veshams to disguise that body. Each

---

2. For further analysis of the vesham sequence, see Handelman 1995.

Figure 2.2. Kaikala *dora* (prince) *vesham* with Chakali minister *vesham*. Photo by the author.

day of the jatara, a different Kaikala man puts on one of these disguises: mendicant, snake charmer, milkmaid, merchant, or sweeper. Finally, in the princely (*dora*) vesham (figure 2.2), Gangamma enacts the beheading of the palegadu. These narrative veshams conceal Gangamma's identity as goddess, but they also reveal the range of left-hand (non-landowning) castes among whom she lives and who serve her.³ Thereafter, over the last

---

3. These double guises, before Gangamma fully reveals herself, are accompanied by a guised Chakali (washer [laundering] caste) male. The paired veshams are said to be the two Gangamma sisters, with the Kaikalas taking the guise of the elder sister and Chakalis taking the guise of the younger sister. (The Chakali vesham accompanying the dora is the dora's minister.) After the dora beheads the palegadu, the Chakali vesham is dropped. Like the Kaikalas, the Chakali families consider Gangamma to be a daughter of their caste. However, the Chakali veshams are performatively secondary to those taken by the Kaikalas. One Chakali twenty-something grandson complained,

three days of the jatara and her last three veshams, Gangamma drops her disguise and reveals her goddess identity.

The sequence of veshams of the first four days are double veshams: through vesham men become the goddess, who herself has taken disguising veshams. The last three Kaikala Gangamma veshams step beyond the narrative and are single guises: Kaikala men in vesham who are simply the goddess. These three are the most powerful forms of the goddess: the *matangi*, who is consistently identified as too powerful (ugra) to bear for long; the split form of the *sunnapukundalu*, or lime pots (lime is believed to be a cooling substance); and finally the *perantalu*, or auspicious woman/goddess. The matangi's ugram is both created and reflected, in part, by the excessive *kumkum* that she is offered by householders, which she subsequently distributes to them from a pouch made by her sari. By midday her hands are dark red and her white-and-red-checked sari is similarly deeply stained. Gangamma's ugram, fully manifest in the matangi, is materially modulated in her subsequent form, the sunnapukundalu, which is split between two human bodies. Venkateshvarlu explained that this vesham assures worshipers that the goddess will not stay so excessively ugra as to become the illnesses against which she has come to protect.

The lengthy preparation of the sunnapukundalu veshams is the only guising creation that takes place in a temple courtyard rather than in the Kaikala home and the only one whose transformation is witnessed by non–family members. The two men chosen to take this vesham grow their hair out in advance so that it is long enough for a few strands to be pulled through a hole at the bottom of clay pots smeared with white lime while still attached to their heads. The hair shank is twisted around and anchored with a small stick that sits at the bottom of the pot. A bamboo frame is attached to the pots, around which strands of jasmine flowers are wound, visually creating a temple structure atop each man's head. As the sunnapukundalu, the goddess is again accessible to her worshipers, and her courtyard is filled with women who have come to witness her material creation.

During the close to one-and-a-half-hour preparation of the sunnapukundalu, Pambala-caste epic singers and drummers perform one of Gangamma's narratives, with the goddess herself as their primary audience.

"We don't get much [respect, from the Kaikalas], but our grandmother is insistent that we take the veshams. . . . [saying]: This is god's work [*daivam karyam*], not something we do for our family [for family respect]."

The story they sing is of Adi Para Shakti, the primordial goddess who ultimately divides into thousands of *gramadevatas*, of whom Gangamma is one. It is as if Gangamma needs to be reminded of her fullest power (shakti, ugram) even as that power is being modulated so that humans can bear to interact with her. And female members of the audience do interact with her, thronging to get the sunnapukundalus' blessings once their vesham is complete (figure 2.3). The veshams then begin their per-ambulations around Tirupati to receive worship of householders; of all the veshams, theirs is the widest spatial circuit in the *uru*, taking up to forty-eight hours.

Males taking stri vesham is common in many Indian ritual and performance contexts: male actors or dancers take female roles through stri vesham in classical dance and village drama performance genres in which women did not (and often still do not) traditionally perform. Baby boys are often dressed in girls' clothing in order to deflect the evil eye from the preferred male child or simply for the enjoyment of "beautifying" infant or toddler sons, as several mothers have told me. In other

Figure 2.3. *Sunnapukundalu* (lime pot) *vesham*. Photo by the author.

contexts, male ritual specialists become the goddess through possession, when they sometimes don the stri vesham of the goddess. Because of their prevalence, occurrences of stri vesham in Indian performance and ritual contexts—like Gangamma Jatara—are not particularly noteworthy for Indian audiences and are, as Harshita Kamath has argued (2019), less "disruptive" to normative gender roles than, for example, the American drag impersonation analyzed by Judith Butler (1990).[4] No one—including the pilgrims who throng Tirupati's main bazaar, bus stand, and train station on their way to or from visiting the famous pilgrimage temple of the god Venkateshvara—pays particular attention to the goddess as she strides down the street, unless they are participating in the jatara and waiting for Gangamma to come to their doorways.

While the Kaikala veshams are worshiped as the goddess, performatively—with their male bodies quite visible—they are also men who have *become* the goddess. This ambiguous identity is performed midday during the matangi's perambulations when she returns to the Kaikala residence for a particularly powerful ritual before resting for a short while. She first sits facing material images of herself and her brother, Potu Raju, that have been set up in the small Kaikala courtyard for the duration of the jatara (figure 2.4). Slowly she begins to stamp her belled feet, moving faster and faster until she is possessed—by still another form of herself. To cool down Gangamma (to dissipate the power of her possession), her tongue is pierced by a tiny silver trident; gradually her stamping slows and she slumps over.

The day I witnessed this ritual and its aftermath, after their possession was cooled, the exhausted matangi was walked to an interior room of the house where the vesham-ed man's wife took off their heavy flower garlands, loosened the goddess/husband's sari a bit, brought him water to drink, and hand-fed him some cooling curd rice. His curious toddler begged to sit on her father's lap. Simply putting on Gangamma's vesham transforms the Kaikala men into the goddess. However, this image of the utterly exhausted matangi, whose high energy on the streets was now totally dissipated, without flowers but still wearing parts of her vesham

---

4. Kamath (2019, particularly chapter 2) demonstrates ways in which stri vesham in the dance tradition of Kuchipudi village actually creates and enables hegemonic normative Brahmin masculinity rather than being a subversive tradition.

Figure 2.4. *Matangi vesham*. Photo by the author.

(sari and ornaments), raises the question of whether the matangi at rest is the goddess or a human male (figure 2.5); performatively, they seem to be both. When I tried to elicit from Kaikala family members how they experience Gangamma's veshams—when a wife worships her husband as

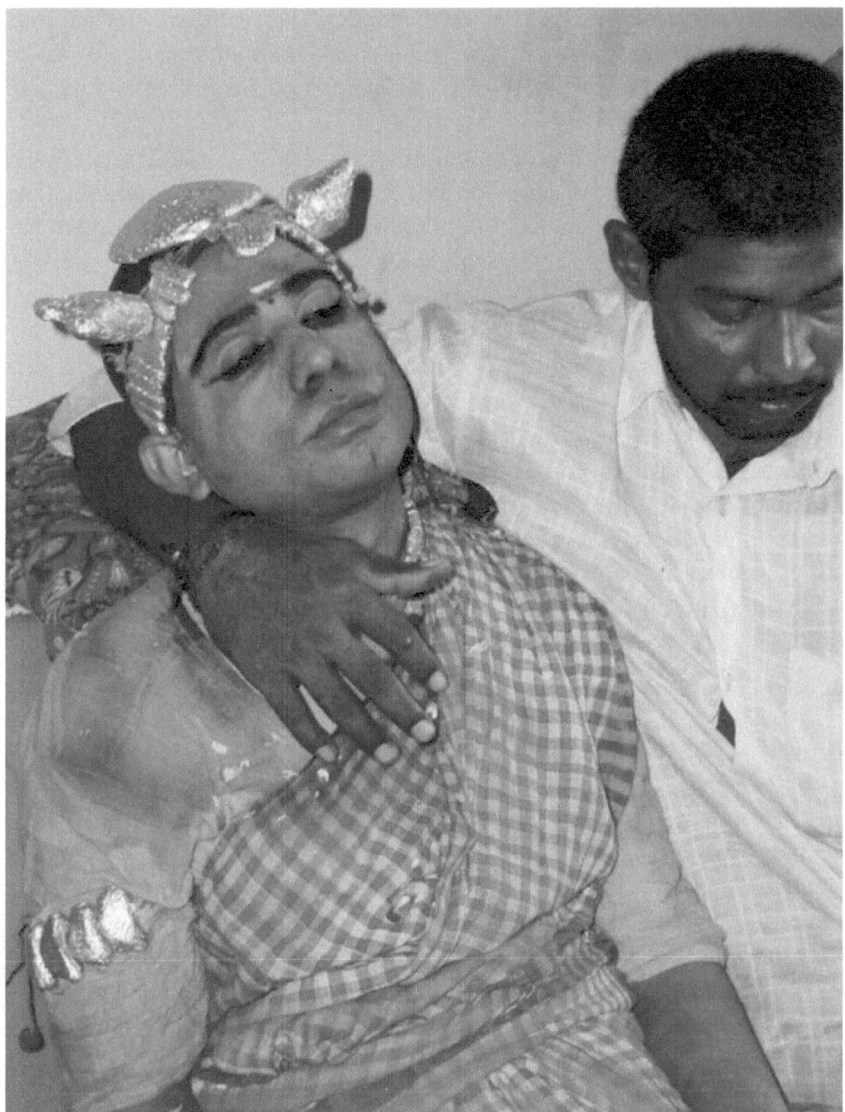

Figure 2.5. *Matangi* at rest. Photo by the author.

the goddess or a toddler sits on the lap of her vesham-ed father—they answered only, "She is Gangamma." Surely the experience is interiorized by Kaikala wives and daughters, sons, husbands, and uncles at a nonverbal, bodily, sensory level that leaves in their imaginations and everyday lives traces of the fluidity of vesham, body, gender, and identity. After an hour of rest, the matangi's garlands were put back on, and she strode out of the house to complete her rounds of Tirupati, again full of energy and fully the goddess.

Through both indigenous commentary and performative analyses, we learn that Kaikala veshams do not simply represent the goddess; they *create* Gangamma and make her tangibly present to the uru outside of her temples and shrines. Women who meet the goddess at the doorways of their homes and apply *pasupu-kumkum* to her feet worship the vesham-ed Kaikala men *as* the goddess, not *as if* they were the goddess. While the goddess possesses some of her worshipers in other contexts, the Kaikala men do not become the goddess through possession but through vesham. Remember Venkateshvarlu's assertion that as soon as he holds the sword and wears the crown, "full ugram comes to me." That the Kaikala veshams literally transform the male into the goddess—and this is readily accepted by jatara participants and most Tirupati residents—suggests the transformative power of vesham in other Gangamma contexts, such as that of laymen taking on stri vesham during the jatara and the turmeric vesham applied to the faces of both Gangamma and her female worshipers.

Lay Stri Veshams

While laymen (that is, non-Kaikalas) who take on stri vesham (saris, female ornaments, breasts, and braids) do not become the goddess or women (they are always identified as stri veshams, not women), their veshams nevertheless transform the men wearing them. However, into who or what these men are transformed is not as explicit as in the case of the Kaikala veshams that create the goddess. I look to broader jatara narrative, ritual, and vesham repertoires for clues of the effects (agency) of stri veshams on the laymen who wear them.

Lay men (or more often their mothers on their behalf) initially take stri vesham to fulfill a vow made to the goddess when they have experienced a childhood illness with which the goddess Gangamma is closely associated. Mothers vow to Gangamma that if their sons recover from their illness, their sons will take stri vesham at least once during the jatara. Other adult males take stri vesham vows later in life for their physical health or educational and business opportunities. Many men take stri vesham only once in their lifetimes; however, some men continue the practice year after year, long after the vow has been fulfilled. Some men are dressed in everyday cotton saris; others are draped in silk or synthetic saris. In earlier days, sari-ed men of left-hand artisan castes wore their saris over their right shoulders—as women of these castes used to do and as pictured in the photograph of an elderly mother with her vesham-ed son (figure 2.6). Today, most men wear their saris in what has become the "standard" style, draped over their left shoulders. In the early days of the jatara, most vesham-ed men and boys who come to Gangamma's biggest temple have taken vesham for ritual reasons. Many of these veshams self-identify as the matangi (taking her vesham), covering their faces with turmeric paste, sandalwood powder, or white ash and wearing

Figure 2.6. Lay *stri vesham* with mother. Photo by the author.

a crown of jasmine flowers, ritual materials dropped by those men who take vesham more "for fun."

The individual male body performing stri vesham—whether it be an elderly male, a young man, or a child—can be considered part of the vesham. I picked up this idea from a female jatara participant who used the word *avatara* (lit., descent; used to identify deities who take form on earth) when speaking of jatara veshams. Seeing my quizzical look, she explained, "You know, Gangamma takes avatara and humans take vesham," equating the two words. Several Gangamma narratives recount the goddess taking a human body as a disguising vesham. Recall that she took the form of a human female baby in the palegadu narrative above, a baby found and raised by a Reddy family that was unaware of her divinity until she showed her vishvarupam as she rounded the fire with the palegadu during her wedding rituals. Another story tells of members of a wedding party traveling by foot when they came across an old woman walking by herself on the side of the road. The women of the wedding party invited her to join them, saying it wasn't right for an elder to be traveling by herself. After stopping to camp for the night, one of the younger women offered to groom the old woman, checking for and picking out the lice from her hair. When the younger woman began to part the elder's hair, she saw on the old woman's scalp the thousand eyes of the goddess and only then recognized her as Gangamma.

Hindu mythology is replete with examples of deities taking a human body guise. Sometimes the human vesham disguises the deity, and other times it enables the deity to become accessible to the humans who would not be able to bear revelation of the god or goddess in their "true" form. In one story, Shiva takes on the vesham of a mendicant to test the loyalty of his devotee, demanding that the devotee make a curry from the body of his own son. After the devotee complies and the curry is served to the god, Shiva reveals himself and miraculously brings the son back to life (Shulman 1993). In the *Bhagavad Gita*, the warrior Arjuna asks Krishna in the guise of his charioteer to show him who he truly is. Krishna reluctantly complies, knowing that Arjuna will not be able to sustain this vision. As the god predicted, Arjuna cannot bear this vision and begs Krishna to return to the form he knows as his charioteer (*Gita* 11:41–46 [Patton 2008, 135–38]). Wendy Doniger suggests that god masquerades as a mortal "to make it possible for us to gaze upon him; he presents us with a shaded lens through which we can view his solar splendor without being blinded" (1980, 69). Understanding the human bodies inhabited by Gangamma and other deities as vesham raises questions of all human bodies and the identities they perform and create.

Part of the ritual fulfillment of a stri vesham vow is display—not only for men to put on a sari but also *to be seen* in a sari, both by the goddess and other festival participants. On the last days of the festival, Tirupati streets become filled with stri veshams whose visual, material, performative effect helps to create a "world become female." Some of these lay veshams try to imitate female body language (but without the nuanced training, for example, of Kuchipudi dancers performing stri vesham), usually exaggerating the swing of their hips or manipulations of their sari ends. Others, like the Kaikala veshams, make no effort at imitation of female body language. While on the first days most stri veshams are accompanied by their mothers or wives, by the last day of the jatara, many men in stri vesham come to the temple and linger on Tirupati's streets in boisterous groups (whose culturally male behavior is often enhanced by alcohol). For these men, vesham seems to take a role of Butlerian masquerade and parody rather than in fulfillment of a vow—what is identified by celebrants as "for fun only." That is, they seem to be self-consciously and with great fun breaking/bending gendered roles and identities. One year I met two men in stri vesham riding motorcycles and stuck in traffic. When I asked whether their mothers had taken a vow on their behalf that they were now fulfilling, they laughed and said no, they were Muslims. They were taking vesham "for fun only." But these parodic veshams are framed by a performance repertoire that includes the Kaikala veshams and stri veshams taken as part of vows, leaving open the possibility of their transformative agency even if the human intention behind them is only fun. This parodic performance of stri vesham constitutes the dominant representation of the festival in the press, whose members write from urban, middle-class, and dominant-caste perspectives on gender and ritual and who decontextualize the practice of stri vesham from Gangamma narrative, ritual, and vesham repertoires.

I asked several jatara participants why it is, for this particular festival, that vows of stri vesham, rather than other kinds of vows, are made to the goddess. One sari-ed man speculated that during the festival, when the goddess is most ugra, "We should not appear before her as men." Another sari-ed man responded, "After all, she's just beheaded a man [the palegadu]." Significantly, lay stri veshams appear on Tirupati's streets in greatest numbers only after the goddess in her princely vesham has ritually beheaded the antagonist of Gangamma's primary narrative, the sexually aggressive palegadu.

The Gangamma narrative repertoire includes another story about the transformation—but, in this case, not death—of men/masculinity that gives us another clue as to what stri vesham may create. In this story, Gangamma in her original form as Adi Para Shakti (lit., primordial goddess) was all alone in the universe. When she reached puberty, she experienced sexual desire and created the three gods—Brahma, Vishnu, and Shiva—one by one, in hopes that he would fulfill her desire. The first word out of the mouths of Brahma and Vishnu was *amma* (mother), which precluded their becoming sexual partners. But the first word out of Shiva's mouth was *eme*, a Telugu pronoun that husbands use to address their wives; he was what one performer called a "candidate" to fulfill the goddess's desire. Recognizing and fearing her superiority, Shiva demanded that Adi Para Shakti give him some of her shakti in the form of her third eye and trident—another example of the agency of materiality, the eye and trident being material forms of her shakti. The goddess thought to herself that only a relationship between equals would be satisfying, and she agreed to give some of her excessive shakti to Shiva. However, Shiva recanted on his end of the deal, thinking that, with the power of the goddess's eye and trident, he now had the upper hand. In her fury at being betrayed, Adi Para Shakti changed the three gods she had created into women—specifically, female servants who massaged her limbs. But then she realized that an all-female world is not *dharmic*—not according to the natural order—and she changed them back into men. But the gods (and their arrogant masculinity) were transformed, now accepting the superiority of the goddess. They agreed to marry her but only if she divided herself into their three consorts (Sarasvati, Lakshmi, Parvati) and 360 (unmarried) village goddesses, so they could "bear her." Both narratively and visually or materially (while not always "in fact," on the ground),[5] aggressive masculinity is transformed: through the narrative destruction

---

5. Many of my middle-class female friends were not willing to go with me on the last morning of the festival to witness the dismantling of the *ugra mukhis* (large clay heads of the goddess that are said to have a particularly powerful gaze), saying they were uncomfortable in the mostly male crowds and feared encounters with increasingly aggressive (often drunk) groups of sari-ed men.

of the threatening palegadu, the narrative transformation of gods into women and back into males, and the ritual proliferation of material stri veshams on the streets of Tirupati.

Male Experience of Stri Vesham

Several male acquaintances in Tirupati remembered taking stri vesham as young boys, and some showed me photographs of their sari-ed selves during earlier jataras. One friend recounted that he had taken stri vesham only once, when he was fourteen years old, "for fun only" and not part of a vow. But then, significantly, he added, "I wanted to see what it would feel like to be a woman. My mother felt very happy to see me as a female, a girl. She said, 'Oh, my lovely daughter.' I wanted to see how I would look as a woman. I felt shy. I felt everything differently in stri vesham." But most of the men I spoke with were surprisingly (from my perspective) unreflective/reflexive about it—perhaps in part because I didn't ask the right questions or because of my own gender or American identity, but perhaps also because stri vesham is an embodied experience about which they had had no need to be verbally articulate.

I heard a more direct comment about male experience of stri vesham when, rather serendipitously, I met a man who had taken stri vesham during Gangamma Jatara every year for thirty-five years. My fieldwork associate and I had stopped at Hathi Ramji Matham (the religious institution that used to administer the Tirumala temple of Shri Venkateshvara) to ask why the *matham* was one of the three sites where, during her perambulations, the matangi's tongue was pierced with a tiny silver trident. Having been directed by a sadhu sitting on the veranda into a large office, at the first desk we were warmly greeted by a Brahmin man whom we came to know as Srinivasan. He answered our questions about the tongue piercing rather cryptically and then surprised us by saying, in English, "Madam, you would be interested to know that I've taken stri vesham every year for thirty-five years" (figure 2.7). Prior to this, I had assumed that Brahmins did not participate in the jatara, except perhaps by sending both vegetarian and nonvegetarian offerings to the goddess through the hands of a non-Brahmin servant. But now, here was a Brahmin male who spoke of taking stri vesham as something quite ordinary, not exceptional for his caste.

Figure 2.7. Photograph of Srinivasan *stri vesham*. Photo by the author.

Srinivasan explained that when he had been a sickly child, his mother had made a vow to Gangamma that if he regained full strength and health, he would take stri vesham during her jatara. At the urging of his grandmother, however, he said he had kept up the tradition for many years following fulfillment of the initial vow. He said his grandmother had told him again (reported in English), "Taking vesham, just once a year, you can get a corner on women's shakti." The use of the term "corner" suggests that stri vesham has the potential to give men just a bit of the experience of being female or access to female shakti. Or if we accept that guising not only disguises and creates but also reveals, then one may speculate that stri vesham reveals the potential of masculinity to include a feminine "corner."[6]

Although taking stri vesham during the jatara may give men access to women's power once a year, photographs commemorate that experience outside of the ritual context. When I went to Srinivasan's for dinner one night after our initial conversation, he showed me a family photo album that held several professionally taken photographs of himself in stri vesham. He explained that he had first taken the guise at about the age of eight, initially wearing a half-sari (a style worn by South Indian young girls); as he grew up, the vesham changed into a full sari. His mother and, after marriage, his wife had carefully chosen his sari, ornaments, and sometimes a fashionable purse. When he was young, he used to go around in stri vesham with his friends: "We would dance. If I didn't dance, they would pinch me. Of course, it's not necessary to dance, but that was for fun only." Srinivasan's two adult sons, who have never taken stri vesham, looked on in some amusement.

Representing another educational, caste, and class level, a tea stall owner, Venkat, answered my question about whether he had ever taken stri vesham by proudly pulling out from under the greasy counter a photograph preserved in a dusty plastic sleeve. In the photograph, he is dressed in an aqua, red-bordered silk sari, posing with two male friends (one also in stri vesham). Venkat gave little verbal commentary to that photographed experience except to say he had taken this vesham several years ago in fulfillment of a vow; however, his smile suggested a memory of pleasure and some pride. That he kept the photograph of his stri vesham close at hand suggests its importance to him.

Many sari-ed, ornamented men, like Srinivasan and Venkat, go to photography studios and pose for formal portraits of their stri veshams

---

6. Some earlier readers of this chapter have suggested that "to get a corner" may mean men who wear stri vesham will gain a measure of control, domination, or advantage over women's shakti, as in the English phrase "cornering the (financial) market." However, placing this grandmother's comment in the context of Gangamma traditions that are female centered, in which the goddess has beheaded an aggressive male, and in which some men are afraid to come before the goddess as men, I do not think this is the meaning of "corner" here. I am also not aware of an Indian-language phrase that idiomatically uses "corner" as advantage or control.

or document their veshams on cell phones. These photographs are still another example of the performativity of materiality in the Gangamma repertoire. Stri veshams are not iterative performances on the male body that "naturalize" and stabilize gender (Butler 2008); rather, their performance is only temporary and periodic (sometimes only once in a lifetime). However, their preservation through photography makes tangible and keeps accessible the memory of that experience and helps to keep open the possibilities for the transformative "work" of the vesham.

In *The Coming of Photography in India* (2008), Christopher Pinney argues that photography is more than simply an index (a "transfer of the real"). Rather, it is an agent that creates, that suggests possibility and impossibility, and that may have "unpredictable consequences" (5), as do all material acts. Pinney suggests that "photographs become 'image acts' which, like J. L. Austin's 'speech acts,' are 'performatives': *in the act of enunciation they do not simply describe the world: they change it*" (145; my emphasis). Photography records whatever appears in front of the camera without distinguishing whether the recorded image has been achieved or is aspirational (137–38). In Tirupati photography studios, vesham-ed men stand in front of generic nature scenes or plain backdrops that give few clues of the contexts in which they live their everyday lives—their domestic or occupational contexts—thus obscuring distinctions of class and caste. The resulting photographs record in a single image the performance of both gender and class, which may be realized or (in Pinney's term) subjunctive, achieved or aspired to.

The veshams that laymen wear in these photographs—silk or polyester saris, pearled or gold-plated jewelry—perform middle-class identity. It is unlikely, for example, that the elder male I photographed dressed in an everyday cotton sari and blouse with ash smeared on his face, without the adornment of costume jewelry, would choose to pose for a professional photographer. Turning to Srinivasan and Venkat, both borrowed saris from females in their own families. However, what the silk or high-quality polyester sari signifies for each family is quite different. Taking into account the class backgrounds of the men who took these stri veshams, Srinivasan's portrait records an achieved middle-class identity, whereas that of Venkat records middle-class aspiration. Photographs of both men record subjunctive gender possibilities.

The stri veshams in professional photographs make permanent a temporary female guise, but the photographed stri vesham is not wholly imitative and the male body is never totally disguised, as it interrupts the female vesham through facial features and body stance. Remember the injunction of Srinivasan's grandmother that he should experience only a "corner"—not the full measure of—female shakti. Lay veshams do not create and are rarely mistaken or viewed by others as fully actualized females. They are seen and experienced, both during their perambulations on Tirupati's streets and in photographs, as veshams, not women. Indigenously understood, while stri vesham "plays with" gender and may raise questions of the nature of masculinity, it does not question its very existence on either a social or an existential level. A subjunctive potential is created. Stri vesham has the potential to change its male actor—not by questioning his gender or transforming him into a female but by transforming the kind of masculinity he performs and embodies, one that embraces at least a "corner" of female shakti.

While writing my book about Gangamma, *When the World Becomes Female* (2013), I realized that I did not know Venkat's caste. I asked a local male anthropologist if he would be willing to find the tea stall and ask Venkat a little more about his background and caste. The anthropologist heard the following: Venkat was a thirty-six-year-old Mudaliar-caste migrant from Tamil Nadu. Venkat reported that he had taken stri vesham four times and had planned to do so again that year (2011). The first time, in 1998 (he would have been about twenty-three years old), he said he took vesham for "fun," joining other friends who were taking vesham. Later, however, when he was experiencing ill health and difficulties in his business, he decided to take the vow to Gangamma of stri vesham. He attributed his return to health and a better economic situation to the resulting intervention of the goddess.

Venkat told the male anthropologist that when he took vesham, he not only wore female garments and jewelry but also tried to enact "the gaze and seductive gait of a woman," approximating a male perception of the body language of a flirtatious woman. He described his male friends' reactions to this stri vesham: they "pulled his hand, kissed him, embraced him, fondled his [artificial] breasts, and pinched his buttocks." His friends took liberties with his stri vesham that they would not have likely felt free to do openly, in public, with female friends. Venkat had started taking stri vesham as a kind of fun masquerade; however, when he was in need, he decided to take the serious vow of stri vesham. He has realized the power of the goddess; at the same time, in stri vesham he enjoys a certain freedom and abandonment of traditional, gendered mores of interactions between men and women in public contexts. We do not know from this narrative or photographs how men may be transformed by stri vesham once they take the guise off. We have to look elsewhere in Gangamma vesham, ritual, and narrative repertoires for clues about the agency of female guising, including the possibility of transformation of aggressive masculinity.

Female Turmeric Veshams

Although rarely mentioned in conversations and press reports about Gangamma traditions, the practice of female turmeric (pasupu) guising—daily or weekly application of turmeric powder on the faces of both the goddess and her female devotees—is much more common than is stri vesham. I was led to identify turmeric as a form of vesham when, in my attempts to verify that women did not take Kaikala Gangamma veshams or stri veshams, one of the women gathered in Gangamma's temple courtyard asserted, "But we do! We wear turmeric every Tuesday and Friday [days special to the goddess], don't we?" In subsequent conversations, Gangamma worshipers were often explicit about what this pasupu "does," thus providing commentary about the agency of other forms of guising in the jatara vesham repertoire.

Gangamma and her gramadevata sisters are often simply stone heads without bodies, whose faces are characteristically covered with turmeric (figure 2.8). The turmeric application is more than superficial; it acts, helping to create the goddesses so closely associated with the substance. In writing about another Telugu gramadevata, David Shulman characterizes her turmeric application as constituting the deity, intensifying her presence, and deepening her self-awareness (2005, 56). But pasupu as vesham goes beyond creating the goddess; it simultaneously hides and reveals her features and transforms her ugra nature. Gangamma's weekly *abhishekam* (ritual anointing with milk and water) in her two largest Tirupati temples, on Friday mornings, is a powerful moment, as her turmeric vesham runs off and her dark, haunting face is revealed. Only now are the goddess's fangs visible, fangs that indicate her demanding, excessive, powerful ugra nature. Her turmeric vesham keeps devotees from regularly coming face-to-face with Gangamma's unguised self, as if this fanged form may be too much to bear on a daily basis (much like the Kaikala Gangamma vesham of the matangi).

Figure 2.8. Gangamma's turmeric *vesham*. Photo by the author.

Venkateshvarlu, who along with his mother serves Gangamma at her Tallapaka temple, has the responsibility to perform Gangamma's weekly abhishekam. After pouring gallons of milk and water over her image until there are no traces of pasupu left, he performs harati and then carefully reapplies her turmeric mask, flicking the dry powder on the wet surface of her face and gently smoothing it over with a feather.

When I asked him the significance of the turmeric, Venkateshvarlu's immediate response was that it made Gangamma *shanta* (tranquil) and a *muttaiduva* (auspicious woman, a term usually associated with married women). Gangamma's turmeric vesham *transforms* her ugra nature, not only hiding it but also making her shanta. However, the turmeric mask does not materially destroy Gangamma's powerful ugram; although hidden, her fangs are still present and their protuberance is barely visible under the turmeric. She is still ugra—as she is consistently characterized by Tirupati residents—but not *only* ugra.

Based on Venkateshvarlu's response, I had initially interpreted the turmeric application as modulating the goddess's ugra nature. But when I ventured this interpretation to the flower sellers at another Gangamma temple, they disagreed. Rather, they explained, the turmeric enabled devotees to see (reveal), quite literally, Gangamma's features, so that she could be "known." Without the pasupu, it can be difficult to distinguish the dark stone's facial features. Other female worshipers likened the turmeric to "makeup," which both beautifies and accentuates Gangamma's features. One female temple employee elaborated: "Turmeric gives beauty and radiance [*kala*; brightness] to the face. Look at this stone. If you leave it just like this, it won't look good [i.e., dry, cracked]. Only when we do alankara [ornamentation; in this case with pasupu] does she look like a muttaiduva. Married women also wear pasupu-kumkum [like the goddess]." The speaker then caught herself, saying, "No, no. Actually, she's not married." This self-correction suggests that the unmarried goddess unsettles the dominant characterization of muttaiduva as a married woman—just as her tali unsettles that ornament's association with marriage. Gangamma's turmeric masking both reveals, in letting us see her features, and conceals, hiding her ugra fangs. Materially, she transcends the traditional dichotomy of ugra and shanta (as a muttaiduva); she is both/and.

Women share the performance of turmeric vesham with the goddess. Many female devotees come to Gangamma's temples on Tuesdays and Fridays with turmeric marks on their cheeks and necks or with their entire face covered with turmeric paste. (Turmeric is also applied to women's feet in some rituals for married women, such as Varalakshmi Puja.) One explained, "We [women] are equal to the goddess . . . so we can put it [turmeric] on our faces," suggesting that men are not equal and thus should not, or perhaps do not have the right to, wear turmeric. Turmeric vesham identifies women with the goddess and materially performs their shared quality of shakti.⁷ A female sweeper at my guesthouse asserted this identification when I asked her if women were afraid of the *ugra mukhis* (oversized clay heads of the goddess constructed on the final day of the jatara), as men seemed be, who told us this form was too ugra to look at directly: "No, we're not afraid. We have shakti and she [the goddess] has shakti, so we're not afraid. But men. They don't have shakti, so they are afraid."

However, one male who consistently wears turmeric is Gangamma's brother, Potu Raju, who stands outside of his Seven Sisters' shrines as a nonanthropomorphic stone form (often a small rounded stone or a conical larger form). He is covered solidly with turmeric, over which are applied vermillion dots. This pasupu-kumkum vesham performatively feminizes him (as turmeric and vermilion are traditionally female-associated substances), materially identifying him with his similarly turmeric and vermilion vesham-ed sisters. He retains his name, Potu Raju (lit., "king of male-ness"), but arguably he is transformed into a different kind of male in the presence of his powerful sisters and by the application of turmeric. Venkateshvarlu identified the turmeric-covered stone facing Gangamma at the Tallapaka temple as both Potu Raju and *shaktiswarupini* (lit., one whose form is shakti; female noun). Potu Raju's female-associated turmeric vesham and appellations (Potu Raju and shaktiswarupini) give us another clue as to how stri vesham has the potential to feminize sari-wearing men, even as they remain men.

Some women take the turmeric vesham daily, along with pronounced, large *bottus* (vermilion forehead markings) and sometimes matted hair. This "excessive" vesham, in relationship to the smaller bottus and restrained, oiled hair most women wear every day, identifies a greater than "normal" religiosity and service to the goddess. This group of women includes those called *matammas*, women who ritually exchange *talis* with the goddess. Thereafter, these women serve as ritual specialists to the goddess and do not traditionally marry human males. Talis are part of their matamma vesham; the tali is particularly significant for women who would not traditionally wear this sign of marital status, such as unmarried women and

---

7. That women appear before the goddess with turmeric vesham suggests it makes the goddess happy/content (*santosham*) to see a reflection of her own shakti identified in women through their turmeric markings—just as it makes her happy to see men-become-female in stri vesham during her jatara.

widows. This was the case for the matamma Pujaramma, who had married a man but continued to wear a tali after she was widowed. In her case, matted hair was also part of her vesham. She told me that she had tried to cut off her matted locks numerous times because of the problems it caused her by "hiding lice." She narrated that she and Gangamma argued back and forth every time she cut off her matted hair, but the goddess always won and the matted hair always grew back. In one conversation, Pujaramma reported a dream in which she saw her matted hair growing back in the form of a serpent's hood, a Shiva *linga* (sign of the god), and Venkateshvara's *jada* (braid). Shiva and Venkateshvara are male gods, and yet here their signs of a linga and jada indicate the presence of the goddess—a play of gender much like stri vesham. Pujaramma specifically identified her matted hair as a kind of vesham, a guise that performs her special relationship with the goddess and Gangamma's presence on/in her human female body.

The performativity of veshams taken by women contrasts significantly from that of men. "Stri vesham" literally means "female attire or guise." This is what women wear every day, and therefore it is unremarkable on a female body.[8] In the context of the jatara, "stri vesham" refers specifically to men wearing female clothing and adornment; men are, quite literally, the marked category in a world that becomes increasingly female as the jatara progresses. Women do not need to take a different vesham than what they wear every day in order to have access to the ugra Gangamma during her jatara, as do men. Similarly, the women assert, turmeric vesham does not transform them; rather, both sari and turmeric veshams recognize them for who they already are. In the same way turmeric lets us "see" the goddess, its markings on female ritual participants reminds both them and those who see them of who they are: powerful women who share the shakti of the goddess.

∽

---

8. For some women in contemporary India, saris have become a matter of both choice and debate. Many women do not begin to wear a sari regularly until they have completed their education, since to begin to wear a sari every day is an indication to her community that she is now ready for marriage. Other professional women may choose not to wear them to work as a matter of convenience. See Zare and Mohammed 2015 for discussion of a debate between two feminist poets on the patriarchal restriction of a sari or its comfort and utilitarian potential.

Female clothing and ornaments, turmeric, matted hair, and photography are all material elements of a performance repertoire of vesham in Gangamma traditions. Each element of the repertoire provides a commentary on the others. Through their juxtaposition, as well as through ritual and discursive cues, we learn that vesham transforms the deity or human who puts it on. While the transformative agency of veshams taken on by the Kaikala men is not discursively questioned or discussed, it is acted upon when women greet the vesham-ed Kaikalas at their doorways as the goddess. This material act provides commentary on the transformative possibilities of other material acts in the vesham repertoire. Similarly, Venkateshvarlu's comment that the turmeric vesham he applies to Gangamma's stone face transforms her very nature, from ugra to shanta, suggests that stri vesham performed by laymen may transform their nature. Stri veshams perform gendered possibilities that are not easily or openly recognized in the everyday social world outside of the ritual contexts. These possibilities—created by material acts of vesham—include recognition of an imaginative reality in which women are the unmarked, encompassing category in a jatara world that at its core is female, and men (or aggressive masculinity) are transformed in order to have access to and a place in that world.

Chapter 3

Material Abundance and Material Excess

Creating and Serving Two Goddesses

Flowers, fruits, grains, turmeric and vermilion powders, oil lamps, human bodies, and other materialities proliferate across Hindu rituals,[1] including the two rituals that are at the center of this chapter: the South Indian women's domestic vow tradition of Varalakshmi Puja and the community-wide festival of Gangamma in Tirupati. In both contexts, the overflow of ritual "stuff" performs—in a J. L. Austin type of way—the very goddesses to whom the materials are offered: the always auspicious (*mangala*), wealth-giving Lakshmi and the both protective and potentially destructive Gangamma. Many ritual material items are shared across the two contexts; however, what they create is quite different, depending on their wider material repertoires and assemblages. In the case of Varalakshmi Puja, the proliferation of materiality creates abundance, whereas in Gangamma Jatara it creates excess. Analyzing the two rituals and their materialities in relationship to each other helps us understand the mangala and *ugra* goddesses who are so created.

---

1. For descriptions of innovative, outsized, elaborate ritual displays (both abundant and excessive) in contemporary Hindu temples in Bangalore, see Tulasi Srinivas's *The Cow in the Elevator: An Anthropology of Wonder* (2018). In these cases, the creative, unexpected ritual displays are indigenously identified as auspicious, but Srinivas argues that they have the potential to become destructive—of traditional aesthetics, social relations, and the environment.

Gangamma is consistently described as ugra, a term I have translated as "excess" (a further discussion of the term follows below). However, there is no single adjective consistently paired with Lakshmi. She may be *saubhagya*, she of good fortune or who brings good fortune, or mangala/shubha, auspicious. Ethnographer Leela Prasad reports that when participating in Varalakshmi Puja, she has most often heard the goddess described simply as "*kala*," beautiful and radiant (oral communication, May 2019). However, what I heard most consistently was simply "Lakshmi," without qualification—an unmarked goddess whom everyone understands to be one who is and brings wealth in all of its forms. Girl babies and brides are often called Lakshmi; ripened harvest is Lakshmi; gold is Lakshmi—all without qualifying adjectives. The goddess is on full display—female bodies, gold ornaments, grain, sweets, turmeric and vermilion, flowers, varieties of vegetables, clay pots, coins, new cloth, oil lamps—in her ritual of Varalakshmi Puja.

Varalakshmi Puja: Material Abundance

On the first Friday following the full moon of the month of Shravan (July–August), at the height of the monsoons, married women from a range of upper castes across South India and its diaspora begin to perform Varalakshmi Puja (also called Varalakshmi Vratam), the annual ritual vow (*vratam*) performed for the goddess. I was first introduced to this vratam when I was conducting fieldwork in Hyderabad in 1999. I had visited a friend, K. Vimala, across town for the day, and as we were walking down her lane, a female neighbor ran out of her house to greet us and asked us to come inside. Knowing that my friend was married, and verifying that I was too, she explained that she needed to give *tambulam* to nine auspicious married women (*sumangalis*; auspicious women) to complete her vratam.[2]

---

2. The number of requisite married participants should ideally be an uneven number: five, seven, or nine. Odd numbers in Indian traditions suggest the possibility of growth rather than completion. Recently I was counted as one of the requisite nine married women to be given tambulam when I visited the Hindu Temple of Atlanta on the first of the four Fridays of Varalakshmi Puja. As I walked into the relatively empty temple, I noticed a line of women sitting cross-legged on the floor with another woman pacing back and forth in front of them, glancing around as if trying to decide what to do. She quickly spotted me as a potential ritual participant and was visibly relieved when I confirmed that I was married. In the US, many Hindu families do not live in

Tambulam is a ritual gift of "women's things" given by a female ritual host to other sumangalis. At a minimum, it includes pasupu-kumkum, betel leaf and nuts, and a piece of fruit, but it may also include uncut sari-blouse material, a sari, glass bangles, a mirror, and other "women's things." Its gifting both performs the shared auspiciousness between sumangalis and transfers that auspiciousness between them. The neighbor asked us to sit down, brought out a saucer of turmeric paste, and applied this to our feet; she then gifted each of us tambulam to complete her ritual.

Later that evening, Vimala, her mother, and I visited several homes of close friends and relatives celebrating Varalakshmi Puja, where we were again gifted tambulam.[3] During our visits, I noticed that several younger women drew Vimala's mother aside to relate some of their sorrows and ask for advice. Almost a decade later, in 2007 Vimala invited me to go with her to her in-laws' home village to celebrate the vratam along with several other female (Velama-caste) relatives living in Hyderabad. She had initiated this city-to-village pilgrimage of sorts, thinking it would be what she called a "feminist act" to create and participate in a "women-only" ritual, and her urban cousin-sisters were game to join her. Creation of female solidarity began days before the ritual as the women who lived in several different neighborhoods phoned back and forth to coordinate who would bring what ritual supplies. While I had initially interpreted one of the vratam's primary purposes to be strengthening of a community of women, during this village celebration I saw that the requisite number of female bodies is also part of a ritual repertoire of abundance that tangibly creates the presence of the auspicious, wealth-bestowing goddess Lakshmi herself.

Early morning on the day Vimala and I went together to the village, we first stopped at a large urban vegetable market, bustling with women carefully fingering and selecting vegetables. Vimala explained that for this ritual, vratam participants would need to cook nine different kinds of vegetables, and she wanted to bring her fair share. Specifically, she was

---

neighborhoods where there are sufficient numbers of Hindu married women, so the ritual is sometimes performed in the temple, where the primary actor knows she will find the requisite number of women.

3. Many middle-class women keep a pile of saris for gifting situations such as this so that when someone unexpected shows up (such as myself on this evening), an extra sari is available. Women keep careful track of which of their friends and relatives have gifted what kinds of saris and how they themselves have reciprocated over the years.

looking for a particular kind of small wild gourd that can be found in vegetable markets only at this time of year and thus is materially associated with the ritual.[4] When we arrived late in the afternoon at the Telangana village a couple of hours away from Hyderabad, we were served tea, and the conversational chatter quickly turned to the next day's demanding schedule of cooking: what time the women would need to get up and bathe (5:00 a.m.); who would cook what; whether or not they had the requisite nine different kinds of vegetables (since so many women had brought vegetables from the city, there were more than enough—eleven varieties in all); what nine varieties of sweets (including coconut-filled triangular pastries that are a "must" for this vratam) they would make; and so on.

The center of activity on the morning of the vratam was the traditional kitchen of the family home. It was the only kitchen of the three households of the extended family hosting the vratam that still retained traditional earthen floors and walls, natural skylights providing the only light, and low, wood-burning earthen stoves (requiring women to squat in front of them to cook, although even this kitchen had one two-burner gas stove set up on a wooden table). When I commented on the simplicity and beauty of the kitchen, one of the elder women explained that this was the center of the home, a space restricted to women, whereas the more modern kitchens with tile floors and gas stoves were open to anyone, including men. By the time I came to the kitchen at about 8:00 a.m., after having been served morning tea—in which the other women did not indulge, since the vratam requires strict fasting from food and liquid until the end of the Varalakshmi *puja* (worship)—the kitchen was bustling with activity and chatter as women cut vegetables and rolled out sweet pastries to fry (figure 3.1). With only four stoves, the cooking had

---

4. For a discussion of embodied material memory, such as that carried by this wild gourd, see Seremetakis 1996. Note that the proliferation of "nines" of vegetables and sweets in Varalakshmi Puja is similar to the "tens" of the Odiya Sudasa Vrat, which also invokes and creates Lakshmi (see chapter 1). The South Indian ritual of Bommai Golu, celebrated during the autumn festival of Navaratri (Nine Nights of the Goddess), also creates and displays Lakshmi. Here, abundance is exhibited through a display and proliferation of dolls. Religion scholar Deeksha Sivakumar quotes a Golu celebrant saying, "You know they say, whatever Lakshmi has given, you have to show. This is how [you] make the boons [prosperity] come" (2018, 45).

Figure 3.1. Women cooking for Varalakshmi Puja, Jupally village, Telangana. Photo by the author.

to be well timed to complete everything before the puja would begin at 11:30 a.m.[5]

In a foyer adjacent to the kitchen, two daughters-in-law to the resident family had been charged to prepare the nonfood ritual items. The elder was decorating nine clay pots with kohl, simple lines creating eyes, nose, and mouth. When the sweet pastries had been fried, one of each kind of the nine varieties would be placed in the pots and subsequently distributed to the celebrants as *prasad* (food items having been offered to a deity). The younger daughter-in-law prepared a simple wooden cart structure that would hold the goddess (in the form of a small wet turmeric mounded form, along with her similarly created husband), seated on a stack of colorful pieces of uncut cloth to be used for sari blouses, toward which each participant had contributed. She marked the cart with pasupu-kumkum and tied small branches of mango leaves to its exterior, interspersing red oleanders (flowers favored for ritual use). A third woman joined them in the foyer to prepare nine small oil lamps made of a mixture of sugar and lentil dough. The flow of ritual preparations felt seamless, each woman knowing her small part.

Throughout the morning while the vratam participants were busy in their preparations, an elderly woman from outside the family went from woman to woman applying turmeric paste to their feet. As in Gangamma traditions, the application of turmeric on both women and the goddess performs their shared female qualities of auspiciousness and *shakti*.[6] In their study of the goddess festival of Paiditalli in Vizianagaram, coastal Andhra, Don Handelman, M. V. Krishnayya, and David Shulman comment on how application of turmeric on human women and goddesses enlivens and adds depth and texture to both classes of females:

---

5. This household was among the fortunate ones visited near the beginning of the presiding priest's ritual rounds, so fasting did not last until late afternoon as was required for households he visited much later. I didn't hear any of the vratam participants discuss the fact that they were not eating; they were fully immersed in the joyful communal cooking.

6. For analysis of similar application of turmeric to the faces of the goddess Gangamma and her female devotees, see chapter 2. In this context, turmeric application is identified as a form of guising that reveals the goddess's features, transforms her potentially destructive *ugram* to *shantam*, and performs the identification between women and goddess.

The essences of the goddess, indeed of all females, are said to be *pasupu* and *kunkum* [sic]. . . . Turmeric, though applied to the exterior of the female, to her skin, enlivens her interior life, *layering* her from within, adding depth and texture. She glows more intensely from within. . . . Her self-shining seems also to signal the *intensification* of coherence and integrity, equalities of selfness, the qualities of depth. . . . Through the essences of turmeric and vermilion, goddess and woman overlap, periodically, momentarily. (2014, 136–37)

So too, here in the context of Varalakshmi Puja, pasupu application on their feet performs women's auspicious, Lakshmi-like qualities.

The men of the family having conveniently absented themselves, the only male I saw that morning inside the house was a male Brahmin *pandit* (priest) who, at about 11:30 a.m., rushed into the home, asking whether everything was ready. It was.[7] Each woman first went to the pandit and extended her wrist, around which he tied several long pieces of red and yellow thread, variously interpreted as marking the intention of the participants, binding them to their vows, and protecting them for the duration of the ritual.[8] For close to two hours, seven married women sat in a semicircle in front of the wooden cart in which the goddess was now housed; other women, myself included, sat behind this circle. This year the chief ritual participant was the youngest woman present, who had gotten married only three months earlier; this was the first year she was eligible to participate in the vratam, now a sumangali. She was dressed in a new sequin-sparkling light-aqua sari and adorned in all of her wedding gold ornaments; the elder participants wore much simpler saris and ornaments. The pandit, sitting at the back of the room behind the women's circle, chanted Sanskrit verses and instructed the women on what to offer and when: water, pasupu-kumkum, coins, fruit, flowers, pinches of uncooked rice kernels, incense, and the dough oil lamps, now lit. The freshly swept and washed stone-tiled floor of the room was soon

---

7. Many female vratam rituals are conducted without the need for a Brahmin pandit. The presence of a pandit at many celebrations of Varalakshmi Puja indicates the middle- to high-caste status of the families that perform this particular vratam.

8. For discussion of these threads as ornaments, see chapter 1.

a riot of material color, texture, and fragrance. This ritual materiality displays and creates wealth not just in quantity but also in variety—the abundance of different kinds of vegetables, sweets, and flowers, and even all the different kinds of containers holding these ingredients (figure 3.2).

The pandit's rushed ten-minute recitation of the *vrat katha* (story of the vow) concluded the festivities, paling in comparison to the elaborate puja aspect of the ritual. He apologized that because he had many other homes to visit, he would not have time to tell the story in detail. The katha sings the praises of the virtuous, truth-telling Charumati, who was devoted to her in-laws and husband. She receives a dream in which Vishnu instructs her to perform Varalakshmi Puja every year during the month of Shravan, assuring her that if she does so, she will receive the blessings of Lakshmi in all of her forms of wealth. While the katha is a crucial element of every vratam, distinguishing it from other forms of puja, on this occasion its recitation was mechanistic and the women seemed to pay it little attention.

Before the pandit left, each ritual participant knelt down in front of him and placed at his feet a stainless-steel platter of uncooked grain, packets of lentils and spices, coins, and a banana, covering the platter

Figure 3.2. Beginning of Varalakshmi Puja (ritual ingredients contained), Jupally village, Telangana. Photo by the author.

with the end of her sari, as he blessed her. The contents of the platters were consolidated by kind (rice with rice, etc.) and put in plastic bags, which the pandit carried home with him. Returning to the goddess, the women cut apart garlands of flattened, turmeric-soaked cotton balls that had earlier been offered to Lakshmi (representing, I was told, clothing for the goddess) and tied one cotton ball to the *tali* of each participant. These cotton balls, like the threads tied to the participants' wrists earlier, were to be worn until they naturally broke and fell off the women's talis. The long ritual sequence concluded when the women went outside to circumambulate the household's *tulsi* (basil) plant (another form of the goddess), pour water at her base, and decorate her with colorful flowers. Now, close to 2:00 p.m., the women could begin to relax. A leaf plate was placed in front of each woman, seated on the floor, on which small mounds of each of the nine cooked vegetables and one of each variety of pastry were placed. This distribution of prasad was followed by a full leisurely meal, lots of conversation, and laughter.

Late in the afternoon, the participating women in the extended family assembled to visit two neighboring families who had also celebrated the vratam, to view their Varalakshmi images and to receive prasad from their rituals. In the gathering darkness, we sat out on the back veranda of one of the homes, which gave me the opportunity to ask about the ritual. Several friends in Hyderabad had earlier explained that Varalakshmi Vratam was the South Indian equivalent of the North Indian vratam of Karva Chauth. Women explicitly observe Karva Chauth for the long life of their husbands, and this was a line of questioning I had pursued throughout the day. Some women had vaguely affirmed that, yes, this was for husbands, but one frustrated woman exclaimed, "Why do you keep asking about husbands? This is about Lakshmi!" I knew she thought this should have been obvious to me, if only I would have noticed who and what was "there"—abundant materiality that did not include husbands.

Traditionally, an auspicious home—a home in which Lakshmi is present—is a home with a living husband, so I thought that while husbands may not be as explicitly referred to in Varalakshmi Puja as they are in Karva Chauth, ultimately the vratam must on some level also be about husbands. However, I learned that Lakshmi is a much broader wealth-giver. I remembered the concept of the eight Lakshmis (*ashtalakshmis*) and thought this would be a good entrée into what it meant to invite Lakshmi home. One woman after another began to list the eight forms of wealth that are Lakshmi, but no one woman came up with the full list. Putting the listings together, the eight included *dhairya*/courage Lakshmi, *dhana*/monetary wealth Lakshmi, *vijay*/victory Lakshmi, *adi*/primordial Lakshmi, *saubhagya*/auspicious Lakshmi, *santana*/child-giving Lakshmi, *vidya*/knowledge Lakshmi, and *dhanya*/grain Lakshmi.[9] One of the elder women commented, "No matter how many Lakshmis we have, what we [women] need, what is 'compulsory' is *dhairyam*. If we lose dhairya Lakshmi, we lose all Lakshmis." Now I was not quite so sure about the centrality of husbands. Lakshmi was being invited into the home as courage, knowledge, wealth, grain, victory, and ultimate reality. Out of Lakshmi's eight forms, only one implied a husband (in a traditional Indian context): santana Lakshmi, she who gives and is the wealth of progeny. In her portrayals on many lithographs (and rice bags, sari labels, etc.), Lakshmi appears alone, without a husband (although mythologically she is the wife of Vishnu), standing on a fully opened lotus with gold coins flowing out of her outstretched hands. Visually, she does not seem to "need" a husband.

Several years after I had participated in Varalakshmi Vratam in the village, I joined the matriarch and two daughters-in-law of my Tamil host family in Hyderabad (a family that does not itself celebrate Varalakshmi Puja) in the late afternoon to visit the homes of several relatives and neighbors who had performed the vratam. In one Brahmin home, instead of being given the form of a turmeric mound as she had been in the village, Lakshmi was present as a silver mask that had been passed down between generations (figure 3.3). Other householders had created Lakshmi by attaching to a coconut a beautifully painted papier-mâché face, complemented by a wig and sari (all available for sale at small local stores selling ritual materials). Few of these urban homes or apartments had a discrete room dedicated to the ritual display, as had been the case in the village. Instead, a wall of the kitchen or living room had been cleared for the goddess in all her abundance, displays that spilled into the middle of the room. In one home the vratam participants included grandmother, mother, and granddaughters, all dressed in silks and gold ornaments, looking much like they were attending a wedding—auspicious female bodies fully adorned. The participants' bodies, as well as ours—as sumangalis—performed Lakshmi's presence. We came home with fancy plastic bags of auspicious tambulam filled with packets of pasupu-kumkum,

---

9. The listing of the names of the eight Lakshmis varies by context; in Odiya contexts, the number of Lakshmis is ten.

Figure 3.3. Varalakshmi silver mask, Hyderabad. Photo by the author.

pieces of fruit, sweets, pieces of cloth for sari blouses in a wide array of colors, and a sari for each of us.

Profusion of materiality and female bodies in Varalakshmi Puja performs the very goddess of wealth (in all her forms) whom the ritual invites and serves. However, the abundance is physically and socially constrained. The vratam is traditionally a domestic ritual celebrated in a bounded space, enclosed by walls. Exceptions to the ritual's domesticity can be found in instances where the ritual is performed in urban and diasporic temples, where the space is, nevertheless, still physically bounded. One year I observed the vratam in a Hyderabadi Venkateshvara temple courtyard where lines of individual women (about thirty in all) performed the puja to their individual small brass images of Lakshmi, offering her kumkum and a few food items brought from home. The social atmosphere was constrained and quiet, very different from the excited hubbub and communal cooking of the village celebration described above.

As with other domestic rituals, the vratam is also traditionally socially constrained. The participants with whom I celebrated in the village were multigenerational members of a single extended family, and the homes they visited at the end of the day were of the same caste or caste level.[10] When I was conducting research for this chapter in Hyderabad and was looking for an urban family that performed the vratam, my friend Vimala told me that one of her Brahmin acquaintances would be celebrating and thought I could participate with her. However, when the friend learned I was not Brahmin, she expressed discomfort; she never specifically mentioned caste, but Vimala interpreted that to be the reason for her ill ease. I did not attend. Instead, I visited several homes of vratam participants with my Hyderabadi Mudaliar host family, but these families too shared upper-class and upper-caste levels (if not the same caste).

Another level of constraint is the fact that Lakshmi's beautifully decorated vratam image to whom offerings are made is singular in each home—in the village ritual I observed, a tiny mound of turmeric, and in Hyderabad, silver heads or decorated coconuts. Both the singularity and (relatively) small, even tiny, size of the image imply that this goddess will not have high ritual demands, that her rituals will be able to be sustained on a daily basis by busy householders, and that abundance will not overflow its boundaries. Once a year, through the materially elaborate vratam that both reflects and (re)creates her presence, Lakshmi is invited to come home—and stay. Whereas the next goddess, Gangamma, is invited to come and leave.

Gangamma Jatara: Material Excess

Gangamma Jatara in Tirupati begins on the fourth Tuesday after the Tamil New Year,[11] when the summer heat has reached its maximum temperatures in mid-May, sometimes as high as 115 degrees Fahrenheit, and fields are bone dry. These are dangerous days that threaten drought and illness. One can almost feel the stirring of the goddess as the days

---

10. Religion scholar Jennifer Ortegren has observed new configurations of vrat communities in the Rajasthani city of Udaipur, where upwardly mobile women who have moved from rural areas may not have family members close by, and so celebrate vrats such as Karva Chauth with neighbors who are of different castes (forthcoming). However, this social mixing is a newly emerging phenomenon when the ritual is performed in domestic contexts.

11. The timing of the jatara is based on the Tamil ritual calendar that governs the Tamil-Telugu cultural region in which the jatara is celebrated.

heat up and hot winds blow, gathering clouds that should release rains on the final morning of the jatara in Tirupati, heralding the approaching monsoons. Whereas Varalakshmi Puja is celebrated at the height of the somewhat cooler monsoon season, when the growing rice fields—a form of Lakshmi herself—are emerald green, watered by auspicious rains, the high temperatures of May are an elemental source of Gangamma's expanding, excessive presence.

Like Varalakshmi Puja, Gangamma Jatara is characterized by a proliferation of materiality, but here the overflow of materials creates excess rather than abundance. The distinction is made, in part, by the very nature of the two goddesses—Lakshmi and Gangamma—but also by the range of ritual bodies (gender, class, and caste), the spatial boundaries of a multitude of distinct rituals performed over a week, and the kinds of materials included in the rituals. Some ritual substances are shared—pasupu-kumkum, fruits, and flowers—but Gangamma Jatara includes *bali* (animal sacrifice), and this element, perhaps more than any other aspect of the jatara, shifts abundance into excess (*ugram*).

Ugram has often been translated as "anger/wrath" or "ferocity" and—when applied to deities—even "malevolence." *Monier-Williams Sanskrit-English Dictionary* offers a much wider range of meanings for the adjectival form, ugra, including powerful, violent, mighty, impetuous, strong, huge, formidable, terrible, cruel, and passionate. In the contexts of Gangamma Jatara, uses and connotations of ugram/ugra are both gendered and specific to context. To account for these differences, I have chosen to translate ugram/ugra as "excess"/"excessive." Ugra is used explicitly in the identification of Gangamma's large clay heads, called *ugra mukhis*, built in her two largest temple courtyards on the last day of the jatara. These heads are literally ugra—that is, excessive in size—but they are also the goddess in her fullest, most powerful form, as her ugram has been built up over the weeklong festival. Several male jatara participants told me that the direct gaze of the ugra mukhis is too powerful to be sustained long by her worshipers, except momentarily when the jute curtain hiding the construction of the faces is drawn back before the face is then dismantled. However, a cue to the gendered experience of Gangamma's ugram was made apparent in the first year we observed the revelation and dismantling of the ugra mukhis when we heard a young mother telling the toddler she was holding on her hip, "Look at her. Look right at her." Another way to think about ugram is its association with heat: the goddess must be ritually heated (aided by the seasonal heat) in order to grow into her fullest (ugra) protective power, but if she becomes too hot, she may become illness or drought itself, the calamities against which she is being beseeched to protect. Therefore, once sufficiently heated, she is ritually cooled or brought down from her fullest ugram.

The multiplicity of sites at which Gangamma Jatara rituals are performed helps to create and display the goddess's ugram. She is, quite literally, expanding and present everywhere in the *uru*, but is also tied to that specific locality. *Gramadevatas* are always "of this place, this very place," with local names and narratives.[12] Each ritual site, each strand in the web of the jatara repertoire, is filled with distinct ritual materials and actors:

1. the Kaikala family home, whose males take on a series of *veshams* that both enact Gangamma's story (see chapter 2) and are the goddess

2. the streets of traditional Tirupati, where the Kaikala veshams wander from doorway to doorway and are met and worshiped by female householders; female householders offer passersby *ambali* (a cooling mixture of yogurt, millet, and onions that both feeds and becomes the goddess); mothers walk with their children to Gangamma's temple, holding protective clay pots over their heads (another form of the goddess); roving bands of young men sing "abusive," sexually explicit songs (*buthulu*) at passersby, accompanied by drummers beating a distinctive rhythm; on the last few days of the jatara, laymen in *stri vesham* linger in order to be seen on their way to the temple (see chapter 2)

3. domestic kitchens, where the goddess is created in several different forms, fed, and distributed

4. the courtyards of the two primary Gangamma temples—Tatayyagunta and Tallapaka—where ritual activity (vegetarian

---

12. Jataras and their goddesses are not transposed to new geographic settings when their celebrants settle in different villages, towns, cities, and countries, such as pan-Indian or pan-Telugu festivals and rituals may be. They do not find their way across the "seven seas" to homes, temples, and high school auditoriums in the United States as do festivals such as Diwali and Ugadi, or as does Varalakshmi Puja.

offerings, cooking *pongal* [a cooked mixture of rice and lentils], animal sacrifice, men in stri vesham presenting themselves to the goddess) builds in intensity until the last day, when the ugra mukhis are built in front of the temples. Many of the ritual actors from across Tirupati come together on the final morning of the jatara to witness the ritual dismantling of the two large clay ugra mukhis.

These spaces and their myriad of seemingly unrelated rituals are held together as a single jatara repertoire through an initiatory ritual called *chakrabandhanam* (lit., tying the circle), performed in the early morning of the first day (a Tuesday) of the jatara, when the boundaries of the uru (village; home place) are sprinkled with rice mixed with the blood of sacrificed animals. (Note that the boundaries of the traditional uru of Tirupati are more restricted than the boundaries of the modern, growing town.) Spatially "tied together," each ritual site and performance genre enters into a relationship with and provides commentary on the others. With this ritual binding, all who reside in the enclosed space become, in some sense, actors in and beneficiaries of the jatara, whether or not they participate directly in its rituals. During the weeklong jatara, no one is supposed to enter or leave the uru. While the prohibition has been lost these days in the bustling modern pilgrimage town, the idea remains. Just as important, the tied boundary keeps the expanding, restless goddess herself inside the uru during this ritually marked time (Handelman 1995). Finally, the boundaries help to consolidate the goddess's ugram that is built up through the jataras, keeping it from dissipating.

Gangamma's ugram grows through the multiplication of her forms within the ritual *chakra* (circle). The assumption would seem to be that the goddess in roadside shrine and temple images of dark stone isn't sufficiently present, intense, ugra enough for the momentous task at hand of protecting the uru from illness and drought (Handelman 1995, 292). During the jatara, Gangamma's stone images inside her temples become secondary to her temporary, fluid jatara forms of human-body guises in the streets, yogurt-millet mixture, diminutive wet turmeric mounds in domestic kitchens, and the ugra mukhis. But this pervasive presence and the potential intimacy with the goddess that it creates, as well as the ritual requirements for this ugra goddess, are too much to sustain throughout the year, so a clear temporal frame (the seven days of the jatara) is established, into which Gangamma is invited and then sent away across the seven seas. Of course, she *also* stays (in her temple and shrine stone forms), but in her ubiquitous jatara forms she is sent away.

On the first Tuesday morning, Gangamma takes her first jatara-specific form in the Tatayyagunta Gangamma temple courtyard as a turmeric-rubbed, sari-wrapped cement pillar (*kodistambham*). The pillar stands permanently in the courtyard, unadorned throughout the rest of the year except with periodic applications of dots of pasupu-kumkum, around which many women perform oil lamp offerings (the lamps being inside-out lemon halves) as part of individual vows. "In the old days," a neem tree was newly cut every jatara and its trunk set up where the cement pillar now stands. A Gangamma devotee whom the goddess regularly possesses in healing rituals told me that Gangamma had come to her one night and complained vociferously about the shift from neem tree trunk to cement pillar, a decision made without asking her permission. The temple priests explained the reason for the cement pillar as being that no one these days has time to go out looking for an appropriate (straight) tree, to cut it down, and to prepare and install it (Flueckiger 2013, 208–9).[13] The cement pillar was simply more convenient.

To transform cement to goddess, Brahmin temple priests (standing atop a temporary platform so that they can reach the top of the pillar) first perform an *abhishekam*-like ritual, pouring pots of turmeric water and milk over the dry cement pillar (figure 3.4).[14] They then rub the entire rough surface with turmeric paste, marking it with dots of vermilion, before wrapping a multitude of cotton saris around the pillar and adorning it with floral garlands. After the pillar-goddess is fully adorned, a yellow cloth holding *vodivalu* (lit., waist/lap rice; a mixture of rice and kumkum along with a coconut that is an embodiment of potential fertility) is tied around the figure's waist, on top of the saris (figure 3.5).[15]

---

13. For what the ritual using a fresh neem tree may have looked like in Gangamma Jatara, see Handelman, Krishnayya, and Shulman (2014, 166–72), who give a detailed description of a cut tree trunk becoming the goddess Paiditalli in a festival of coastal Andhra.

14. The Brahmin priests only began to serve Gangamma in Tatayyagunta temple in 1993, when they replaced a Mudaliar-caste family, which had built up the temple from a tiny open-air shrine and served the goddess since 1913 (see Flueckiger 2013, chapter 8). Presumably, the Mudaliars performed this or a similar ritual before they were evicted.

15. Vodivalu is similarly tied around the waists of brides of some castes, as well as around the waists of the *matangi* and *perantalu* jatara veshams.

Figure 3.4. Transformation of cement pillar to goddess. Courtesy of K. Rajendran, K. R. Studio, Tirupati.

Figure 3.5. Wrapping saris on *kodistambham*. Courtesy of K. Rajendran, K. R. Studio, Tirupati.

Finally, the priests perform *harati* (flame offering) to the pillar-goddess. It is ambiguous whether the turmeric-sari vesham has fully transformed the cement pillar into the goddess (as the Kaikala veshams transform men into goddess; see chapter 2), which the harati acknowledges, or if the harati itself is the final step in calling Gangamma into the pillar. By this time the courtyard is crowded with (mostly) women who, as harati is waved before Gangamma, raise their arms in *namaskaram* (greeting). One woman standing next to me exclaimed, "She's beautiful! She's come!" The goddess is in her interior temple form, but she has now come in the first of her many jatara-specific forms. The temple courtyard activity of the first few jatara days flows back and forth between this pillar-goddess and the goddess's large cement feet close by, to which piles and piles of food, flowers, and pasupu-kumkum are offered.

Almost simultaneously to the creation of the pillar-goddess, Gangamma comes (through possession) to her other jatara-related temple, Tallapaka Gangamma, where the goddess is served by members of the Kaikala family. For the week of the jatara, the Kaikalas bring out from an interior room of their home a metallic face of Gangamma to live temporarily in their courtyard. Here she is joined by a brightly painted, papier-mâché image of her brother, Potu Raju; but he must be brought from the dusty corner of the temple where he is stored throughout the rest of the year.[16] The ritual sequence begins with the family matriarch preparing a stainless-steel pot, rubbing it with turmeric, applying vermilion lines and dots on it, filling it with curd rice, and placing neem leaves at its opening. Lifting the pot on her head, she walks from her home to the temple, ceremoniously accompanied by Pambala drummers. Her son Venkateshvarlu, a ritual attendant at the temple and key actor in the Kaikala vesham sequence, performs harati to Gangamma's stone temple form and then offers the curd rice to Gangamma and audience members observing the ritual. He told us that if the curd rice loses its savory flavor (sourness), "We know that Gangamma has come from beyond the seven seas to attend her [own] jatara." The year I observed this ritual sequence, Gangamma's presence was intensified through her possession of the Kaikala

---

16. Venkateshvarlu explained that his domestic Gangamma doesn't require the presence of her brother throughout the year but that during the jatara, "when she is moving around," quite literally (through her perambulating veshams), she needs Potu Raju's protection.

matriarch at the very moment Gangamma's stone image was being fed the curd rice. With confirmation that the goddess had arrived, Venkateshvarlu placed Potu Raju atop his head and made his way from the temple back to the Kaikala home. The next day (Wednesday), Gangamma, through her Kaikala veshams, began her perambulations of Tirupati's streets, making herself accessible to residents of the uru.

While the Kaikala veshams are perambulating Tirupati's streets, the courtyards of Gangamma's two major temples are alive with rituals that would seem to have little to do with the narrative that the Kaikala veshams enact over the first four days of the jatara. In fact, many female celebrants I spoke with did not know the details of Gangamma's story and often confused the names and identities of the Kaikala veshams; they suggested that if I wanted to know the story, I should ask the Kaikalas. Temple courtyard rituals, in which women *are* experts, are motivated by another rationale: to satisfy the ugra (excessively hungry) goddess through feeding. During the first several days of the jatara, her ugram is satisfied through profuse feeding of vegetarian items, offered at the base of the kodistambham and at her oversized cement feet. Throughout the week, family groups of women also build individual small fires along the walls of the temple courtyard, over which they cook pongal—which should, according to custom, boil over, creating and reflecting plenty, fullness, and abundance.[17] But pongal and offerings of flowers and fruits would seem not to fully satisfy the expanding, increasingly ugra goddess. As the week progresses, nonvegetarian offerings of sacrificial chicken and goats begin to take the place of vegetarian offerings. One female participant explained that "nonveg" is more satisfying when someone (in this case, the goddess) is "really hungry."

On the final Tuesday, the penultimate day of the jatara, Tatayyagunta Gangamma's courtyard is filled with families (men now accompany the women) performing individual chicken (and a few goat) sacrifices, feathers and blood covering the earth, mixed with ritual leftovers of flowers, neem leaves, and pasupu-kumkum. (I was told by several participants that buffalo bali used to be offered—and that surely, somewhere in Tirupati, at least one buffalo would be offered under cover of night—but that these

---

17. Overflowing pongal pots of the festival of the same name perform the abundance of the winter harvest that the festival celebrates.

days, this was against the law.[18]) The goddess's hunger—perceived by her worshipers to be literal, not symbolic—has grown to its ugra maximum and can be satisfied only with ugra bali, not vegetarian offerings. Families build small cooking fires right where they have offered the chickens, in order to prepare the meat for their own consumption. The material excess of sacrifice is accompanied by a gentle flow of moving bodies as families spatially negotiate, and small children run between, the products of excess. This temple courtyard bali atmosphere contrasts to the more ugra (in both size and atmosphere) buffalo sacrifice I witnessed during three different jataras in the neighboring village of Avilala (1992, 1993, 2000), where the jatara organizers continually yelled out instructions to the four Madiga-caste male sacrificers, who themselves shouted loud exclamations as they caught hold of the buffalo by its legs and laid its head over the sacrificial pit.

While the media and male commentary on the jatara focus on the drama of male transformation through stri vesham and the Kaikala vesh-ams making their rounds on Tirupati's streets, women are actively—and intimately—creating Gangamma in their homes. The goddess is too ugra—demanding of too many rituals to be kept satisfied—to keep in domestic shrines throughout the year, but she comes home during the jatara, when women have set aside time to serve her. Many female householders first bring Gangamma into their kitchens or sitting rooms by drawing three simple lines of pasupu, with dots of kumkum between them, on a wall or turmeric-smeared wooden board propped up against the wall. Once here, the goddess needs to be fed. The first ritual feeding is a pot of ambali. A stainless-steel or clay pot sitting on a bed of cooling neem leaves is marked with pasupu-kumkum and filled with ambali before the women of the home perform puja to it (her). This puja suggests that ambali not only feeds the goddess but also *is* the goddess, another example of

---

18. The government of Andhra Pradesh outlawed animal sacrifice in 1950; however, it is still performed in some villages throughout the region. For discussion of efforts by animal rights activists, particularly People for Animals (PFA), to stop bali in the Himalayan region of Kumaon, see Govindrajan 2018 (35–36). In response to litigation filed by PFA, the Uttarakhand High Court ruled that animals could no longer be sacrificed for "*explicitly* religious reasons" but only for human consumption. Specifically, animals may no longer be sacrificed on temple premises and the resulting meat must be consumed by the sacrificers. Govindrajan emphasizes the intimacy between sacrificed goats and the women who offer them in sacrifice. Intimacy and relatedness between animals and humans does not preclude sacrifice.

materiality instantiating the goddess. Before the householders themselves partake of the ambali mixture as prasad, one of the female householders takes a ladle or pitcher of ambali to her home's front door to distribute to any (male) passerby. And, I was told, there always is someone, or two or three men in a group, waiting. The women explained that these men come to their neighborhoods specifically to receive this blessing. It is a moving sight to witness the small lanes of Tirupati lined by women distributing the goddess. Through this ambali ritual, women both feed and satisfy Gangamma and actively multiply and distribute her.

On Friday, midway between the beginning Tuesday and ending Wednesday morning of the jatara, female householders create Gangamma in three tiny mounds of pasupu. Each mounded goddess is placed on a new piece of cloth atop a fresh green banana leaf, again marked with pasupu-kumkum. Large plates of cooked rice and vegetables are placed in front of the goddess, after which the women of the home in which I observed this ritual went into the next room. On this occasion, after photographing the goddess in her diminutive form, I had remained standing at the doorsill between the kitchen and living room, where the rest of the women had moved. They called me to follow them and gently chastised me for continuing to watch the goddess as she was eating. The goddess should be left alone to eat in privacy. The pasupu forms are subsequently placed in the domestic shrine; they are now no longer the goddess but rather material that has been infused with her blessings, bits of which may be ingested throughout the year for healing purposes. While on the streets, the Kaikala veshams are growing in ugram, in the home, Gangamma is created in a particularly intimate form.[19]

Later this same Friday, mothers walk their children to the temple, holding small clay pots over their heads. These "thousand-eyed pots" (*veyyikalladuttas*) with small holes cut into them hold a camphor flame, small black glass bangles, and often a flower and coin. Remembering one name of the goddess to be "the thousand-eyed one," I asked the women with whom I was walking, holding such pots on the heads of their children, if these pots were themselves the goddess. They paused before answering, "Yes, they could be," but they were more assured of the outcome of the

---

19. Women who have a particularly close relationship to the goddess may create Gangamma much more elaborately in their homes for this ritual, by drawing a face with charcoal onto a coconut, placing the coconut in the mouth of a brass pot, and draping a sari around her.

ritual that would protect their children from Gangamma-related illnesses. The belief that Gangamma is both the protectress from these illnesses and, if not satisfied, may become the illnesses themselves, is materialized in this ritual: she is the protectress as she is held over the child's head walking to the temple and her illnesses when mothers smash the pots violently against the ground behind the temple.

Throughout the jatara, women do what they do every day—cook—but their cooking is now intensified and focused on the goddess rather than their families. When I once asked whether Kaikala women take the goddess's veshams, knowing that they did not but seeking an indigenous explanation, a Kaikala male gave as reasons both menstruation and women's lack of the physical stamina to walk the streets as the veshams are required to do. But the elderly Kaikala matriarch who overheard this comment protested that, on the contrary, it was because women are too busy cooking for the goddess. She considered the two activities equally necessary to creating and satisfying the ugra goddess: vesham and cooking.

The perambulating Kaikala veshams connect the multiple sites of the jatara: they are met by female householders at the doorways of their homes; they walk the streets; and, on the final morning of the jatara, the *perantalu* vesham begins the dismantling of the ugra mukhis that have been

Figure 3.6. Gangamma's *ugra mukhi* on final day of *jatara*, Tatayyagunta temple. Courtesy of K. Rajendran, K. R. Studio, Tirupati.

built in Gangamma's two temple courtyards (figure 3.6). Venkateshvarlu asserted that anyone other than the goddess who might attempt to tear apart her clay face would be burned to ashes: "Only a shakti can touch shakti." (His comment recalls that of the guesthouse cleaning woman who asserted, "She [the goddess] is shakti and we are shakti; so we're not afraid [of the ugra mukhi]"—by which she may have argued that a human woman *would* have the shakti to dismantle the ugra mukhi.)

At this final moment of the jatara, it is the goddess herself who breaks the cycles of building and satisfying her ugram. The ritual cycles have reached the limit of their productivity: the illnesses have been defeated (in one ritual, literally smashed) and the rains are coming (if not this final morning, then surely in the coming days). Having become sufficiently ugra to fulfill the primary purpose of the jatara—to protect the uru—and with ugram now fully satisfied (culminating with bali), Gangamma returns to her stone forms in temples and shrines and at uru boundaries where her now-diminished needs can be more easily managed. Much as she is already in Tirupati but also arrives at the beginning of the jatara, at the end she both leaves and stays.

Jataras are characterized by material multiplicity, distribution, and intensity as well as expansive spatial and social boundaries. Over the period of a week, an elaborate web of celebrants perform diverse ritual activities at different sites (home, street, temple) that sometimes intersect and at other times are relatively independent—all held together by the temporal limits of the jatara and the chakrabandhanam. Participants span a wide range of castes: Kaikalas who perform Gangamma veshams, Chakalis who accompany Kaikala veshams, potters who make the ugra mukhis, householders from left-hand (non-landowning, primarily artisan) castes who meet Gangamma (the Kaikala veshams) at their doorways and create her in their kitchens, Pambala drummers, some higher-caste men who take stri vesham, and, more recently, Brahmin priests who serve and politicians who attend as chief guests at Tirupati's largest Gangamma temple. Not all celebrants participate in all rituals, and some may not know much, if anything, about the rituals in which they do not directly participate. Nevertheless, each ritual participant plays a part in creating, managing, and satisfying Gangamma's ugram.

Jatara ritual sites proliferate throughout the uru, and at each site Gangamma takes different material forms, each requiring unique rituals: cement pillar to goddess, ambali, pasupu-kumkum wall markings and tiny mounds of turmeric, thousand-eyed clay pots, ugra mukhis, Kaikala

Gangamma veshams, and Gangamma's presence through possession of human bodies. (Possession itself can be characterized as ugra, when the possessed human body can become unpredictable.[20]) Gangamma quite literally expands throughout the uru through this proliferation of her forms. Once created through excessive forms at numerous ritual sites, celebrated by excessive numbers of participating human bodies, the increasingly ugra goddess needs to be satisfied, first through vegetarian offerings and finally through bali. However, Gangamma's ugram is not totally dissipated; she is consistently characterized as ugra, too demanding of ritual service, for most householders to keep her at home throughout the year. As one female celebrant told me, "By the last day [of the jatara], we can't bear her anymore. We would have to give her piles of food [*kumbham*] every day; we wouldn't be able to bear that. So saying, 'Next year we'll worship you,' we send her off."

Returning to Abundance and Excess

The shared proliferating materialities—turmeric and vermilion powders, flowers, fruits, grains, oil lamps, and auspicious women's bodies—of Varalakshmi Puja and Gangamma Jatara suggest that there is a material continuum, rather than a dichotomy, between abundance and excess, auspiciousness and ugram, and the respective goddesses, Lakshmi and Gangamma, associated with these ritual traditions.

However, they are also distinct. Lakshmi is always auspicious; her abundance is never potentially threatening. Her only threat is to leave if she is not periodically invited into, created, and served in the home. A home without Lakshmi is vulnerable and unstable. Gangamma is more complicated. After having been brought home as a baby by a Reddy family, as one female narrator recounted, "as soon as she entered the home, the milk began to overflow." That is, her very presence brought fullness and auspiciousness, as indicated by the overflowing milk. Gangamma can be

---

20. Over my many years of fieldwork, several middle-class women have asked me if I'm not afraid to attend festivals where possession is common. They've told me they're afraid to attend on the chance that they themselves will become possessed, and then they have elaborated: "Who knows what you will do and what will happen: your sari may come loose; you may say something. Who knows?" Varalakshmi Puja carries with it no possibility of possession.

auspicious in certain contexts, but she is not only auspicious; she is also ugra, excessively powerful and with excessive ritual demands, which, if not met, may result in illness and even death. And yet this same ugram is needed to protect the uru against the same, particularly in the dangerous days of the hot season. The aesthetics and rituals of the jatara perform this fine calibration of eliciting and building up the goddess's ugram and satisfying it, keeping it from spinning out of control and becoming dangerous.[21]

The performance of materialities in Varalakshmi Puja and Gangamma Jatara reveal that abundance and excess are distinguished, in part, by the ways materialities are circumscribed—or not. One might say that in the context of these rituals, excess is abundance unbounded. The materialities of Varalakshmi Puja are abundant but constrained—at least spatially and socially—with no suggestion that they may become dangerous or disruptive. Gangamma's ugram is more volatile. The goddess is called out of her dark stone forms to take residence in a wide range of forms and multiple sites throughout the uru that are served by men and women from a wide range of castes. The only constraint of proliferating materialities and human bodies is, ultimately, the uru boundaries that are marked by the chakrabandhanam ritual. Within this expansive social and physical space, the jatara's materiality is unbounded, augmenting Gangamma's ugram until it grows sufficient to vanquish illness and drought. But this same protective ugram has the potential to become dangerous if not materially managed—if the goddesses' growing hunger (ugram) is not satiated.

Gangamma's ugram disrupts a commonly drawn distinction in Indian studies between auspiciousness and inauspiciousness—*shubha/mangala* and *ashubha/amangala* (Madan 1985; Narayanan 2000; Pintchman 2005). While Lakshmi is the epitome of auspiciousness (wealth and prosperity at all levels), Gangamma is both auspicious (associated with auspicious turmeric and boiling-over pots of milk and pongal) *and* ugra. But her ugram doesn't make her inauspicious; she is the goddess, after all. Rather,

---

21. An example of this calibration occurs when, on the first days of the jatara, young boys use neem branches to beat the cement feet of the goddess at the entrance to her Tatayyagunta temple while singing sexually explicit songs. The physical beating and songs are said to heat the goddess and call her out of her dark stone temple form, while the neem leaves cool her at the same time. For a discussion of this balance between heating and cooling as performed in Tamil Hindu, see Dennis McGilvray's photo essay, *Symbolic Heat: Gender, Health, and Worship among the Tamils of South India and Sri Lanka* (1998).

she is simply ugra—excessive. A profusion of ritual materiality creates Lakshmi and Gangamma and performs their shared female qualities of shakti and beauty (particularly through pasupu). However, their bounded and unbounded materialities also distinguish them, causing them to act in particular ways and to have particular needs, determining whether householders invite the goddess home to stay—or invite her, feed her, and then ceremoniously send her off.

Chapter 4

Expanding Shrines, Changing Architecture

From Protector to Protected Goddesses

The rapidly shifting urban landscape of Hyderabad is punctuated by small but physically expanding cement shrines of village goddesses (*gramadevatas*).[1] Whereas these goddesses used to live in open spaces at village boundaries or next to bodies of water, now they are enclosed by four walls and a roof. The exterior walls are often painted with images of puranic goddesses, and boundary walls are erected around the land surrounding many gramadevata shrines. In a few cases, full South Indian–style enclosed temples typical of those enclosing puranic deities have been constructed—domed roofs decorated with plaster images of puranic deities, and a few bigger ones with a *gopuram* (tower gateway) leading into temple courtyards.[2]

These shrines are ubiquitous along Hyderabad's major traffic arteries as well as its small lanes and gullies. Some are right in the middle of major thoroughfares that have been built around them; others have been

---

1. Worshipers at these shrines do not commonly use the term "gramadevata"; rather, they simply call these goddesses "Amma" or "Ammavaru" (mother).

2. The expansion of simple, originally open-air shrines like these is common throughout India, but their histories in particular places and their material performativity can be quite different. See Elison (2018) for the transformation of *kaccha* (temporary or made of impermanent materials) shrines to *pakka* (made of bricks, stone and mortar, or cement) ones in Mumbai and Gold (2008) for transformation of village goddess shrines in Rajasthan. The shrines Elison analyzes are newly created, "encroaching" on public space (streets and sidewalks), whereas these Hyderabadi goddesses and shrines were there first, before the roadways that threaten to encroach on the gramadevatas' space.

submerged when the road level has been raised by the city government in its efforts to maintain a major thoroughfare—sites now difficult for worshipers to access, causing some to have fallen into disrepair. By their very presence, gramadevata shrines are traces of a material history of the urban landscapes of Hyderabad; they are testament to the destruction of water tanks, dissolution of village boundaries, and merger of villages that have been swallowed up by urban expansion.[3] Many water sources, such as tanks, that are traditionally protected by goddesses such as Pochamma have been filled in for developing neighborhoods, and the only trace of the lost water source is the goddess who has stayed her ground. Goddesses who once protected (now lost) boundaries or village crossroads are now surrounded by bustling streets and commercial and residential neighborhoods (figure 4.1).

Most worshipers and shrine caretakers I talked with about the newly enclosed goddesses and the expansion of their shrines ventured that the primary purpose of these changes was to protect the goddesses from the traffic that threatens to run them over or from land encroachment, against which all urban dwellers must be constantly vigilant. However, some Hyderabadis (specifically, I heard this from some university professors) objected to the expanding shrines as a reflection of Hindutva (political Hinduism) expansion—literally, taking up space and displaying Hindu power. But it is not only Hindu shrines that are expanding in this way and "intruding" on traffic; numerous Muslim *dargahs* (shrines to saints)—particularly in the Old City—and some Christian shrines have also expanded into major thoroughfares. Most Hyderabadis simply maneuver around those shrines that extend into or are in the middle of the roads they are navigating—as they do other vehicles, dogs, and cows—without paying particular attention to them.

Space is not an inert phenomenon. Doreen Massey's seminal work, *Space, Place, and Gender* (1994), argues that space both enables and shapes human activity within it. Dick Pels and his colleagues elaborate: "People perform objects, but especially buildings, by moving through and around them; but these objects also *perform people* by constraining their movements

---

3. Folklorist Pulikonda Subbachary took me on a tour of several such shrines in fall 2014, during which he identified each shrine by the name of the old neighborhood or village of which it used to be a part: Aminpur village, Gangaram village, Medinaguda, Alvin Colony, etc. See Anand Taneja (2013) for analyses of lost Muslim shrines and landscapes (and lost archival records of same) in post-Partition Delhi.

Figure 4.1. *Gramadevata* shrine in middle of major Hyderabad thoroughfare. Photo by the author.

and by suggesting particular encounters between them and others" (2002, 13; my emphasis). Analyzing three shrines with different histories and at different stages of transformation, I demonstrate that space as marked by architectural structures has the potential to "perform"/transform not only humans but also deities. While explicit human intentions behind these gramadevata architectural changes may be to honor the goddess, modernize her abode, keep traffic from running over the goddesses, or to stave off encroachment into the land she inhabits (all of which I have been told), the effect of the expansion—that is, the *agency* of the new architectural features—has the potential to change, and is changing, the identities and theologies of the goddesses housed inside.[4]

---

4. Art historian Annabel Jane Wharton argues for the agency of material architecture (2015). However, the agency she analyzes is deeply rooted in the human historical contexts that both motivated and are embedded in particular buildings. Her analyses of the effects of human or social contexts read similarly to Appadurai's "social life of things" (1986) or Hoskins's "biographical objects" (1998).

Most of the gramadevatas known as the Seven Sisters, housed inside the shrines, are roughly hewn, small—even tiny—images or an uncarved rounded rock covered with vermilion and turmeric powders, although some are (more recently) full-body dark stone images.[5] Their single brother, Potu Raju, is present as a turmeric-vermilion-covered stone outside the shrines, facing his sisters.[6] Many shrines have painted on their exterior walls dramatic, colorful images of the puranic goddesses Durga and Kali. One Pochamma temple has been expanded by building a second story where Durga is housed, above the original shrine where the gramadevata sits. So while Pochamma has not lost her unique name, here she is a "sister" to Durga rather than to the other Seven Sister gramadevatas, and this familial association has the potential to change who she is.

The doorways of many shrines are flanked on one side by an image of a woman carrying Bonalu festival offerings on her head, and on the other side by an image of Potu Raju holding his braided-straw whip as he takes form in human male bodies when he leads Bonalu processions (figure 4.2).[7] Bonalu is a Telangana goddess festival celebrated during the month of Ashada (July–August) that is most publicly visible by processions of women carrying on their heads clay, turmeric-smeared pots filled with jaggery-sweetened rice as they make their way from smaller gramadevata shrines to larger goddess temples for four consecutive Sundays.[8] The doorway paintings of Potu Raju and the Bonalu-celebrating woman are

---

5. The names of the Seven Sisters vary from village to village, region to region, and villagers can rarely name them all—in part, because particular villages/neighborhoods rarely, if ever, host all seven. Nevertheless, the idea of the seven is widespread.

6. For discussion of the feminization of Potu Raju in Tirupati, see Flueckiger 2013, 10–13. Whereas in Telangana (where Hyderabad is located), he often appears in paintings at the doorways of gramadevatas shrines and in Bonalu processions as "hypermasculine," bare-chested, wearing a tightly wrapped loincloth, and swinging a braided-straw whip.

7. The only gramadevata whose image is painted on the outside walls of her own shrines is Yellamma. At many Yellamma shrines, chickens and goats are still offered, and she seems to be retaining her unique gramadevata persona longer than some of her sisters.

8. The state government of Telangana (formed in 2014) has identified Bonalu as a festival that represents the unique culture of the state; and state officials attend the final ritual at the Ujjaini Mahankali temple in Secunderabad, where most Bonalu processions make their way.

Figure 4.2. Potu Raju and female Bonalu festival celebrant flanking doorway of Nalla Pochamma shrine, 2014. Photo by the author.

cues that the interior goddesses are not exactly the same as the puranic Durga or Kali painted on the outside walls.[9]

The South Indian Seven Sisters have not always been so enclosed by permanent structures. Rather, most gramadevatas have traditionally stood watch in open spaces, at the boundaries of villages or on the banks of a water source, as protectors of the *uru* (home place; village), protecting its inhabitants from disease (such as hot-season poxes and fevers) and drought. Here, they may simply appear as an uncarved rock, carved stone head, or a line of iron tridents, standing in the open air, under the shade of a tree, or under a loosely woven thatched roof held up by bamboo poles.

---

9. The bamboo and paper constructions (*tottelus*) that often hang on trees next to the temple—offered by infertile women in hopes of a child—are also indications that a gramadevata lives inside.

Gramadevata narratives and rituals characterize the Seven Sisters as fluid and moving, goddesses who do not like to be closed in, who want to be free to wander (Flueckiger 2013, 6–10). Oral narratives circulate about human efforts to enclose gramadevatas with permanent structures whose roofs or walls subsequently fall in, indicating the displeasure of the goddess. However, more and more of these open-air shrines *are* being enclosed as urban neighborhoods grow up around them. If the permanent structures stay standing, perhaps the goddess has given her permission implicitly or explicitly to be enclosed; some shrine caretakers tell stories of asking for and receiving this permission.[10]

Nalla Pochamma Temple, Tarnaka

Each shrine has its own oral narratives and spatial, family, and divine histories that are, quite literally, being built over and around by urban development. Nonetheless, many of these stories share a narrative and material grammar with those of other shrines. Let me start with the transformations of one shrine—that of Nalla Pochamma (lit., dark [beautiful] Pochamma). Some transformations were narrated by members of the family that served as its primary caretakers until 2016, and other transformations I have witnessed myself. As mentioned earlier, Pochamma traditionally resides on the banks of rivers, lakes, or water tanks, bodies of water that she protects. A trace of this association with water sources remains at this site through the bore well and public tap (whose dated formal installation

---

10. The Mudaliar-caste family that established the first enclosed temple for Tatayyagunta Gangamma in Tirupati recount asking the goddess for permission before closing her in. The current family patriarch told the story of his grandfather asking Gangamma (who was only a head under a tree) to heal his ailing wife and daughter. When they recovered to full health, he thought such a great goddess should not be left without shelter over her head. He asked for her permission before building an enclosed shrine. If her answer was yes, the neem branch placed on her head would fall to the ground; if her answer was no, the branch would stay put. The branch fell and he built the shrine (Flueckiger 2013, 184–90). Ann Gold writes of certain Rajasthani goddesses who forbid temple construction over their heads, conveying their displeasure through dreams or divination. Gold was told many times that the goddess Sundar Mata, for example, proclaims, "'I make shade; no one may shade me'" (2008, 160).

in 2002 is commemorated by a plaque embedded in one of its boundary walls) that sits at the entry to the shrine's courtyard.

The shrine lies on the side of a long, paved, cement-walled lane that connects the main road of Tarnaka (Secunderabad) to the neighborhood interiors. Its single doorway is flanked by a mustached, hemp-whip-wielding Potu Raju and a woman wearing a red sari and holding a Bonalu festival pot on her head (figure 4.2). One exterior wall has painted on it an image of Durga, and Kali graces another wall. Although two large, black stone plaques embedded in the courtyard wall identify the temple as that of Pochamma, several worshipers identified the interior goddess as Durga, perhaps because embedded on the back wall of the interior of the shrine is a large tile picturing Durga riding her lion[11]. The shrine caretaker's own thirty-year-old, MA-graduate daughter (who used to work as a flight attendant for Singapore Airlines and was working in a call center when I met her in 2014) thought the interior goddess "must be Durga." She then admitted that she really didn't know, since she hadn't come to the shrine regularly for many years due to work time pressures. One young male worshiper—who stops for a few moments at the shrine on his way to work every morning, whispering some prayers as he does *namaskaram*—identified the goddesses painted on the outside as the gramadevatas Pochamma and Maisamma. When I told him that the signboard identified the goddess inside as Pochamma but that the outside paintings had the iconography of Durga and Kali, he said, "Yes, yes, all the sisters are the same: Pochamma, Maisamma, Mahankali, Mangalamma, Durga Mata, and Yellamma."[12]

On the ground in front of the wall-tile Durga and a framed lithograph of Durga sits a tiny, uncarved rock covered with *pasupu-kumkum*: the gramadevata goddess Pochamma (figures 4.3 and 4.4). The shrine is

---

11. These tiles of images of deities are also embedded in compound boundary walls of other temples and secular buildings, in part to keep male passersby from urinating against the walls and to keep others from spitting red *pan* (betel nut) juice against them. The strategy seems to be largely effective.

12. Note that Durga and Kali are not traditionally named as one of the gramadevata Seven Sisters in villages; however, I often heard them included in Hyderabadi listings. Another young male worshiper surprisingly identified the interior goddess as the North Indian goddess Vaishno Devi. This identification suggests that the worshiper either is from North India or has made pilgrimage to Vaishno Devi in the Himalayas.

Figure 4.3. Kumhar matriarch, 2014. Note Durga tile image on wall and tiny stone Pochamma at ground level. Photo by the author.

Figure 4.4. The goddess in Nalla Pochamma shrine, 2014. Photo by the author.

surrounded by a stone-paved courtyard, with a high wall on one side separating it from an adjacent college and a lower wall on the other side separating it from the narrow traffic lane. On the courtyard wall facing the goddess are two black inlaid plaques: one reads (in English) "Nalla Pochamma Youth Association . . . Inauguration of the Renovation Programme" and lists the names of the chief guests, with a date of November 19, 1999. The other reads "Nalla Pochamma Temple Bore Well Inauguration," with the date February 24, 2002, and includes the names of those responsible for the same. The use of English rather than Telugu is an indication of the class, or aspirational class, of the chief guests and organizers of these renovations, which was quite different from that of most daily or weekly worshipers and the primary caretakers of the shine (the latter were Telugu-educated only through third and fifth class and are introduced below). The dates of the renovation and inauguration of the tube well fall within the broad parameters of dating (when available) of many other gramadevata shrine expansions, from the late 1980s through the present.

I had passed this Pochamma shrine many times over the years during which I had conducted fieldwork in Hyderabad in the 1990s and early 2000s, walking to the main road to catch an auto, but I rarely saw anyone serving the goddess and only an occasional worshiper standing in front of the shrine entrance. In the fall of 2014, by which time I had begun my research on gramadevata shrines, I noticed a middle-age man sweeping the courtyard of the shrine and stopped to ask if he was the caretaker. Yes, he said, his family had built and taken care of the shrine, but his wife was the primary caretaker; he gave me a phone number to arrange to meet her. He assured me that he could always be found on the sidewalk of the main road around the corner, where he sold clay pots—returning to his Kumhar-caste and family occupation of potter, which he had taken up only upon retirement from government employment.

I met the family matriarch on a Friday, a day special to the goddess, when the matriarch comes to clean the shrine's interior and to serve Pochamma (figure 4.3). She wore a green cotton sari with a turmeric-colored blouse (colors said to be pleasing to the goddess) and an unusually large dark red forehead marking, which the matriarch made a point to say was also pleasing to the goddess. Both of her forearms were encircled with red glass bangles, interspersed with silver ones, marking her auspiciousness, and her graying hair hung loosely (rather than being tied up in a bun or plaited in a braid)[13]—all traditional signs of a woman in a particularly close relationship with (often possession by) a gramadevata goddess.[14] I introduced myself as someone who had written a book about the gramadevata Gangamma in Tirupati and who was interested in similar gramadevata shrines in Hyderabad. She interjected, "Oh, she's truly the goddess [*ammavarich hai*]; she's very beautiful, very powerful."

Guessing, correctly, what I might want to learn from her, the matriarch immediately launched into the story of "her" *gudi* (shrine), a performance punctuated with laughter that was characteristic of her subsequent conversations with me. Speaking in Hindi, since that is the language in which I first addressed her, although Telugu is her mother tongue, she began: "We made all of this—*all* of this. In the beginning, she [the goddess] came to me in my sleep; she told me to light her a *chiraq* [oil lamp]. . . . I said, 'OK, Amma.' . . . She was a little, little girl. She said this in my sleep, to light a chiraq; then she said, 'Everything will go well for you, *beta* [dear child].' . . . After that, we made all this." I heard similar intimate narratives of the establishment of several other shrines: the gramadevata goddess comes to someone (usually a woman) in a dream, often as a little girl, a beautiful little girl, to make her wishes known.[15]

---

13. When I visited the matriarch at her home, her hair was bound in a bun. I had thought she left her hair loose at the shrine with an expectation or possibility of possession by the goddess, when a woman's hair should be loosened so that the goddess can more easily enter her body. However, when I asked if the goddess came to her in that way, the matriarch responded, "No. I see her, but she sits quietly [*khamosh*]. She's happy with me and sits quietly. She comes inside, but she's quiet; she's happy." Her answer implies that possession is an indicator of the disquiet, and perhaps dissatisfaction, of the goddess.

14. When I got home from the shrine and showed the digital picture I had taken of the matriarch to the female Muslim cook of the household where I was staying, she immediately pointed out her large *bottu* and said (speaking Urdu), "Oh, she's someone who gets *haziri* [becomes possessed]."

15. Such dream narratives/messages are common across India. Ann Gold tells the story she heard of the Rajasthani goddess Parliya Mataji: a nondescript stone was used by some pilgrims to fix the wheel of their ox cart and upon their return home carelessly tossed aside. That night, the goddess appeared to one of the pilgrims in a dream and chastised him: "'You brought me here, so you have to take care of me! . . . You brought me, how did you throw me down like this, you threw me there!'" The man and his traveling partners found the rock they'd thrown down and established it as the goddess and began to worship her (2008, 158–59).

The matriarch explained that she had first dug a hole in the earth under a tree, put bits of gold and silver and pasupu-kumkum powders into the hole, and covered them up with soil. She then set up the rock (presumably the same uncarved one that was now housed in the shrine) that became the goddess (without a particular ritual of installation, such as is performed in puranic temples): "We put the rock there and then she was there." It was next to a big well where a big snake and her six babies used to live, but she wasn't afraid, the matriarch asserted, knowing she would be protected by the goddess. After that, the matriarch continued, "She [the goddess] gave all these good things, and then my husband got government employment." Shortly after their wedding, he had suffered a severe accident at work in a factory that had resulted in the loss of most of his hearing, so his permanent employment thereafter, first as an employee of the Employee State Insurance Corporation (ESI) and then as an "office attender" to a series of government officials, was experienced as a miracle of the goddess.

In a later conversation, the matriarch and her husband determined that they must have established the goddess and built the first shrine in 1987. Others in the neighborhood tell a different history, of a water tank at the site that was filled in with rocks and dirt and a junior college built over it (now on the other side of the boundary wall of the shrine, into whose yard the boundary wall of the shrine itself extends). Another neighbor remembered that when she moved to Tarnaka in 1985, a shrine was already sitting at this location next to what was then a large, open, empty field where the junior college now stands. The divergent narratives share a story of urban growth over and around the shrine, a history that will soon be lost with the passing of the elders' generation.

Since establishing the shrine, the Kumhar family has regularly served Pochamma at this site and gradually made improvements to the shrine. The matriarch explained that the neighborhood association had told them they should wall in the shrine and its courtyard to protect it from traffic and potential land grabbing, but, the matriarch complained, the association had given no money toward the cause. She emphasized that her own family had paid for all the expansions with funds saved from offerings made to Pochamma.

I asked the matriarch about the relationship between the interior Pochamma and the exterior puranic goddesses, Durga and Kali—who has more shakti? Her answer, like many I received to similar questions, was that all goddesses are the same, and then she laughed, adding, "She

[Durga] is Ammavaru [the goddess] herself; after all, she sits on top of Pochamma [referring to the tile image on the back wall above the small stone Pochamma]" (figure 4.3). She then explained that the tile Durga and paintings of puranic goddesses on the outside had been added to "make the shrine look good" but that the real goddess was the tiny stone inside. However, many middle-class passersby, whose families or castes do not traditionally participate in gramadevata traditions but who may make namaskaram as they pass, do not know who is inside—and even those who do identify the goddess as a gramadevata may misidentify which of the Seven Sisters she is.

Many gramadevata shrines are only two feet high, requiring worshipers to kneel down to see the interior goddess, something many worshipers do not do unless they have time to sit in front of the shrine. The metal gates to the interior shrines are often locked during the day, suggesting that seeing the enclosed deity herself is not the primary mode of interaction with the goddess for the passersby for whom the visual connection to and identification of the goddess is with those painted on the outside—Durga or Kali. However, this (what we may call) misidentification does not seem to bother the caretakers of these shrines, and—unless the anthropologist is asking—they may not even know of it. After all, worshipers and caretakers frequently assured me, when I mentioned the discrepancies, "All goddesses are the same."

The year after I had first met the Nalla Pochamma caretakers, I returned to Hyderabad and was surprised to see the original shrine razed and a much larger temple being built at the site. The only sign of worship was a lithograph of Durga propped up against a wooden chair, a burning oil lamp in front of it, in the middle of the construction site. In front of the bamboo construction scaffolding hung a large banner that pictured what would be the end product: a puranic-style temple. The name of the temple president and his phone number were printed at the bottom of the banner; however, during the two weeks I was in Hyderabad on that visit, he never picked up the phone. By the time I returned to Hyderabad eight months later (August 2016), the colorfully painted, fully enclosed temple was complete (figure 4.5). But the gate to the courtyard and the wooden door to the temple interior were locked each time I passed by for the next several days. It was such a contrast, I thought then, to the open fields and village boundaries where such a goddess would be always available, or to the shrine that used to stand there where worshipers could enter the courtyard at any time of day. Only later did I notice a small signboard

Figure 4.5. Nalla Pochamma new temple, 2016. Note *tottelus* (bamboo structures offered in vows) hanging on an exterior wall. Photo by the author.

on the boundary wall of the new temple that gave the visiting hours of the temple to be 7:00 to 11:00 a.m. and 6:00 to 8:30 p.m.

Finally, one morning the gates were open when I passed by, and there was a flurry of activity in the courtyard, where a young family was offering a *tottelu* (bamboo–tissue paper structure) to the goddess in fulfillment to a vow they had made to her.[16] Pochamma was being served by a Brahmin *pujari*. I introduced myself to a man standing at the temple entrance, who I learned was the temple "maintenance manager." He was curt and seemingly irritated with my questions about who had sponsored the major renovation of the temple, how a Brahmin pujari had been installed, and what had happened to the earlier Kumhar-caste caretakers.[17]

---

16. Normally this vow offering would have been brought to a gramadevata temple during Bonalu, but the family had been unable to do so then and was bringing it now at their "own convenience."

17. Although the Kumhar daughter had given me both her cell phone number and

He refused permission to take any photographs, even of the outside of the temple, although the pujari listening to our conversation had no objection to photographing the outside and tried to persuade him otherwise. The temple president later explained the photography prohibition: "We're very strict [about taking photographs of the temple interior and deity]. It's like when a woman is pregnant and shouldn't have x-rays—like that. It takes away *shakti*." However, he gave me permission to photograph the temple exterior.

While the signboard outside the temple still identifies the goddess to be Nalla Pochamma, she is now a three-foot-tall dark, anthropomorphic stone—a four-armed body and turmeric-covered face to which has been applied silver metal eyes. She sits on a tiger (Durga's traditional animal mount) whose face peeks out from the goddess's brightly colored sari. The original tiny stone Pochamma—still covered with turmeric but now with a pearl necklace around her neck and a cloth wrapping her lower half—sits at the new image's feet. In front of this tiny goddess is a three-dimensional *stri chakra* (geometric design of the goddess) with kumkum sprinkled over it—"a must for any shakti [goddess] temple," the pujari explained. To the right side of the full-body image of Pochamma is an image of the elephant-headed deity Ganesha and to her left Subramanyam, the two sons of Shiva and Parvati. Pochamma's brother, Potu Raju, who had kept her company in the earlier shrine, was nowhere to be seen (either in the form of his small turmeric-covered stone or his painted image by the shrine doorway). When I asked the maintenance manager about Potu Raju's absence, he simply said, "We took him out." The goddess's family had been dramatically altered; she had no brother but seemingly two sons who are traditionally associated with another goddess altogether.

Like many gramadevata shrines, one of the exterior walls of the temple is still decorated with a painting of the puranic deity Durga riding her tiger. But, unusually, two other wall paintings are of goddesses not traditionally found on gramadevata shrine walls: Lakshmi (goddess of

---

email address, she never answered my calls or emails on this or my previous visit to Hyderabad (when I had first seen the new temple construction), or several times from the US. Although her father's clay pots were still stacked on the sidewalk on the main road, every time I passed by at different times of day, they were covered with a tarp and he was never there. I was not sure how to interpret the daughter's lack of response and her father's absence. While meeting this family and our initial interactions seemed serendipitous, now their absence and lack of response was similarly so.

wealth) sitting on a lotus and Sarasvati (goddess of learning and music) holding her *vina* (stringed instrument). The temple committee has posted several signs on the exterior walls of the compound. One advertises a range of services of (and prices for) an astrologer (*jyotish*); another sign lists the costs of special individual *archanas* (offerings) and sponsorship of *abhishekam* (ritual anointing with a series of liquids), along with timings of particular daily, monthly, and periodic festival temple rituals. The term "archana" and the ritual of abhishekam are traditionally associated with puranic, not gramadevata, temples, and these are indications of the brahminization of the temple's rituals. Finally, another signboard prohibits activities that *are* often associated with gramadevatas. It pictures a chicken and goat standing side by side and, in an adjacent image, an alcohol bottle, each image with a big red "X" over it, indicating prohibition of animal sacrifice and alcohol on the premises.[18]

After several phone calls, I finally met the temple president, Uday Kumar (a fortysomething, English-speaking businessman), who proudly narrated the history of the recent temple renovations. Three years earlier (2013)—at his suggestion, he emphasized—the local temple committee of the earlier shrine and some neighborhood elders had decided to undertake the renovation. Mr. Kumar hired a traditionally trained puranic-temple architect to draw up a plan for the new temple, whose building cost nine to ten *lakhs* of rupees (equivalent to about $15,000 in 2015). Mr. Kumar himself had committed to donating Rs. 1.5 lakhs and raised the rest of money from friends (who, he said, "wouldn't be able to say no"), as well as smaller amounts from the local community. The groundbreaking for the new temple was on August 19, 2015, and building began that November. The goddess was installed in her new temple on February 13, 2016.

Mr. Kumar emphasized that he and the temple committee wanted everything to be (speaking in English) "systematic," with no animal sacrifice or alcohol, so that it would be "accessible to all," including, he specified, Brahmins, Gujaratis (from the western state of Gujarat), and Rajasthanis (from the northwestern state of Rajasthan)—an interesting collective,

---

18. The same prohibition against animal sacrifice is displayed on a signboard outside a shrine to the gramadevata Yellamma situated in the middle of a wooded crossroads at Osmania University, only a couple miles away from the Tarnaka Pochamma temple. However, here the prohibition is often broken. Since the early 1990s when I began coming to Hyderabad regularly, I have frequently seen goats being led to the shrine entrance and signs of sacrifice on the shrine's earthen courtyard floor.

indeed. Brahmins are traditionally vegetarian; his mention of Gujaratis may have implied strictly vegetarian Vaishnavas or Jains, since many who have migrated to Hyderabad come from Gujarat. But the significance of Rajasthanis is unclear, since there are also local goddesses in Rajasthan who require *bali* and to whom alcohol is offered. He emphasized that the clientele of this new temple was much broader in caste and class than had been the mostly lower-caste and lower-class worshipers at the earlier shrine. He seemed unaware or unconcerned that the latter may now feel out of place in the new temple.[19] Perhaps, I thought, Pochamma herself feels out of place in her new abode.

I asked Mr. Kumar who had decided—and why—to have Subramanyam and Ganesha stand to each side of Pochamma. Initially, he explained, they had wanted to change the name of the goddess herself so that the temple wouldn't attract alcohol and bali. He explained, "If you keep the name Mata [mother—referring here to gramadevata], then the same bali and alcohol will keep happening." (Traditionally, gramadevatas require bali at certain times of year, such as Gangamma in Tirupati does by the end of her jatara.) He consulted with his guru (whom he did not name), who told him they should keep the name Pochamma but that they should add the presence of the two male deities, "*who would protect her*" (my emphasis). Potu Raju, the brother of the Seven Sisters, is also said to be a protective "watchman," facing his more powerful sisters in front of their shrines; however, it is also clear that he is at the "beck and call" of his sisters. When I suggested that the presence of brothers Ganesha and Subramanyam (inside the temple rather than outside, where Potu Raju traditionally stands) suggested the goddess was Parvati, the brothers' mother, Mr. Kumar assured me that "though her forms and names are many, she's only Mata."[20]

Mr. Kumar further explained the reason for the absence of Potu Raju and the paintings of Potu Raju and the Bonalu participant that had

---

19. With caste being the sensitive issue that it is in contemporary India, I did not feel free to ask worshipers whom I was meeting briefly at the temple, for the first and only time, their castes, so I cannot verify if caste members traditionally associated with gramadevatas continue to worship at this new temple, with its new Sanskritic rituals and Brahmin priest.

20. Mr. Kumar's use of the term "Mata" here is interesting, since he had just told me that this appellation suggests a gramadevata, who requires or attracts bali—something the new temple prohibits.

flanked the doorway of the original shrine: their absence would deter alcohol and bali. Were bali to be performed or alcohol consumed on the premises, he asserted, the ritual installation of the goddess would need to be performed again—according to "*shastric* [brahminic, textual] requirements"—at a cost of two or three lakhs. He quickly added, "It's not a matter of money—we could collect that easily—but you shouldn't redo this ritual [of installation]."

By this time, I felt I could broach the sensitive matter of what happened to the Kumhar family that used to serve the goddess. Mr. Kumar's account of the history of the temple was quite different from what I had heard from the family. He did not know the origins of the temple, but "in his earliest memory" an old woman used to serve Nalla Pochamma until about twenty-five years earlier, at which time the Kumhar family began to come regularly to serve Nalla Pochamma. (This is only a three-year difference from the date the Kumhar family had estimated they had established the shrine—from the ground up.) A neighborhood temple committee had already been formed by this time, and it had no objection to the Kumhar family serving the goddess, even if they were not from the local neighborhood. But, Mr. Kumar insisted, "They never had any rights over the temple. . . . Later, they caused a lot of problems. [When they were removed,] they complained to officials at various levels." I asked if they still come to the temple, if they could still serve the goddess if they wanted to. "No," he said,

> They could come sweep the outside if they wanted, but they don't. They used to go inside and touch the goddess; now, after the [brahminic] installation ritual, only Brahmins can go inside; no one is allowed inside, including Kumhars [implying that they aren't being discriminated against simply because of their caste status]. . . . Just last week that Kumhar family offered to buy the temple for ten lakhs, to have control. But it's not a matter of personal power or control; it's the will of the goddess. She wouldn't have let this be built without her approval.

Nalla Pochamma has kept her name, but for many of her worshipers, including the temple president, her character has changed. The transformations began as seemingly minor architectural ones: an enclosure over the place where she resides and a boundary wall. Eventually, to "please her," according to the Kumhar matriarch, the shrine's outside walls were painted with images of Durga and Kali. These transformations (and perhaps the growing value of the land itself) motivated other architectural changes and eventually an entirely new temple. The gramadevata has lost the company of her brother and been given "protection" of two "sons." She seemingly no longer requires, and is not permitted, animal sacrifice. Architectural and iconographic changes were accompanied by changes in personnel serving her: taking the place of the Kumhar matriarch, a male Brahmin pujari now chants Sanskrit to the goddess (chants that are broadcast across the neighborhood through big speakers) and performs brahminic rituals. Most worshipers look like they are middle class and middle caste rather than from the lower castes who traditionally served her.[21] One can imagine Nalla Pochamma thinking to herself, experiencing all of these changes, something similar to what the Tirupati gramadevata Gangamma said to one of her devotees (in a vision) upon the substitution of one of her annual festival forms from neem tree to cement pillar, without being asked her permission for the change: "What significance do I and my *shulams* [tridents; one traditional form of gramadevatas] have?"—suggesting the existential question, who am I; who have I become?

Critically, the identity and nature of Nalla Pochamma began to change before a Brahmin priest began to serve her in the renovated temple. The Kumhar family had already enclosed her within four walls, built a courtyard boundary wall, and added paintings of puranic deities as decoration on the shrine's external walls. Even then, passersby and many worshipers did not recognize the interior goddess to be a gramadevata or confused her identity with those of her sisters. But the puranic-style architectural renovation, introduction of a Brahmin priest and Sanskritic rituals, explicit prohibition of bali, change in the goddess's physical form, and addition of Ganesha and Subramanyam by her side have accelerated changes in the goddess herself. She is no longer an independent, fierce, and protective goddess free to wander at will. Her needs and desires (for bali) are being ignored or suppressed, and she has been given a new family—sons whose protection she is said to need.

On the other side of the city, another temple has undergone transformations similar to those of the Nalla Pochamma shrine, with the addition of puranic-style architecture and a Brahmin pujari. However,

---

21. See Flueckiger 2013a, chapter 8, for a similar history of architectural, personnel, and ritual changes at the Tatayyagunta Gangamma temple in Tirupati, where a Mudaliar family of caretakers was evicted and replaced by Brahmin priests.

here, the goddess's name itself has changed, indicating an identification between the gramadevata Maisamma and the puranic deity Lakshmi. The signboard above the temple entrance reads "Maisamma Lakshmi." But for at least some worshipers, the transformation is not complete. I provide a lengthy personal narrative of one of these devotees that reveals that, for her, the goddess is not contained in that transformed architectural space and that she is still the *ugra* Maisamma, who is both protective and demanding in ways that the always *shanta* Lakshmi, with whom she has been paired, is not.

Maisamma-Lakshmi Temple, New Santosh Nagar

The Maisamma-Lakshmi temple sits among the inner narrow lanes of New Santosh Nagar, a neighborhood adjacent to Hyderabad's Old City, on land that used to mark the boundaries of the city but is now a neighborhood filled with immigrants from the surrounding countryside. The heavy wooden, carved door to the temple was locked when I first visited one early afternoon with my friend K. Vimala, who lives several lanes over. As I was photographing the temple exterior, a middle-age woman entered the crossroads where the temple sits. She was dressed in a red sari, her arms loaded with glass bangles, wearing a large red bottu—signs that indicated she may have a special relationship with the goddess (like the matriarch of the Pochamma temple discussed above). We stopped her to ask what she knew about the temple and its goddess. She bemoaned, "Why didn't you come at 11:00 a.m., when the temple was open and you could have talked to the pujari? But it's the grace of Ammavaru [the goddess] that I walked by at just the right time, to meet you."

When we tried to clarify who was dwelling in the temple, since the signboard gave two names, she asserted (mentioning Durga, however, and not Lakshmi, whose name is paired with Maisamma on the signboard): "Durga and Maisamma are one [*ekhich hai*; she was a Telugu speaker speaking Hindi for my benefit, since I had initially addressed her in Hindi]. Kalika, Yellamma, Durgamma, Kanaka Durgamma—they're all one; they've just been given different names. Kali Mata is on top [on the cement-casted images on the top of the temple exterior]—see? They're all one.... Durga came to me just the day before yesterday. There was no one at home; my sister held on to me." We asked, "It was Durga, not Maisamma?"—"No! They're the same." Vimala again pushed for clarification: "But how are Maisamma and Lakshmi the same?" "They are *all* the same; we only name them differently. Actually, she's [the goddess dwelling here] Dhana Lakshmi [Lakshmi of wealth]; [that's because] there used to be money under the image of the goddess." We were not going to get an easy answer.

I looked for a Potu Raju stone, but on our initial visit to this temple, he was not visible.[22] So I asked the devotee, whom we came to know as Sandhya, "If the goddess is Maisamma, where is Potu Raju?" and her immediate reply was "*I* am Potu Raju." Seeing our perplexed expressions at her response, she confirmed that she is regularly possessed—by the goddess, however, not Potu Raju. Here, she may have been identifying with Potu Raju as someone who serves and bears witness to the goddess. She told us that in Bonalu festival processions, there are six Potu Rajus with whips (processions are led by male bodies who are Potu Raju). Again she implied she was one of them, saying, "There are six of *us* [my emphasis] with our whips." However, when pushed again—"Are *you* Potu Raju, then?"—she answered, "No, no, I'm Talli [the goddess]. . . . My eyes get big like Ammavaru. When they play the drums, Ammavaru comes and we dance [in possession]. Some people may ask questions, and, if they do, I answer [i.e., the goddess speaks through her]."

Sandhya intimately experiences the goddess primarily outside of her material stone form in the temple, as an ugra gramadevata and not the pacific, auspicious Lakshmi, which the narrative that follows confirms. This goddess has had dramatic material effects in her life. Sandhya reported that the goddess had first possessed her only five years earlier, and then she told us a painful, fragmented, and quickly moving story in which this possessing goddess had protected *her* but not her daughter. She began by telling us she had moved to Santosh Nagar from the nearby neighborhood of Narayanguda, where she had lived in a multistory apartment building. There, Mata (the goddess) used to regularly come to her in possession.

---

22. The temple president told me they were waiting until all innovations and expansions were completed before installing a Potu Raju outside the entrance. When I returned the next year, a rectangular two-foot-high cement column painted a deep yellow had been set where Potu Raju traditionally stands, facing his sister. However, painted in red on the column were images not traditionally associated with Potu Raju: an Om (symbol for sacred sound, associated with sanskritic rituals rather than those to gramadevatas) on one side, and a female face—with a large nose ring—on another side, which neither the temple president nor pujari could identify.

But her middle-class neighbors (whom Sandhya characterized as "worshiping Santoshi Mata," a goddess who became popular, particularly among Indian middle classes, in the 1960s) were unhappy with her possession. They had asked her, "Why Yellamma, why Maisamma, why Durgamma, why Kanaka Durga? Why do all these [gramadevatas] come to [possess] you?" Sandhya reported that they threatened, "We're going to kill you on Sunday; we won't let you stay." She explained, "You know the *jadu* [black magic] of Hyderabad; they did that. But Amma [the goddess] wouldn't let it stick. I begged Amma, 'Give me shakti, give me shakti,' and I ate neem leaves [which are cooling; implying cooling down the goddess, becoming unpossessed]."

Sandhya's regular possession by the ugra goddesses named by her neighbors was seemingly disruptive to the middle-class ethos of their apartment complex, much as bali and alcohol would have been disruptive to the middle-class clientele of the renovated Nalla Pochamma shrine. Sandhya had felt her neighbors' disapproval and experienced it as threatening to her very life, so she moved to small rental quarters near the Maisamma-Lakshmi temple. This recent move may help to explain her continued identification of the temple goddess as a singular gramadevata, with little knowledge of the Lakshmi part of the name.

At this point in Sandhya's narration, a man she identified as the temple president passed by on a motorcycle and stopped to find out who I, as an obvious outsider to the neighborhood, was. He asked us to wait there while he ran a small errand. Sandhya said his unexpected appearance, as hers had been, was the grace of Ammavaru. Then she continued her disrupted narrative: "I was wearing a red sari—this sari I'm wearing today—with a blue blouse. I had bolted the door and was sitting in the house. Ammavaru came. Hearing the sound of the drum—*dum dum*—I came running out. Ammavaru came onto me. I didn't know what was happening to me.... The [neighbors'] *jadu mantra* [black magic incantation] didn't hit me, but it hit my daughter. My daughter died. She was only sixteen.... Ammavaru was coming on me, right?" The neighbors "tried to do something to me," Sandhya said, "but it hit my daughter." Worried that "the police would take them away," the neighbors suggested that Sandhya's daughter had committed suicide because she failed her exams. But Sandhya said she and her husband had asked their daughter directly about her grades, and she had told them that she had not failed. Sandhya shifted back to the complaints of her neighbors: "'Why is she doing this [becoming possessed]? She is supposed to be worshiping Santoshi Mata;

why is Durga Mata coming?' They did something. . . . At that time we were living in a good apartment in Narayanguda; only later we came here. My daughter had lost only two [grade] points in her exam. She was eating. But then she poured kerosene and started a fire." Her daughter had self-immolated. "I was calling out to her, "Sarupa, Sarupa." But she wasn't responding. She was burning, but she wasn't saying anything, just standing like this. She wasn't coming toward me; she was moving back. My daughter was running. Someone wrapped a bedspread around her and she fell down."

Sandhya explained that nothing else in the house burned—"no saris, no bedding, nothing." In her anger at the goddess's failure to protect her daughter, she banished a material representation of the goddess that she had served in her home:

> I was so angry [*kopam*] at Ammavaru, and I took her out and left her somewhere. But she came back. At Bonalu she came into my dream, so I went and brought her back. The goddess protected me but not my daughter; she couldn't protect my daughter. I ate this many neem leaves and lemons [cooling substances] and asked her, "Give me shakti, give me shakti, give me shakti." She gave *me* shakti but not my daughter. She was so beautiful; she was my youngest child, only sixteen. I left my own house and came here; we rented it out and came here.

By this point Sandhya was weeping. She was clearly identifying her narrative with a gramadevata who had high demands, and not the pacific Lakshmi whose name now joins that of Maisamma at the temple.

The temple president returned, hearing only the last few words of Sandhya's narration. He asked her where she lived but did not recognize the house she named. She explained the situation: "My name is Sandhya, but they're asking about Potu Raju and I'm telling them." The president cut short the conversation, clearly annoyed with Sandhya's fragmented, indirect speech patterns. He first called the temple secretary on his mobile phone and then the pujari, who did recognize Sandhya as someone who frequently visited the temple. I asked the three men about the hyphenated name Maisamma-Lakshmi. The president laughed, "She's Lakshmi 350 days a year, and for two weeks during the month of Ashada, for Bonalu, she's Maisamma." The temple secretary ventured that she was "three-quarters Lakshmi and one-quarter Maisamma;" and the pujari quickly added,

"She's Maisamma at night, when she wanders around the neighborhood," implying that by day she was Lakshmi. Listening to them, Sandhya again insisted, "They're all the same."

I explained my interest in changing Hyderabadi gramadevata shrines and the impact of these changes on the goddesses they house. The men gave an abbreviated history of the temple since the time they had become involved with it: Santosh Nagar used to be on the outskirts of the city, which over the last few decades had grown rapidly around it. Literally to protect the land around the tiny gramadevata shrine—and the goddess herself—the neighborhood association had built up the permanent temple in front of which we were standing. The temple president pointed out the original structure across the lane from the new temple: a stack of four bricks forming three low walls, covered by a stone slab, sitting on a small cement platform under the shade of seven auspicious intertwined trees, backed by a large poster picturing the goddess across the lane (figure 4.6).

After performing puja to the goddess on our behalf, the pujari handed me his calling card, which gave his name as G. Venkataramana Panthulu and advertised his services in a range of associated ritual systems (numerology, astrology, and *vastu* [a Hindu system of architecture]) whose prescriptions help to deflect negative forces. Nowhere on the card were listed his priestly services at the Maisamma-Lakshmi temple; presumably the services he offers here as a pujari are only a small portion of his professional activities. On a subsequent visit to the temple, Vimala learned from the pujari that in 1982, the Pushpagiri Peetham (religious center of learning in the town of Kadapa, 425 kilometers from Hyderabad) took over this shrine, replaced the simple rock form of Maisamma with a three-foot-tall carved image of Lakshmi, appointed a Brahmin pujari, and changed the name of the temple. The pujari could not tell Vimala why a Brahmin matha at such distance from the current temple was motivated to take over administration of the temple or what its associations were to this gramadevata site.

Like Nalla Pochamma, this Maisamma-Lakshmi temple has undergone architectural change, transforming from a tiny shrine to a puranic-style temple; the goddesses of both temples now inhabit anthropomorphic images rather than tiny uncarved stones. In both cases, resulting changes in the identities and theologies of the goddesses have been initiated but are not yet fully complete, and the trajectories of their transformations are quite different. Through her personal narratives, we learn that Sandhya experiences the goddess outside of her material form and that she has not

Figure 4.6. Sandhya standing in front of original Maisamma shrine. Photo by the author.

internalized the addition of Lakshmi's name to that of Maisamma. Even as she asserts "all goddesses are the same," she knows and experiences the goddess as an ugra gramadevata, who has a personality and ritual needs that are unique from those of Lakshmi. The temple personnel also acknowledge that the transformation is not complete: by night the goddess is Maisamma, and she retains her unique gramadevata identity for the two weeks of the Bonalu festival.

The Goddess Who Lives at the Charminar: Bhagya Laxmi

In the middle of Hyderabad's Old City, at the base of its iconic Charminar, another shrine's transformations have become highly politicized and the name of the goddess has changed fully. The Charminar is a heritage site with four minarets (its base open on all sides), built on the banks of the Musi River in 1591 by Muhammad Quli Qutb Shah to commemorate the end of a virulent plague that had struck Hyderabad. Many Hyderabadis attribute the end of the plague to the powers of a gramadevata, although her name varies depending on who is telling the story; some worshipers at the Charminar shrine told me the goddess housed there was this very gramadevata. However, as indicated on the shrine's signboard—Shri Bhagya Laxmi Temple—the name of the goddess has dropped any association with a gramadevata.[23] With numerous Hindu-associated saffron-color flags flying above it, the shrine stands next to one of the four *minars* (towers) of the Charminar (figure 4.7).[24] On the other (inner) side of this same minar is a Shi'i shrine (*chilla*) flying Islam-associated green flags, which draws many fewer worshipers than does the goddess. (Interestingly, this Islamic shrine does not seem to be part of the politicized discourse around sacred space at the Charminar.) Perhaps it is the contentious recent history of unrest surrounding the Bhagya Laxmi temple and the involvement of politicians of Hindu organizations such as the Bhagya Laxmi Temple Protection Samithi (Committee) that has

---

23. In India the name "Lakshmi" is sometimes spelled "Laxmi" when written in English lettering. Bhagya Laxmi is the official name of the goddess at this shrine when written in English, so I have retained this transliteration, Laxmi, to refer to the goddess Lakshmi at this site.

24. It is difficult for a casual onlooker to discern whether the shrine is actually touching the minar, and many supporters argue that it is not actually on the property of the Charminar itself (Hindu Janajagruti Samiti 2015). The banner of the website of the Hindu Janajagruti Samiti (Committee to Awaken Hindus' Awareness), above the organization's name, reads, "For the Establishment of the Hindu Rashtra [Nation]." This organization, among others, has helped to politicize the Bhagya Laxmi temple site.

Figure 4.7. Bhagya Laxmi shrine at base of Charminar, with flags flying, 2011. Photo by the author.

caused some Hyderabadis to generalize about other expanding shrines to be explicitly (Hindutva) political acts, claiming literal space in the multireligious landscapes of Hyderabad.

Although I had seen the shrine many times on visits to the Old City and Charminar, I had never stopped to find out who was housed inside until fall 2011, a few days after Diwali. For this festival, over the entryway of the shrine, temple personnel had hung a large blue plastic tarpaulin that had been covered with strings of (now-fading) flowers. The head of the Bhagya Laxmi Temple Protection Samithi is reported to have said that the purpose of the temporary cover over the shrine was only to give protection from heat and rain to worshipers, and not to expand the temple, as critics had asserted (*Times of India* 2012b). When I returned in fall 2014, the shrine was surrounded on the street side by blue metal barriers on which were printed in white paint the word "Police," with only a small entrance for worshipers to access the goddess—the police presence a reminder of both past and potential communal unrest.

Many oral narratives circulate about the origins of the shrine. In 2011 an elderly pujari at the shrine explained to me that the shrine was over five hundred years old—older than the Charminar itself, he asserted. When I asked whether the goddess had been a gramadevata before becoming Bhagya Laxmi more recently, a male worshiper jumped in, saying, "Yes, you're right. The goddess was first named Maisamma,[25] but 'locals' [using the English word] took it over and built up the temple and renamed it for the goddess Bhagya Laxmi." He elaborated that the locals were, specifically, Marwari- and Agarwal-caste jewelers whose families had come from Gujarat and whose shops line one of the artery streets leading up to Charminar. When I asked who Maisamma was, both he and several other onlookers asserted that everyone knew that story: she was the goddess who had saved Hyderabad from the flooding Musi River.[26] She had blessed Hyderabad, saying, "Let Hyderabad grow like fishes in the ocean." Thereafter, the Muslim ruler (nizam) of Hyderabad and his family had continued to worship her.[27]

Returning to the reason for the goddess's name change, the elderly pujari rejoined the conversation. Several years earlier, he explained, the previously identified Gujarati jewelers had donated a pure silver *kavacham* (silver covering), giving the uncarved stone goddess an anthropomorphic form whom the Gujaratis had identified Bhagya Laxmi. The caretakers of what until then had been identified as a gramadevata had agreed to use the kavacham and to make a signboard naming the goddess to be Bhagya Laxmi. But, the elder continued, under the kavacham was a tiny stone that was a gramadevata (not specifying her name). When I returned to the shrine a few years later, a young pujari (who spoke on his cell phone even as he accepted offerings to the goddess) asserted, "No, no, there is no gramadevata here; it's only, and has always been, Bhagya Laxmi." He was the grandson of the elder I had spoken to earlier but seemed not to know (or want to acknowledge) the shrine history that had been related earlier by his grandfather. The young man pointed out the white marble image of a goddess who is clearly Lakshmi, standing behind the (presumed)

---

25. The Hyderabadi friend who had accompanied me to the Charminar on that occasion corrected the worshiper in an aside to me: "Not Maisamma; she's Pochamma."

26. This narrative is also attributed to Maisamma housed in the Katta Maisamma temple at the outside base of Tank Bund, which dams, on one side, the lake Hussein Sagar. This shrine too is rapidly expanding, but its growth is limited by the Tank Bund against which it is built, on one side, and a major thoroughfare road on the other; its expansion has been primarily horizontal.

27. The nizams were hereditary Muslim rulers of Hyderabad from the eighteenth century until 1950.

gramadevata stone covered by the metallic kavacham (figure 4.8). That the murti is white marble is indicative of the Gujarati community, immigrants from western India, who had donated it; South Indian temple images of deities are black granite.

Figure 4.8. Bhagya Laxmi marble image behind silver *kavacham*, 2014. To the right of the *kavacham* is a silver plaque on which is imprinted Lakshmi seated on a lotus. Photo by the author.

My Muslim auto driver had another story of the establishment of the shrine. There was not a goddess there "from the beginning"; rather, what has become the goddess was simply one of several cement posts erected to keep traffic from hitting the minars of the Charminar. Someone began to put kumkum on it, people began to make offerings, and then "the story came" and a goddess was created. The material act of kumkum is ambiguous here. Did the kumkum itself sacralize the cement post—that is, create the goddess? Did it identify a goddess already present? Or was it a political act to Hindu-ize an Islamic architectural heritage site? Materiality can hold this ambiguity. The caretaker of the chilla on the other side of the same minar told me that a similar process had threatened to start when kumkum began appearing on one of the other minars only a few months before our conversation. The kumkum had been quickly wiped off by city workers before worship could begin at that minar.

The basic contours of this narrative are repeated in various media reports: that the shrine originated in the late 1960s through application of kumkum on a stone or traffic marker near the Charminar (*Times of India* 2012a). In a 2012 article, *The Hindu* newspaper published two undated photographs, with no visible temple at the base of the minar in one and a more recent one that shows the temple structure but without the large sign and expanded temporary covering that now protects the permanent structure (Srivathsan 2012). Some readers of the original article questioned the authenticity of the older photograph, which they said looked like a painting; this elicited a response from *The Hindu*. The follow-up article explained that the older published photograph had been "colour-touched," a common practice in the days before color photography. This article published two more photographs from the newspaper's archive, dated 1957 and 1962, that show no temple structure (*The Hindu* 2012). The dating of the photographs and, thus, the date of the establishment of the shrine have become important in the debate about the right for the goddess to live there.

I thought perhaps some shopkeepers in the crowded Laad Bazaar (lit., lacquer bazaar, well known for its unique lacquer bangles), located on one of the four roads converging at the Charminar, may remember some of this history of the Bhagya Laxmi temple. However, in 2014, a longtime owner of a shop selling Hindu ritual paraphernalia was reticent to talk with me about the shrine. He volunteered that the shrine had been there for at least sixty years, before he was born, but then he quickly cut off my questions by asserting that the goddess had always been Bhagya Laxmi and that she had never been a gramadevata. Perhaps his reticence was due to a recent history of communal violence around the shrine. While after the destruction of Babri Masjid in Ayodhya in December 1992, some Hyderabadis identified the existence of the Charminar Hindu and Muslim worship sites side by side as evidence of the city's peaceful interreligious history, by that time there had already been violence around the Bhagya Laxmi shrine. On November 23, 1979, in a disagreement about whether Hindu shopkeepers could keep their stores open during a strike (*bandh*) called by the Majlis-e-Ittehadul Muslimeen (MIM) political party, some Muslims not only set fire to stores that had remained open but are said to have also desecrated the shrine (Ghosh 1997, 23). Subsequently, the site has remained politically volatile. The most recent significant violence occurred in 2012, when, as mentioned above, the caretakers of the shrine expanded the literal space of the shrine grounds in preparation for Diwali celebrations—without the requisite permission of the Archaeological Survey of India, which has identified the Charminar as a protected heritage site. This led to cars and buses being set on fire or otherwise damaged (Srivathsan 2012).

The controversies over the Bhagya Laxmi temple do not concern the identity of the goddess herself or the architectural style of the shrine. None of my interlocutors or newspaper articles found her transformation from gramadevata to Lakshmi, or the assertion that she had always been Bhagya Laxmi, to be particularly contentious. Rather, reference to the goddess's gramadevata identity is primarily evoked to establish the historical presence of the shrine and give it legitimacy. The controversy centers on the very presence of the shrine—its material presence and expansion interpreted by some as indicative of expansion of "Hindu" space and political power. Seemingly forgotten in the political upheavals and discourse about the shrine are the initial motivations of the Gujarati jewelers' offerings of a silver kavacham and their insistence that the goddess be named Bhagya Laxmi. It is possible that the initial kavacham offering was an act of devotion, or it may have been a material means to transform the "original" gramadevata, a local goddess, into Lakshmi, thereby bringing into their neighborhood a goddess whom the jewelers (as "outsiders" to Hyderabad) recognized. However, given the political significance of the Charminar and the multiple communities sharing the urban space of the Old City of Hyderabad, the material presence of a Hindu shrine at the base of one of the minars—no matter which goddess lives there—gave opportunity for devotion to be usurped by politics.

From Ugra Protector to Protected Goddess

Hyderabadi gramadevata shrines and temples exhibit architecture, personnel, and goddesses that are at different stages of transformation. Some tiny open-air shrines have added cement exteriors to protect the goddess from traffic, without paintings of the puranic deities Kali and Durga; other, larger shrines have these goddesses painted on their exterior walls, suggesting to passersby that the interior goddess is, indeed, a puranic one. By including the names of two goddesses on its signboard, the Maisamma-Lakshmi temple explicitly identifies a goddess in transition, still incomplete, from a gramadevata to a puranic one. Sandhya's narrative suggests another way in which this transition is incomplete and the limits of architectural agency: the goddess continues to exist outside of her material abode, making herself known as an ugra goddess through dreams and possession. And finally, the Charminar shrine is an example of the goddess's identity (if she was, indeed, originally a gramadevata) having changed completely from that of a gramadevata to Bhagya Laxmi. In each case, the transformation begins with a material transformation: a cement boundary wall or enclosure, or in the case of the Charminar shrine, the simple application of kumkum on one of the minars and, subsequently, the addition of the silver kavacham that changed the identity of the goddess from gramadevata to Bhagya Laxmi.

Each shrine holds personal and spatial histories that, with the passing of the generations that established and served the goddesses as gramadevatas, may soon be lost. Many current caretakers of Hyderabadi gramadevata shrines are women who have little formal education, and whose life work has been to serve the goddess and their own children. However, as these children become educated—like Nalla Pochamma matriarch's daughter—many, even most, of them are losing personal association with the goddesses, particularly as she reveals herself to humans through dreams and possession. They do not know the gramadevatas' traditional protective powers against drought and illness and have little interest in serving as their primary caretakers. Just as memories of village boundaries and bodies of water have been erased through urban expansion, memories of the gramadevatas' unique personalities and ritual requirements are being erased by their conflation with and transformation to puranic deities. This change in identity or personality does not, however, seem to be of concern to most worshipers and caretakers who serve and worship these goddesses. "They are one," they commonly assert.

The frequently repeated phrase that "they're all one" or "they're all the same" warrants some elaboration. In fieldwork with gramadevata traditions in Tirupati, I often heard the phrase used in relationship to the Seven Sister goddesses, particularly when a speaker could not name all seven sisters. In any case, when relating their experience of a particular gramadevata, speakers most often refer to her as Ammavaru or Amma rather than by her distinct name. More broadly, I have heard the phrase used to identify goddesses in general as singular (and have never heard from worshipers in India a similar phrase characterizing all male deities as "one").[28] In this context, the phrase is used to characterize the diversity of goddesses—the elasticity of the idea of "goddess"—without implying exclusion of any one of them. However, when used by interlocutors in this chapter, the phrase usually refers to identification between puranic goddesses and gramadevatas. The implication is that names do not matter: they're all one. Within an increasingly dominant (and dominating) middle-class and brahminic culture in India, it may be that traditional worshipers of gramadevatas use the phrase "they are all one" to retain conceptual/imaginative space for themselves and their experiences of their gramadevatas. We have seen that materially and ritually gramadevatas and puranic goddesses *are* distinguishable; and once their material abodes and forms change, so too do their rituals and clientele. The unique powers, duties, personalities and needs of the gramadevatas, now equated with or transformed into puranic goddesses, are being lost; indeed, a wider culture of gramadevatas is being lost.[29] Many Hyderabadis now encoun-

---

28. I specify "in India" because I have heard many Hindus in America assert that all gods are one, when they are attempting to explain what looks like worship of multiple deities to non-Hindus visiting a temple, whom the Hindu speakers assume are monotheists and likely to be judgmental of polytheistic traditions.

29. Note that many upper-caste, middle-class Hindus may still call poxes of various kinds "Ammavaru," referring to the gramadevatas with whom poxes were traditionally associated. They may even engage in traditional rituals to Ammavaru, employing neem leaves to cool her, to mitigate the poxes. During my fieldwork with Gangamma in Tirupati in 1999–2000, my fieldwork associate, a PhD candidate in American literature, contracted chickenpox. The flower sellers at one of Gangamma's temples teased her, saying she should have expected that Ammavaru would visit her, since she spent so much time at her temple with me. Her mother dutifully hung neem leaves outside my associate's bedroom door and fed her cooling foods; but before working with me, my associate knew little about Gangamma except her name. However, gramadevata

ter gramadevatas through their new puranic forms residing in their middle-class renovated shrines.

We have seen that a primary reason for making permanent, enclosed, and expanding gramadevata shrines, from the perspective of the humans who serve the goddesses, was to protect the goddess. Secondarily, the forms of architecture, and more specifically the paintings on the outside walls, are to please the goddess; and "they look good." But as Rohan Bastin (2005) argues, in his study of the Munnesvaram temple in northwest Sri Lanka, temples are not simply representations of their respective deities; rather, their architecture is active in creating (what he calls "capturing or ensnaring") the deity. Material architecture has agency. In the case of Hyderabadi gramadevata shrines, their material changes are initiating changes in the nature of the goddesses themselves—from gramadevatas who protect to goddesses who need protection, quite literally.

---

culture is much broader than association with illness, a culture with which these same families do not engage: they do not know the gramadevatas' narratives or their desires; the goddesses don't visit members of these castes in possession; nor do most upper-caste, middle-class Hindus participate in their jataras.

Chapter 5

Standing in Cement

Ravana on the Chhattisgarhi Plains

For a child growing up in Chhattisgarh, the often tedious four-to-six-hour journey on the narrow national highway between our village and the railway station in the city of Raipur was marked, in part, by the ten-to-twelve-foot-tall cement Ravana image in the village of Tumgaon, visible from the main road; it meant we were either one-third or two-thirds through the journey (figure 5.1). Ravana is the antagonist (*rakshasa*, often translated as "demon") of the Ramayana epic. As a child, I did not realize how unique the phenomenon of a permanent Ravana image was in the broader Indian landscape nor that this was one of many sprinkled across the Chhattisgarhi heartland.[1]

Most Chhattisgarhis themselves do not find these cement Ravanas remarkable. In the course of my fieldwork, I often heard assertions like "There's a Ravana in every village," although, in fact, there are not. Some

---

1. In Chhattisgarhi and Hindi, names such as Ravan, Ram, Lakshman, and the narrative Ramayan are pronounced without a final "a." However, for this chapter, I have used the Sanskrit transliteration of these terms for ease of recognition by non-Hindi readers (Ravana, Rama, Ramayana, etc.) except when these terms are part of a Chhattisgarhi name, such as Ravan Bhatha (an open field in Raipur upon which a cement Ravana stands).

When I began my research on Ravana, I searched the internet for "Ravana temples" and found several sites that list the same five temples scattered across North India. None of the websites mention Chhattisgarh's permanent images, which stand outside of temples.

Figure 5.1. Ravana, Tumgaon village, 2014. Photo by the author.

of my interlocutors thought that these kinds of images could be found in the "south" (implying Tamil Nadu), although I have not heard of or seen such Ravana images there;[2] perhaps they were thinking of Sri Lanka (after all, Ravana is the king of Lanka).[3] There seems to be, for some Chhattisgarhis, an assumption of a southern "Ravana culture," at whose northern borders lies Chhattisgarh. Others characterize the region as the jungle through which Rama wandered during his fourteen-year exile, or

---

2. The association of Ravana with the "south" can be attributed, in part, to the political pro-Dravida movement (Dravida Munnetra Kazhagam, or DMK), which celebrates Ravana as a "southern" king who was defeated by the "northern" king Rama. Activist Periyar E. V. Ramaswamy campaigned against Rama and the Tamil Ramayana from the 1920s until he died in 1973 (Pandian 1998). DMK leader M. Karunanidhi famously declared, "If you insult Ravan, you are insulting me." See Kancha Ilaiah's similar argument against burning Ravana images at Dussehra (Diwali) (2013).

3. For contemporary revitalization of Ravana (including new temple images) among Sinhalese Buddhists in Sri Lanka, see Deborah De Koning 2018. She analyzes the phenomenon as part of a nationalist agenda glorifying the "ancient past" of Lanka.

they identify Lanka with Chhattisgarh and Lanka-dwellers with the original inhabitants of Chhattisgarh.

Chhattisgarhi cement Ravanas stand at village and town centers or on open fields at their outskirts. While their styles differ significantly, the images share a basic visual grammar: Ravana has nine or ten visible heads[4]—most with a donkey head atop his crowned middle head—and he is always mustached, as is every rakshasa in Chhattisgarhi local dramatic enactments of the Ramayana. He may have two arms or numerous arms on each side of his chest and usually holds one or more weapons; he may have a sword tucked into his cummerbund. The rakshasa king is often depicted wearing a royal knee-length coat—blue or red—and gold-colored pants or a *dhoti* (traditional male garb; a single cloth tied around the waist and drawn up between the legs); fewer images depict him bare-chested. A brahminic thread crossing his torso from left to right is often clearly visible—even outside his coat, whereas traditionally it would be worn inside—overperforming his Brahmin identity. Some images wear shoes (often slippers with upturned toes), while others are barefoot. Ravana often wears a fancy gold pendant, or he may be graced with a floral garland. The images are consistently light-skinned; this may be an aesthetic preference, a choice to distinguish him from dark-skinned (blue) Rama images, or to perform his Brahmin identity.

The Ravana image found in the village of Tari uniquely wears a dark blue suitcoat (in the color and style of the suitcoat worn by images of Ambedkar, a Dalit activist and one of the primary writers of India's constitution), a striped tie, a gold shirt, and modern blue pants held up by a belt (figure 5.2).[5] In the early 1980s, when I first met the Tari Ravana, he was wearing a suitcoat and dhoti. In 2014, when I asked village elders why the change from dhoti to pants, they laughed and said that Ravana was changing according to fashion, "just like we are."

---

4. Presumably, those with only nine visible heads imagine a tenth on the back of the large central head.

5. A 2014 newspaper article dates this Tari image to the 1930s. Very few Chhattisgarhi Ravana images are close to Rama temples, but Rahul Bhutra (2014) writes that a Tari village community organization, seeing puja performed to Ravana's image every Dussehra, decided to build a Rama temple right across the street. They thought god too should be worshiped. Village elders had initially resisted the Rama temple, explaining that it was because of the presence of Ravana that the village had been a peaceful place all these years; after all, they said, he was a wise man and an ascetic.

Figure 5.2. Ravana, Tari village, 2014. Photo by the author.

Throughout most of the year, cement Ravanas are unattended, gathering the dust of passing vehicles, serving as a rest stop for goat herders, or whose pedestals serve as a climbing apparatus for young children at play. Once a year, in the weeks preceding the festival of Dussehra (which in Chhattisgarh and North India celebrates Rama's destruction of Ravana), the images are swept off with brooms tied to long bamboo poles, and their row of ten heads and clothing are repainted. Ramlilas (dramatic performances of the Ramayana) are held in front of many of these cement Ravanas during Dussehra, at the end of which a fire-lit arrow is shot toward the Ravana image, or firecrackers are set off around it to indicate his destruction. However, while narratively Ravana is killed by the hero-god Rama, materially he remains, standing in cement throughout the year on the Chhattisgarh plains—albeit with his painted clothing a bit worse for wear after Dussehra celebrations.

These images are material actors, creating alternative possibilities to dominant narrative conclusions regarding Ravana, possibilities that human actors and communities may not have consciously intended when they built the permanent images. A 2001 volume titled *Questioning Ramayanas* presents a range of what Paula Richman calls "oppositional tellings" but considers only narrative and discursive forms of questioning. This chapter introduces the possibility of material questioning.

In what follows, I describe images, rituals, and conversations related to three different cement Ravanas and one effigy. Each of these figures stands amid or has been built by a different clientele or community, which leads me to at least one conclusion: that the material acts of cement Ravanas do not create a single ideology or theology but that they open up possibilities for a range of alternative ideologies, including a Ravana-dominant subculture and (often unarticulated) identification with Ravana.

Ravan Bhatha, Raipur

The Ravana constructed by the Dudhadhari Math (*matha*; a Vaishnava monastic center and temple), on the open field called Ravan Bhatha, is the most famous in the Chhattisgarhi plains. The *bhatha* field is identified with the physical form of Ravana standing there rather than the Rama-centered Ramlila that is performed in front of him.[6] Oral histories told by the chief priest and administrator (*mahant*) of the Dudhadhari Math assert that theirs is the largest and oldest cement Ravana, built by the (brahminic) matha about 150 years ago at the site where it still

---

6. Elsewhere in North and Central India, Ramlila grounds are called Ramlila Maidan. Chhattisgarhi *bhatha* and Hindi *maidan* both translate as "open field."

stands, on the outskirts of Raipur, at the same time the matha itself was established.[7] (It is likely that the first permanent Ravana images were not made of cement but rather the earlier-used mixture of lime, mud, and pebbles for large images such as this.) This same history—that the Ravan Bhatha image was the oldest in Chhattisgarh—was reasserted with great pride by the chair (an influential land developer in Raipur) of the 2014 Ravan Bhatha Ramlila organizing committee when he addressed a burgeoning crowd to introduce the afternoon's program and announce the kite-flying competition.

The mahant speculated that other villages had copied the Ravan Bhatha image, and many, but not all, village Ravanas do share a dress style similar to that of the matha Ravana: gold pants or dhoti and a red jacket with white patterning. Most cement Ravanas have been constructed much more recently. I remember seeing the above-mentioned Ravana of my childhood since the 1950s and heard from my interlocutors similar dating of the 1950s and 1960s for most of the other Ravanas I have documented. Before that time, and still in some villages on the peripheries of the central Mahanadi River plain, many simple Ravanas were built of mud or clay, formed around a central wooden pole. These too are not destroyed at the end of Dussehra but left to melt away in the rains. Cement Ravanas continue to be built, depending on individual communities' financial and social resources.

Above and on one side of the Dudhadhari Ravana's heads are painted the words *ahamkari ravan*, prideful Ravana; above the middle head is a small donkey head. The latter feature marks most Chhattisgarhi Ravanas, although the animal represented is often barely recognizable. A unique feature of the matha's Ravana is the painting of his son Meghnath (also known as Indrajit) on the smooth back side of the image, a lithe delicate figure compared to his imposing father on the front side. No one I initially asked, including the organizer of the Ramlila, knew who this back-side figure was, and many interlocutors said they had not even noticed it. Ultimately, it was the mahant of the matha who identified him as Meghnath. When I asked about the donkey atop this Ravana's middle head, most people said they had not noticed it and did not know what it might signify. Others who also had not noticed it (and who had earlier identified Ravana as a

---

7. The Balaji temple at the matha is widely believed to have been built in the early seventeenth century CE by Raghu Rao Bhosle, king of Nagpur, in whose jurisdiction Raipur was located.

vidvan [wise one]) suggested the donkey might signify obstinance, ignorance, or stupidity. "Donkey" is a common appellation in Chhattisgarhi used to refer to someone who the speaker perceives to be ignorant or stupid, as in "What a donkey [*gadha*] you are!" Two Ravana *murtikars* (image makers) with whom I spoke had no answer to the significance of the donkey; they simply said, "This is what we were taught."

That most people I spoke with had not noticed Meghnath on the Dudhadhari Math Ravana or the donkey atop his head (nor had I noticed it, to my chagrin, until I showed some of my early photographs to an art historian, who immediately asked what was atop Ravana's head) raises the question of what these material features create if no one "sees" them. However, the material Ravana's agency is created more through his *presence* in human communities than through specific elements of his iconography that may or may not be seen by members of the communities among which he stands. Not only the donkey but also Ravana himself, as a full figure, is often not "noticed" outside of Dussehra celebrations. In her study of oversized (up to twenty feet high) Christian roadside crosses, Hillary Kaell calls such objects, seen and unseen at the same time, "ambient" objects, objects that are embedded in "assemblages" that may foreground or background the crosses, causing them to be seen or unseen (2017, 144). Some caretakers of these crosses told her that people can look right at a cross and, literally, not see it—until they are called by and respond to the cross itself (137–39, 154). Similarly, Ravana images are more often simply present than "seen."

Noticed or not, the donkey iconography is worth further consideration (figure 5.3). I have been unable to locate any narratives that describe the donkey atop Ravana's middle head, but in visual representations of Ravana, the donkey is not unique to Chhattisgarh. While I have not seen this feature on other kinds of Ravana sculptures (primarily on the exteriors of temples), there are many examples of miniature paintings that depict the donkey head.[8] We have already noted the association between a donkey and ignorance or stupidity, but this association is visually at odds with a royal scholarly Ravana described in both textual renditions of the

---

8. An example of such a miniature (ca. 1750) can been found at the Brooklyn Museum (www.brooklynmuseum.org/opencollection/objects/127224). Portrayal of a donkey atop Ravana's head is not limited to miniature paintings. In tiny wooden Benarsi-style figurines of Ravana, he is also portrayed with a (barely decipherable) big-eared donkey atop his head.

Figure 5.3. Ravana with visible donkey atop his middle head, Ghirola village, 2014. Photo by the author.

Ramayana and by many Chhattisgarhis. It is possible, of course, that his stupidity is his arrogance and pride.

Christian Novetzke has observed what he calls a "donkey curse" at the end of some eleventh-to-twelfth-century Marathi (western India) inscriptions and sometimes as visual images (2016, 78–86). The inscriptions warn that the curse will afflict anyone who would defile or dishonor a particular donation, Brahmins, or brahminic activity or institution: may the person who would dare do so become a donkey (78–79). Many of the donkey images were erected at the boundaries of donated lands, and Novetzke suggests these were created to both divert the envious evil eye and, at the same time, draw attention to the donor (82–84). It is, of course, impossible to draw a direct connection between these inscriptional curses and the donkey on the top of Ravana's heads. However, they raise the possibility of the donkey to both draw attention to Ravana and protect him, deflecting the evil eye. While visually fascinating to those of us noticing it for the first time, what the material presence of the donkey may create remains an enigma.⁹

The 2014 Ramlila at Raipur's Ravan Bhatha was an open-air performance and the conclusion of an indoor, nine-night recitation of the poet saint Tulsidas's Hindi *Ramcaritmanas* text, sponsored by the same organizing committee of the Ravan Bhatha celebrations. When I arrived at the bhatha at about 3:00 p.m. on Dussehra day itself, the puja at the feet of the cement Ravana that I had been told would start the entire celebration only in late afternoon had already taken place. The few remnants of coconut, marigold garlands, and now-extinguished oil lamps lay rather unceremoniously scattered at Ravana's feet. I was in time, however, for a lively kite-flying competition, one announcement after another of lost children or mis-parked cars, felicitation of and speeches by luminaries and members of the organizing committee, and a highly anticipated musical performance by a Chhattisgarhi movie star. Several speeches by chief guests noted that the burning up of Ravana's effigy was the burning up of *pap* (sin), mentioning specifically the sins of drinking and dowry.¹⁰

Following these events, the attenuated Ramlila that night comprised of Rama's and Ravana's armies (with five warriors per side) fighting each

---

9. An obscure reference to Ravana's association with donkeys is found in the tantric text of *Kriyakalagunottara*, translated by Michael Slouber (2017, 174–78). One chapter addresses the treatment of bites from "insect-like demon-donkeys whose bite causes skin inflammation" (46). Shiva explains the flame donkeys as originating when Ravana lifted up and shook Mount Kailash and Shiva pressed the mountain down with his big toe. At that time, "a subterranean flame emerged. [Which] . . . was worshipped at Gokarna in the form of a donkey." In the same text, Shiva prescribes various donkey products as appropriate treatments for spider poxes (174). While the goddess of poxes, Shitala, rides a donkey in some iconography elsewhere in India (Ferrari 2015), in Chhattisgarh she is most often an uncarved stone or takes form through white flags as a Gond deity.

10. In responses to public lectures I have given about Chhattisgarhi Ravanas, several Indian and non-Indian audience members have suggested that the burning of Ravana's effigies is equivalent to his funeral pyre; others have suggested the purificatory qualities of fire rather than its destructive ones. However, none of my Chhattisgarhi interlocutors has made similar observations. In this chapter I am juxtaposing Ravana's narrative destruction with his permanent cement images; the burning effigy would materially support Ravana's narrative destruction.

other in various configurations until Rama finally shot a fire-lit arrow at Ravana's effigy to begin its destruction by fire. When speaking with me about the Ravana cement image and his straw effigy, the *lila* organizer distinguished the two as *murti* (permanent material image; the word also used for worshiped material images of deities) and *putla* (doll; effigy), respectively. Although he could not specify when, he said that the addition of the effigy was relatively new—"according to fashion"—and that before effigies had begun to be used, a fire-lit arrow simply hit the cement image to indicate its (narrative) destruction.[11] The crowd of thousands of celebrants quickly dissipated (as quickly as that many people can move) as the effigies of Ravana, his brother Kumbhakarna, and son Meghnath burned to the ground. As I left on the back of a friend's motorcycle and looked back, the performative image was striking: the imposing cement Ravana, lit by the light of the dying fires, looking down on his own burning effigy—the materiality of two ideologies (figure 5.4).

I returned to the Dudhadhari Math after Dussehra to try to learn from the mahant why the matha had first constructed their cement Ravana.[12] While he was very talkative when it came to the various images of deities in the temple complex, the mahant had little to say about Ravana. His initial answer was simply, "This is a matha for Vishnu, right? We worship Rama [one of Vishnu's incarnations] here, right? This matha celebrates five Rama festivals a year: Ramnavmi, Krishnashtami, Vijay Dashami, and Deepavali, and Holi—Krishna is Vishnu, right?"—then, changing the flow of thought—"We paint Ravana every year, as if he's ready for war." I probed a little more, asking why theirs was a permanent cement Ravana, now accompanied by an effigy on Dussehra. He first speculated that the matha had erected Ravana on its empty lands to protect against encroachment. Pausing to reflect, he added, "If we burn down the putla one day of the year and remember, then we forget 364 days a year. Ravana was so truthful [*satyasali*], but all his good qualities [*gunas*] were erased by his *ahamkar* [pride]; you must have seen that painted on the murti: 'ahamkari Ravan.'" How was Ravana understood, I asked, given that puja was performed to him? Was he a god? No, the mahant answered, "No, he's not a god. But he was very wise; that's why we do puja," suggesting

---

11. Much smaller effigies, two to three feet high, are sold on some of Raipur's back streets for domestic use. The man selling them told me some families buy these for their children to burn and "to have fun."

12. The mahant self-identified as the ninth in line after the founding Dudhadhari saint (*sant*) himself.

Figure 5.4. Ravana cement image and burning effigy, Ravan Bhatha, Raipur, 2014. Photograph courtesy of Akhilesh Nand.

that in this context, puja may not be worship but a ritual of honor. The mahant suggested the permanent image was an ethical reminder, although one could interpret his material royal permanence more positively, as are other Chhattisgarhi cement images of politicians, military martyrs (*shahids*), and often elaborate images of ancestors atop their *samadhis* (death memorials; graves). Then we remember the donkey. There is an ambivalence around the images: Ravana is a model of both truthfulness/wisdom and ego/pride.

A retired matha administrator listening to our conversation—who had lived in Raipur for only twenty years and is therefore not considered a "local" Chhattisgarhi—added the explanation that Chhattisgarh was the northern border of Dandaranya, the forest where Rama, Lakshmana, and Sita lived during their exile and from where Ravana had kidnapped Sita, and that he was a good and great king, after all. He explained that Ravana only kidnapped Sita to bring Rama to Lanka so that he could be killed by god and achieve liberation. Ravana's status, the administrator continued, was displayed in the fact that after Rama killed him, Rama had to perform purificatory rituals to atone for the sin of killing a Brahmin.

Further, Rama had ordered Ravana's brother, Vibhishana, to honor Ravana by performing death rituals of both a brother and a king. "All this is why," he concluded, "we have these Ravanas in Chhattisgarh."

Throughout the year, outside of the festival days of Dussehra, the Ravan Bhatha image is, most simply, present, without discursive meaning given to it. Raipur residents often refer to the bhatha as a geographic marker when giving directions to that part of the city, much like a movie theater or hospital is used to identify a neighborhood. Young goat herders climb atop the platform on which Ravana stands with barely a glance to the image looming above them. Only during Dussehra is focus given to Ravana himself. This particular Ravana carries the authority of both the brahminic matha that constructed it and its age. Several chief guests at the Ramlila I attended at this bhatha made explicit the burning of the effigy as a symbol of the destruction of sin; they did not seem to notice that the cement Ravana stayed standing. Whatever symbolic significance some humans may read into the burning effigy, the cement image is not destroyed and thus offers a material alternative to the dominant Ramayana narrative.

Ravana as Brahmin Neighbor

We move now to the town of Dhamtari, 65 kilometers south of Raipur. I first came across this Ravana image quite by accident, as he stands on a road I rarely travel, tucked away between houses rather than on a large field or in a commercial area of town. Built in 2005, he has a distinctive look—dressed in a gold "silk" dhoti and scarf (one year white, another year painted saffron color) draped across his lower back and over his arms, a gold pendant and belt, a Brahmin thread crossing his bare chest (figure 5.5). While he has multiple heads (the middle one marked by a vermilion Shaiva forehead mark), he has only two arms. Bare-chested like a Brahmin priest, he wears royal ornaments (necklace, belt, armbands, and bracelets) and carries the sword and bow of a warrior king.

I knocked on the door of a house only about fifteen yards from the image and was greeted by a Chhattisgarhi Brahmin woman, Maheshwari.[13] She was taken aback by a visitor like me, but quickly invited me in for

---

13. I distinguish her as a Chhattisgarhi Brahmin, since, she told me, "Our families have always been here" and that her mother tongue is Chhattisgarhi. Brahmins whose families immigrated from Uttar Pradesh several generations ago still identify and are identified by others with their northern origins.

Figure 5.5. Ravana, Dhamtari, 2015. Photo by the author.

tea, no matter why I was there. I explained that I had stopped to ask about the distinctive Ravana standing outside her door and eventually asked how she understood the fact that physically he is not destroyed but stands there all year. Maheshwari responded with a lively half-hour Chhattisgarhi retelling of the story that provided little description of Ravana, and she had little else to say about the image. Her response to my question about the permanent images of Ravana two years later was similarly a retelling of Ramayana narrative episodes, many of which are not found in the sixteenth-century poet Tulsidas's Hindi *Ramcaritmanas*, the dominant textual Ramayana tradition in Chhattisgarh.[14] My direct questions did not elicit direct answers.

On this subsequent visit, Maheshwari's husband (a *pandit* who regularly performs rituals for other families and at several nearby temples)

---

14. One episode Maheshwari performed that is not found in the *Ramcaritmanas* related how Ravana had buried a clay pot filled with blood that he had demanded from a group of imprisoned *rishis* before he would grant them their freedom. This pot became Sita and was plowed up by her father, Janaka.

joined us after she had retold the narrative. He proudly told me that it was he who had caused this Ravana to be built when he was the neighborhood headman (*sarpanch*)—at the urging of the neighborhood council (*panchayat*)—and that his intention had been to provide a designated space for the local Ramlila. This intention had been contradicted, however, by his wife on my first visit when she said that this small area in front of their house was not, in fact, the site of a Ramlila; there is a nearby, large bhatha for that, with no cement image. Rather, around Dussehra time, she explained, small groups of neighbors gather across the road from the Ravana to recite Tulsidas's *Ramcaritmanas*.

Maheshwari and her husband grew up in households that had actively participated in learning and reciting the *Ramcaritmanas*, although Maheshwari was equally fluent in Chhattisgarhi oral versions of the epic. She described how her paternal grandfather had made all of his grandchildren read the *Ramcaritmanas* for a half hour every day before they began their homework. And today she regularly participates in Brahmin female *Ramcaritmanas* recitation groups that, she explained, gather on special occasions such as a grandchild's birthday. She and her husband know the narrative well, but their conversations—only hinting at coexisting, alternative ideologies—vacillated between the narrative and the murti standing outside their door. Although they characterized Ravana as a vidvan, the most learned of men (from whom Lakshmana learned the art of warfare, Maheshwari's husband specified), the pandit explained (when asked) that the donkey head had been attached by Shiva as a sign of Ravana's *lack* of wisdom.

Maheshwari asserted that even when an effigy is burned at the bhatha, it is not Ravana himself who is destroyed but rather "all bad things" (*burhai*), including consumption of alcohol. After all, she continued, "Rama killed Ravana once; there's no need to kill him over and over." Discursively, the couple confirmed Ravana's narrative death. During the lively conversation in which husband and wife vied for the performance floor, Ravana's Brahmin identity came up several times; and this identity, rather than king or rakshasa, is materially performed outside their doorway. Maheshwari's husband speculated that many passersby—particularly members of lower and adivasi castes who don't know the Ramayana—may not recognize the murti as Ravana,[15] but "they pay respects (do *pranam*,

---

15. In my fieldwork over many years in Chhattisgarh, I have found that many non- or low-literate members of lower and adivasi castes know only a minimal Ramayana narrative, if any at all, which was confirmed by the pandit's comment.

a bodily gesture of respect with hands pressed together and raised] to it nevertheless, as they *should* to a Brahmin." The pandit assumed that Ravana's Brahmin identity would be recognized by this particular image's bare chest, clearly visible sacred thread, and his upper cloth (which does not explain how his ten heads would be interpreted).

Later in our conversation, the pandit answered my question as to whether or not they offer puja to the murti: "No, no we don't. But we light diyas and offer coconuts [a ritual that other Chhattisgarhis had identified as puja, at Ravan Bhatha], because, you would know, he is a Brahmin." That a Brahmin, who regularly performs Sanskritic rituals as a self-identified pandit for others in his neighborhood, and for several nearby temples owned by his own family, commissioned this image may help to explain its unique visual features and the pandit's primary identification of Ravana as a Brahmin. This Ravana proudly stands among Brahmin households as a highly respected neighbor of the same caste, materially unfettered by the narrative in which he is god's antagonist and is killed by Rama.

Ravana as Gond Ancestor in the Company of Gond Deities

Cement Ravana images are found in a relatively bounded geographic area in the heartland plains of Chhattisgarh, fed by the great Mahanadi River—with Raipur at its center—and not on its jungle and hill peripheries where adivasi populations are in greater proportions than they are in the plains. Many Chhattisgarhi interlocutors asserted that such Ravana images would obviously not be found in adivasi-majority areas such as the south Chhattisgarh district of Bastar, since these communities have not incorporated the Ramayana into their traditions as either performers or audiences. The social networks of the central Chhattisgarhi plains, however, include many adivasis who have been "Hindu-ized" and incorporated into local caste networks—that is, Gonds living in the plains function like a *jati* (endogamous caste group), observe many Hindu festivals, and perform puja to Hindu deities. Many of these same families, however, also keep a shrine to the Gond deity Burho Dev (in the form of iron tridents) in their homes. Other Gond song and festival traditions are also performed throughout the plains and help to give identity to Chhattisgarh as a cultural region (now a state, as of 2000) unique from surrounding regions (Flueckiger 1996). Adivasi presence and significant influence in Chhattisgarhi life is one factor that may have supported the tradition of cement Ravanas and the possibility of performative, alternative ideologies that they create.

On the full-moon night *after* the tenth day of the lunar month on which Dussehra is celebrated in Raipur—and elsewhere in Chhattisgarhi towns and cities, as well as the North Indian plains[16]—I visited the Gond-dominant village of Pirhapal, about a half-hour drive from the royal center of Kanker. The village sits at the edge of the jungle and at the base of some hills where, I was told, Naxalite (Maoist) activists live and from where they were likely to come down to witness the Dussehra celebrations. Pirhapal has no cement Ravana, but I went there to meet a thirty-one-year-old Gond activist, about whom I had heard in Kanker, whose parents had given him the name of Ravan: Kishan Ravan Mandavi (a matter of some joking when his "rakshasa" name came up in conversation among some of his non-Gond acquaintances). He works as an office attendant in the local high school, but his passion is his activist work with a Gond service organization, whose seven-colored flag flies above the doorway of his home. As an example of the kind of *seva* (social service) this organization performs, Kishan mentioned helping to support weddings for poor families, but its primary purpose, he told us, is to increase pride in Gond culture, for which the organization runs workshops in which Kishan has participated. On one wall of the front veranda of Kishan's simple home were several posters distributed by this Gond organization. These included one that pictures a royal man wearing the *singmohur* Gond headdress of bison horns (which the Gond ancestor-hero Lingo also wears in visual representations of him); he is bare-chested, wears a dhoti lower cloth, is heavily ornamented, and holds a sword. The wording on the bottom of the poster identifies him as "Prithvi ke Maharaj, Koyavamshi, Lankapati, Gond Raja Ravan Mandavi" (The Great King of Earth, [from the] Koya Lineage, Lord of Lanka, Gond King Ravan Mandavi). Ravana, explicitly named and visualized as a Gond king, shares Kishan's Gond-associated name Mandavi.

---

16. When I visited the village of Chilhati in 2013, in the company of the *raja* of Kanker Aditya Deo, we were told by a passerby that this village celebrates Dussehra after the tenth lunar day so that the raja can attend—which he cannot do on the tenth day itself, given his royal responsibilities on Dussehra. Not recognizing who he was standing in front of, our interlocutor explained that this custom started with the grandfather of the current raja. We later learned that Dussehra is celebrated on different days, in rotation between villages in this area, so that villagers can attend one another's celebrations.

When I asked Kishan about the inclusion of "Ravan" in his name—Kishan Ravan Mandavi—he explained, "Our dharma guru [religious teacher] told my parents to give this name, because we Gonds are in the lineage [*vamsha*] of Ravan."[17] When I asked about his father's name, which did not have "Ravan" in it, Kishan explained that they did not know "back then" about the Gond connection with Ravana. That Kishan's father, a *bhagat* (ritual specialist) of the royal family and a practicing *baiga* (priest to Gond deities) did not "know of these things" suggests that this particular mode of Gond activism and honoring of Ravana as an ancestor is relatively new in Chhattisgarh and postdates the first constructions of cement Ravanas.

We were served tea while waiting for the Ravan Vadh (lit., defeat/killing of Ravana; significantly not called Ramlila) to begin, and Kishan explained what we could expect. First, he said, they would conduct puja to the Ravana effigy. I tried to elicit from Kishan what this ritual, in this context, could mean. Did this mean that Ravana was considered a god? I wondered about the significance of worshiping someone you were about to kill or whether puja is considered "worship" in this context. Kishan's first cryptic response was "It's like you do puja to an animal before sacrificing it," presumably honoring the life one is about to take. After the puja, the Gond-associated goddess Shitala and her entourage of Gond deities (who take form through white flags held aloft on tall bamboo poles and possessed human bodies) came to greet Ravana as he was present in his effigy (figure 5.6). Shitala shares the name and some characteristics with the goddess associated with illness in North and Central India, but in Chhattisgarh she has uniquely been integrated into a Gond cosmology of deities (*devi-devtaon*).[18] As is appropriate for a king or honored guest, the goddess applied a *tilak*

---

17. He did not identify the dharma guru but said that he lived in a village about fifty kilometers away.

18. See Aditya Deo 2013 for descriptions of the pantheon of Gond deities, which includes Shitala, into which Ravana in this village is incorporated. Religious studies scholar Fabrizio Ferrari cautions against generalizing Shitala across cultural regions: "Goddesses like Shitala should be studied as integral to the vernacular tradition they belong to and discussed as local products of that variegated knowledge which constitutes folklore" (2010, 145). While it may be tempting to associate Ravana's donkey head with Shitala's donkey mount (*vahana*) as is found in many parts of India—and hence the donkey would be one material link between the two—here in Chhattisgarh she is not associated with the donkey. Her Gond material forms are white flags and the human bodies that she possesses.

Figure 5.6. Shitala greets Ravana, Pirhapal village, 2014. Photo by the author.

(vermilion powder marking) on his forehead. This ritual greeting between the Gond goddess Shitala and Ravana creates a relationship of respect that draws Ravana into a Gond imaginative, ritual field. Significantly, Rama is absent. Ravana continued to the open dusty field that would become the lila site of battle between human actors of his and Rama's armies. Shitala returned to her temple; the Ramlila is outside of her world.

At the bhatha, pair by pair, a warrior from each side first used their wooden weapons in a ritualized dance-like movement; then, dropping their weapons, they wrestled one another before one of the two battling warriors admitted defeat and ran back to his side of the field. Finally, Rama and Ravana met face-to-face, their battle looking the same as those of their armies. I was sitting on Ravana's side of the battlefield, where the audience cried out with great enthusiasm through the battle, "*Jai* Raja Ravan! *Jai* Raja Ravan!" (Victory to King Ravan!) Rama had his supporters on the other side of the field, but their cries of support were drowned out by those for Ravana. When Ravana was finally defeated, Rama held up a lit arrow and struck the effigy standing nearby. On this particular night, the straw in the effigy was wet and it took considerable effort to get a fire going, creating an interesting performative moment suggesting that Ravana may not be so easy to destroy.

With Ravana's effigy nearly burned to the ground, we regathered at Kishan's home, and he expanded on what Ravana puja might mean: "Actually, we shouldn't burn Ravana, because he is the god [*bhagvan*] of the Gond vamsha."[19] He told us about a village nearby that had not burned Ravana for the last two years for this very reason and speculated that in eight to ten years from now, Pirhapal too would no longer be burning Ravana: "It was Devi [lit., the goddess; i.e., Shitala] herself [presumably through possession of her ritual specialists] who has been saying we should not kill him, but it will take a few years before everyone understands and agrees." He clarified again that this association between Gonds and Ravana was relatively new, something that had come up in Chhattisgarh only in the last fifteen to twenty years.[20] I wondered then if that village might build a cement Ravana if it continues to no longer burn the effigy.

---

19. Gond deities are commonly called "devi-devtaon," distinguished from puranic deities who are identified as bhagvan (god) and devi (goddess), so it is unusual that Kishan uses the term "bhagvan" to identify Ravana as a Gond deity.

20. Gond activism is more established and widespread elsewhere in the Central Indian region identified as Gondwana (lit., land of Gonds), which crosses six political states (Patankar 2017; Rashid 2015; Dasgupta 2014). Gond activists are building new Ravana temples as Gond pilgrimage sites; some villages have begun to celebrate a Ravana festival to generate pride in the king, who is believed to be their ancestor; Ravana is given a unique Gond iconography of a king wearing a horned headdress; and Gond histories are being reconstructed. Mayuri Patankar describes the promotion through these means of a unique religion called Gondi Punem (Patankar 2016, 2017).

Another village, Chilhati—which lies in the same south Chhattisgarh cultural area as Pirhapal (also with a majority of Gond inhabitants)—hosts two cement Ravanas. One of these is incorporated in their Dussehra celebration held the night after that of Pirhapal. This Ravana stands at the edge of the village, across a small lane from a Shiva temple built by a now-deceased Brahmin, Pandit-ji Devlal Maharaj. One of our village guides explained that the pandit had built the Chilhati Ravanas (not giving any date) so that people who would come to see them would also come to the temple, suggesting that at that time such images were not as common as they have become today. The implication is that the images initially had little ritual significance but had first been built as tourist attractions. The two Chilhati images are distinctive in that Ravana does not appear alone. The Ravana incorporated into Dussehra celebrations is accompanied by his wife, Mandodari, kneeling at his feet in a gesture of supplication. The other is accompanied by Mandodari sitting cross-legged at her husband's feet and his brother Kumbhakarna reclining lethargically, holding his head up, as if just awakened from the long, six-month-per-year sleep to which he has been destined (as the result of his misarticulated request for a boon from Brahma) (figure 5.7).

Chilhati's Dussehra rituals began with a male villager pouring red paint into the navel of one of the cement Ravanas, into which Rama (embodied in a man dressed as the god) then rather unceremoniously stuck an arrow and "blood" poured out. (Some Ramayana narratives identify the site of Ravana's power as his navel rather than one of his heads—a secret that Ravana's brother, Vibhishana, revealed to Rama.) Soon after Ravana's navel had been pierced (an act that narratively would have killed him), Shitala (again in the form of her white flags and possessed human male bodies) left her temple to greet Ravana, who materially/performatively had not died (as becomes evident when the Ravana effigy and Shitala walk in procession through the village). She first stopped at the cement image, where her priest performed puja to Ravana (breaking a coconut, lighting incense and an oil lamp), as the goddess bore witness. She then went to greet Ravana's effigy that had been prepared close by and applied a vermilion tilak on his forehead (as she had done in Pirhapal). Both Shitala and the effigy Ravana proceeded through the village in the company of other Gond deities in the form of white flags and possessed human male bodies, drummers, and a small group of male villagers. The Ravana effigy was carried by a man standing inside of it, and Ravana "danced" (*nacna*, one of the words used for deity possession)—a performance villagers said was unique to Chilhati.

Figure 5.7. Ravana, Mandodari (*right*), and Kumbhakarna (*left*), Chilhati village, 2014. Photo by the author.

As Ravana and Shitala walked slowly through the narrow village streets, a female from every household on the route came out to perform puja to them while other females in the families, dressed in their finest festival saris, stood at their doorways watching—a procession and ritual common in many Gond festivals during which the devi-devtaon process through village streets. Having accompanied Ravana to an open field where villagers had gathered—a journey of about one and a half hours—the goddess returned to her temple, a village baiga performed a final puja to Ravana, and the humans acting the parts of Rama, Lakshmana, Hanuman, and Ravana bowed down to his feet. Significantly, during this ritual and following lila, no puja is performed to the Rama human-embodied character. Performatively, unlike Shitala and the Ravana effigy in this context, he is not god but rather a human actor.

I was expecting, minimally, some dramatic battle enactments, but a lila organizer (rather than the Rama character) lit Ravana's effigy almost immediately after the puja had been performed, before the subsequent lila. In fact, not many villagers were watching this sequence of events after the procession. One of the evening's organizers told the actors to make the subsequent lila short so that audience members could go home to eat and come back in time for the evening's (seemingly more important) cultural program of Chhattisgarhi song and dance, to be performed by a traveling professional troupe. The actors/characters of Rama, Sita, Lakshmana, and Hanuman went to a side stage, away from the burning effigy, where the male actors engaged in some lackluster fighting with a few actors from Ravana's army. In this village, I was told, the lila part of the celebration is relatively new and for this reason did not command attention of the growing crowds waiting for the musical event.

In Chilhati's Dussehra celebrations, the procession of Ravana and Shitala through the village streets is ritually and performatively the most important part of the evening, while the Ramayana narrative enactment is underplayed, and it is unlikely that many of the villagers know more than a very basic outline of the narrative. Ravana has been materially and ritually drawn out of the Ramayana narrative into a Gond pantheon of deities led by the goddess Shitala.

Why a Permanent Ravana?

When I began to investigate Ravana cement images, I asked neighbors to the Ravanas and community leaders who were responsible for the annual Ramlilas held in front of some of the images why the cement figures are not destroyed like his effigies are at the conclusion of Ramlilas in so many parts of North India. Was there, I asked, something unique to Chhattisgarh that accounted for the differences? Having lived most or all of their lives around these Ravanas, most of my interlocutors had not pondered this question before. Some urban middle-class Chhattisgarhis found it difficult to understand why I was so interested in Ravana's image rather than the narrative epic itself—and god. One airport bus passenger asked with some exasperation, "Are you interested only in Ravana or also in Ramayana?" But others caught my enthusiasm about the seeming discrepancy between Ravana's narrative death and his permanent material image.[21] A few respondents answered my question by simply telling a short summary of the Ramayana narrative, as if the story itself would make self-evident the answer I sought. Other responses were initially rather utilitarian: it was cheaper and more efficient to build a permanent image that simply had to be repainted every year than to spend money on effigies (made of bamboo and tissue paper) that would simply be burned up. Still other respondents thought the cement images kept people from encroaching on the open (but private) lands on which they stand. While these responses are, of course, significant, initially they were not very satisfying; they did not answer my question "Why Chhattisgarh?" These motivations would presumably be true of many other regions and communities where there is no cement Ravana and where he is present only as an effigy that is burned at Dussehra. And there are many other possibilities for preventing land encroachment other than this particular image. (For example, an over twenty-foot-tall Hanuman was built on lands belonging to ISKON [International Society for Krishna Consciousness], next to their temple in Secunderabad, Telangana, to prevent—successfully—the aboveground metro line under construction from crossing their property.)

In the village of Girhola, at the southern edge of the geographic area where such images can be found (Kanker District), an elder told us he was the person responsible for their Ravana. In 2005 he had sponsored, with the support of the village headman, the erection of the permanent image to commemorate his own participation over many years as Ravana in the

---

21. When I checked into a hotel in the industrial city of Bhilai on a different mission altogether, I asked two young male hotel staff members if there was a cement Ravana in their city. They both knew it existed but said they would have to ask their parents where it was. The next morning, they reported the location of the image and the lively conversations among their family members about the seeming contradiction between narrative and the cement image that I had mentioned the day before. They laughingly said that now I had everyone in their families thinking about Ravana.

local Ramlila. Subsequent questioning about the village Ravana resulted in a lively discussion. A Yadav-caste patriarch of this village asserted that erecting such Ravanas was a recent "fashion." He felt that since such images have started being installed, there has been a steady decline in social morals—itself an indigenous commentary on the agency of materiality. He reminded those gathered to hear our conversation that until the 1960s, Dussehra in this part of Chhattisgarh had been celebrated only in the royal center of Kanker (with the raja in attendance), and that this royal celebration is not Rama-centered but instead focuses on the goddess.

A visiting Yadav relative speculated that the permanence of the Ravana statue showed that only those who died at the hands of gods achieved *moksha* (liberation). He pointed out that the monkey deity Hanuman and others from Rama's side of the epic battle were not celebrated or memorialized in the same way as Ravana, because they did not die such a glorious death at the hand of god. The few massive (twenty feet or so tall) Hanuman and Shiva statues that have begun to appear in the Chhattisgarhi landscape in the last ten to fifteen years, increasingly common throughout the Indian landscape, would seem to belie this suggestion, but his comment also suggests that Ravana images have been around much longer.[22] In further conversations, other reasons emerged for not destroying Ravana. He is a Brahmin and thus it would not be dharmic (ethical) to kill him. One respondent asserted, "He is a Brahmin; that's why we do puja [to him]." Others said that he is a vidvan, the wisest of men, and that we should honor such wisdom, or that he is a king and one should honor the same.

Chhattisgarhis identify Ravana's single downfall to be his ego or pride: *ahamkar*, a word painted on several of the Ravana images I have documented. He is characterized as flawed but not evil. Some interlocutors reminded me that, after all, he did not touch Rama's wife, Sita, when he kidnapped her (an act that set off events culminating in the great war between Rama and Ravana and, finally, Ravana's death) and thus was an honorable king.[23] Ravana is identified as a rakshasa, which we often (mis)

---

22. For discussion of these contemporary massive sculptures, see Lutgendorf (1994) and Jain (2016). Jain characterizes these sites as "assemblages" between these massive sculptures, the post-liberalization boom in automobile production, and attendant "resignification and revaluing of land" (1).

23. In April 2018, death threats were made against cartoonist Swathi Vadlamudi, who used this assumption that Ravana did not touch or rape Sita to critique Hindutva

translate into English as "demon"—a term associated with evil; "anti-god" or "anti-hero" may be a better translation. I now see that one of the problems I had identified in beginning my research on cement Ravanas—that they were permanent images of a rakshasa—may have been a different kind of problem for English-speaking scholars than for Indian participants in Ramayana traditions. Rakshasas in Hindu mythologies and epics are not evil in the way we may think of a devil or demon in English; rather, they are flawed. They have their own dharma and even devotion to a deity; after all, Ravana himself was an ardent Shiva devotee and is said to have gained his power through this devotion.

It was only when I went to Pirhapal that I heard a Chhattisgarhi reason for the preponderance of permanent cement images of Ravana in the region: that Ravana had been a Gond tribal king and therefore that Gonds should not participate in his immolation. "We shouldn't burn our ancestor," Kishan Ravan Mandavi asserted.[24] In retrospect, I am a bit chagrined at my initial fieldwork goals—looking for someone to say something specific about what the cement Ravanas "mean"—and the fact that Kishan's explanation for Ravana's permanence as an ancestor was initially more satisfying to me than other seemingly mundane explanations, such as cost or land protection. I was subverting my own intuitions that the materiality of the images may perform possibilities that remain unarticulated or are unintended. At least some oral histories identify the Ravana of Raipur's Dudhadhari Math to be the oldest in the region, built by the matha long before any Gond activism developed that would discursively identify Ravana as a Gond ancestor, so this explanation has limits. Why Ravana entered that institution's imagination as a permanent image over

---

(Hindu right-wing) support of men accused of rape in two different incidents. She portrayed a conversation between Rama and Sita in which Sita says, "I'm so glad I was kidnapped by Ravana and not by your *bhakts* [devotees]" (BBC News 2018). Another social media example of Ravana's dharmic action came across a 2014 WhatsApp viral message on the occasion of the festival of Raksha Bandhan, a festival celebrating the relationship of brothers and sisters. The text asked, "Who would you like your brother to be like? Ram or Ravan?" A sister answers, "Ravan, because he defended his sister Surpanakha; further, he didn't touch Sita without her permission."

24. This is a similar argument used by some activists in Tamil Nadu who identify Ravana as Dravidian. In 2016 the Chennai-based organization Thanthai Periyar Dravida Kazhagam (TPDK) announced celebration of what they called "Ravana Leela" to protest what they consider the anti-Dravidian ritual of burning an effigy of Ravana at the end of Ramlilas (Dabas 2016).

one hundred years ago remains an enigma. However, when there was one permanent image, installed by an authoritative brahminic matha, these images became possibilities.

Chhattisgarh's adivasi population is surely significant to the possibility of permanent Ravana images. Ravana images are not found in Bastar, south of the central plains I have been focused on, where adivasi inhabitants have not been incorporated into a "Hindu" jati system and where they do not perform, nor are they audience members to, the Ramayana narrative. The narrative is necessary to Ravana's permanent (cement) existence on the plains but is not determinative of what the material images create. Except for the day Ramlilas may be performed in front of Ravana, he stands all year without narrative (or ritual), independent of the god who narratively destroys him.[25] This material presence creates possibilities of alternative histories and ideologies. While, in Chhattisgarh, Ravana has been identified as a Gond king and ancestor only relatively recently, Gonds may have consciously or unconsciously earlier identified with him as an authority associated with the jungle that is their inheritance. Gond activists have picked up on these imaginative possibilities when they declare Ravana as their ancestor/king, creating a distinct identity from that attributed by dominant Hindu castes of the Chhattisgarh plains.

The burning of Ravana effigies is a relatively recent custom at those sites that already had a cement image, and many village interlocutors reminded me that the proliferation of Ramlilas is also a recent innovation in many villages that now host the dramatic performances. The lilas can be interpreted as a kind of "Hindu-ization" of adivasi communities in Chhattisgarh's heartland. And yet this process is not complete. In the villages of Pirhapal and Chilhati, Ravana is drawn into a Gond family of deities when Shitala comes out of her temple to greet him, and he joins her in her traditional processions through village streets to be worshiped

---

25. Of course, being India, there are exceptions. In 2017 I came across a five-year-old cement Ravana standing to the side of a public square. Across the square stands a cement Rama with his bow held up, ready for battle.

See Lutgendorf 1994 for a discussion of similarly narrative-independent images of Hanuman, who often appears in small shrines or under peepal trees (shrines that are also ubiquitous in the Chhattisgarhi landscape), without the presence of the god Rama, with whom Hanuman is narratively associated. The difference, of course, is that in small shrines, Hanuman is regularly worshiped. However, his more recently established tall, imposing images are similar to cement Ravanas in that they are not actively worshiped.

by female householders—from which Rama is absent. Rama resides in some urban Chhattisgarhi temples, and their numbers have increased in the last decade, perhaps due to growing immigrant communities from elsewhere in India or to the current political strength of Hindutva, for which Rama is a central deity. However, his temples are uncommon in villages, and Rama does not commonly reside on domestic puja shelves of "native" Chhattisgarhis.

Permanent cement Ravana images are sometimes neighbors and other times guardians of property and boundaries. They are part of the everyday landscape for those who live nearby and are barely noticed by travelers who pass by them. The images are not objects of worship or explicit human action throughout the year, until they are newly painted for Dussehra and puja is performed to them before Ramlila performances.[26] Although once a year Ravana dies narratively/dramatically, materially he stands and visually dominates a landscape from which Rama is materially (relatively) absent. Standing in cement, Ravana's presence on the Chhattisgarhi plains opens up alternative imaginative, ideological, theological, and even political possibilities to those of more dominant verbal Ramayana narratives.

---

26. The images are not constrained by regular ritual requirements of murtis in shrines, temples, or domestic puja shelves. Since the late 1980s, similarly large (or larger) images of deities, such as Hanuman and Shiva, in particular, have begun to be built in public, open grounds in Chhattisgarh, "according to fashion," as one of my interlocutors explained.

Afterword

Returning to Material Acts

The purpose of this book has been to bring materiality to the center of our understanding of everyday Hindu worlds, to cause us to notice materials, and then to analyze the creative agency of these materials in specific ethnographic contexts. While I draw the term "material acts" from J. L. Austin's "speech acts" (performatives) (1975), I take the agentive potential of these acts further than Austin himself does—that is, beyond the human intention of the speech or material act, beyond what he calls the "right conditions" for "successful performance" that fulfills human intention.[1] While human intentions behind material acts may create certain effects (or those acts may "misfire," to quote Austin, and fail to create what humans intend), I have observed that the agency of materiality is not limited to those intentions or their failures; other effects or possibilities may also be created.

In the progression of the chapters in this book, the distance between human intention behind creation of materialities and their potential effects grows. We begin with indigenous understandings of the ways in which material ornaments have particular desired effects on the women who wear them: ornamentation is protective and generates auspiciousness. Subsequent

---

1. See Amy Holliday's 2002 essay about performativity, subjectivity, and agency, in which she summarizes Austin's argument for the necessity of intention and "right conditions" (certain speakers to certain audiences) for a speech act to "work." She brings into her discussion Jacques Derrida's and Judith Butler's counterarguments that make space for the performative to create unintended consequences when it "misfires," not fulfilling the intentions of the human speaker.

analyses nuance this indigenous model of material agency by bringing in examples of materiality that are agentive beyond human and discursive intentions. The sites of agency also shift—from effects of materiality on humans to its cosmic effects. By the final two cases of architecture and cement Ravanas, the materialities under consideration widely exceed human intentions of their creation. Enclosed and expanded shrines built to protect Hyderabadi goddesses from urban growth and crazy traffic change the nature and potentially the identity of goddesses who used to stand as *ugra* protectors at village boundaries. The very presence of permanent, cement Ravanas—and the material absence of the god who narratively defeats him—performs alternative theologies and ideologies. Between these ends of a spectrum of intentionality, repertoires of Gangamma Jatara *veshams* and material offerings to two goddesses expand upon, but do not subvert, human intention. The veshams act upon both humans and the goddess: male *stri veshams* transform aggressive masculinity so that men have a place in a female-dominated festival world; female *pasupu* guising both performs the shared *shakti* between women and goddess and modulates Gangamma's excessive nature. In Varalakshmi Puja and Gangamma Jatara, two very different goddesses are instantiated through displays of abundant and excessive offerings, respectively. We have seen that material acts create and change the world and its human and divine inhabitants.

Some upper-class Hindus educated in English and others who live in the diaspora may describe a very different material world in which material does not *act* but is symbolic. In their visits to Hindu temples in Atlanta, my American students have often been told by Hindu worshipers (speaking in English) that they do not actually worship the physical image of a deity but that it gives a focal point for concentration. Or the Hindu hosts have explained that the *murtis* do not actually eat food offerings made to them; rather, the offerings are symbolic of worshipers' devotion. A priest at the Hindu Temple of Atlanta explained that each substance of the *abhishekam* "stands for" something that humans desire (sprinkled sugar, for example, the sweetness of life)—he did not address what the abhishekam may create for the deity upon whom it is performed.[2] These too are indigenous discourses of materiality, which may be shaped, in part, by the very language being spoken and its non-Hindu English-speaking

---

2. For a video clip of abhishekam to Ganesha, see the Michael C. Carlos Museum's (Emory University) Odyssey website: http://carlos.emory.edu/htdocs/ODYSSEY/SOUTHASIA/ganesha.html.

audiences. My emphasis in this book, however, has been less on what forms of materiality "mean" than on what they do, perform, and create.

When I have spoken in various academic forums about this project, some audience members have pushed back against my use of the term "agency," agreeing with the above-mentioned Hindus at American temples that the work of the materials I analyze is metaphoric and that these materials do not actually cause something to happen.[3] This is where ethnographic and phenomenological questions and goals may differ from philosophical ones. When I began this book with indigenous articulations of the agency of ornaments, I was less concerned with whether a *tali* actually creates auspiciousness or kinship ties than with what a world looks like in which it does—that is, a world in which application of turmeric paste on a tali renews and maintains its agentive strength to positively affect a woman's marriage. Or one in which the absence of glass bangles on a Gond married woman's arm may affect the very life and death of her husband. Or a world and its afterlife in which tattoos survive the body on which they are inscribed.

This indigenous theory of material agency decenters many dominant assumptions—shaped, in part, by Protestant worldviews and poststructuralist theories—about the symbolic or metaphoric ways material "works" and gives us analytic frameworks through which to recognize, in new ways, the potential for material agency. Having ethnographically observed the ways materialities shaped the everyday worlds of my interlocutors, I shifted to an analytic, performative lens through which to look at ways in which other materials, not so discursively identified, may be agentive. For example, Telugu women cooking for and making material offerings to Lakshmi and Gangamma told me that they did so to please and satisfy these goddesses and to invite them to be present. I took my analysis one step further (outside of an indigenous framework) when I concluded that these auspicious and excessive offerings, respectively, materially *created* the two goddesses to whom they were made.

We are left with a question about whether particular materials have inherent agency or if how they work depends on their human, social,

---

3. Enid Schildkrout writes about her experience of similar pushback to her work on tattoos from some post-structural scholars. Arguing against the "'disembodied' poststructuralist body," she asserts that "these practices, including tattoos, branding, and piercing, may be highly *symbolic*, but they are not *metaphorical*" (2004, 320; my emphasis).

and physical contexts. Does turmeric as a powder create the same thing independently of where it is located, on the face of a goddess or in a spicy vegetable dish? Do toe rings have the same creative agency in Hyderabad as they do in Atlanta?[4] Would a cement Ravana standing in the Gangetic plains have the same agency as it does in Chhattisgarh? As I hope to have shown, context and material assemblage are crucial to understanding the potential agency of materiality through both indigenous and performative lenses. The materiality of a sari will create differently if the garment is worn on a male or female body, or if it is worn by a woman working in the fields or a woman at an upper-class wedding.

In a well-known essay, A. K. Ramanujan articulated this assumption of (what I am calling) the agency of context to be an "Indian way of thinking" (1999). He identifies space and time, for example, as agentive: a raga of classical Indian music creates different moods or emotions (*rasas*) depending on the time of day it is performed and is composed with this knowledge, so the morning song of *suprabhatam* should be heard or performed in the morning to experience its full intended effect (49–50). That human intention will not be fulfilled when an Indian living in Atlanta plays the suprabhatam on her phone during an evening commute home, but something *else* will be created.

Performance contexts of material acts include human actors and their narratives and discursive commentary, but equally important are their *material* repertoires and commentary. We learn about the agency of Chhattisgarhi tattoos through ethnographic observation and indigenous discursive commentary but also by placing them in a wider material repertoire of other auspicious, agentive ornaments. Narratives of Gangamma taking vesham give us cues as to what vesham creates, but female turmeric guising is just as important to understanding what and how stri veshams may transform masculinity (something participants did not articulate directly).

---

4. When I started to conduct fieldwork in South India, I began to wear traditional Telugu silver toe rings. During my first year of teaching at Emory University (1992), in a class on performance and religion, a student wrote a final paper on Grateful Dead concerts as pilgrimage. The next semester the Grateful Dead performed in Atlanta, and the student invited me to go to the concert with him. When he told his roommate that he had invited me, the roommate exclaimed, "You invited a professor?" The student reported that his immediate response was "Come on! She wears toe rings, doesn't she?" He had interpreted my toe rings as performing alterity and resistance to dominant American culture, not knowing that in India toe rings perform traditional gender expectations of a married woman.

While human intention behind expanding gramadevata shrines was most often articulated to be to protect (literally) their enclosed goddesses and please them with more permanent and decorated abodes, an assemblage of architectural features and the growing dominance of middle-class, upper-caste aesthetics and ideologies have begun to transform the enclosed goddesses in ways beyond what their creators initially intended.

While arguing for material agency, I have also included examples of its limits. Observation and analyses of material transformations of gramadevata shrines do not tell the "whole story" of the goddesses so enclosed. Sandhya's personal narratives alert us to the presence of the goddess outside of her new physical forms and abodes. Cement Ravanas need the context of the Ramayana narrative for them to be identified as Ravana, although we have seen that the narrative is not determinative of their material agency. A Ravana in the company of Gond deities creates differently than the cement Ravana who was created by a brahminic institution or one standing next to a burning effigy. In each case, materials may tell us something about the humans with whom they interact, human actors may have their own intentions in creating and interpreting these materialities, the intentions may fail or be fulfilled, and material agencies may both exceed and be dependent on those intentions.

To bring materiality into the center of religious studies, and the study of Hindu worlds more specifically, necessarily changes definitions for and means of study of "religion." A reader may argue that if ornaments, for example, count as religion, then religion as a field of study has no boundaries. However, I take my cue for what counts as religion from an Indian-language term often used to translate "religion": *dharma*. The term is derived from a Sanskrit verbal root *dhr* that literally means "to hold." Thus, dharma can be interpreted as "what holds [the world] together," what makes the world meaningful—that is, religion. Most Hindus I have worked with do not themselves use the term "dharma" to identify "what they do" religiously as individuals, families, and members of particular castes; rather Telugu speakers may use the term *matam*, or Hindi speakers may refer to the frameworks and actions that hold their social and physical worlds in place as *achara* or *dastur*. I use the term "dharma" analytically,[5] as a framework to identify material acts that help to shape and hold together

---

5. Jennifer Ortegren (forthcoming) similarly uses the term "dharma" analytically in her book on class as a religious (dharmic) category that shapes the lives of upwardly mobile Rajasthani women.

the worlds we live in, often creating possibilities that human actors do not imagine. To leave out everyday materiality from the study of religion is to leave out significant ways in which religious worlds are shaped and experienced. We end with the epigraph with which this book begins: "To be accounted for, objects have to enter into accounts" (Latour 2005, 79), which we may now articulate slightly differently: to account for objects as material actors will change our accounts—of religion itself.

Glossary of Key Terms

(with diacritics provided in parentheses)

abhishekam (*abhiṣekam*)	ritual anointing of image of deity with series of liquids
achara (*ācāra*)	conduct, custom, tradition
adivasi (*ādivāsī*)	tribal; first inhabitant
ahamkar; ahamkari (*ahaṃkār; ahaṃkārī*)	egoism, pride; egotistical, proud
alankara (*alaṅkāra*)	ornamentation
amangala (*amaṅgala*)	inauspicious
ambali (*ambali*)	mixture of cooling yogurt, heating raw onions, and cooked millet
archana (*arcana*)	temple ritual; *puja* offering made by priest on behalf of worshiper
ashtalakshmi (*aṣṭalakṣmi*)	eight Lakshmis
ashubha (*aśubha*)	inauspicious
avatara (*avatāra*)	lit., descent; incarnation
bali (*bali*)	animal sacrifice
bhagvan (*bhagvān*)	god
bhatha (*bhāṭha*)	open field

bottu (bŏṭṭu)	auspicious forehead marking (often vermilion powder or stickers)
churi (curī); churi pahinana (curī pahināna)	glass bangle; to put on glass bangle
darshan (darśan)	sight, taking sight of a deity
dastur (dastūr)	custom, customary practice
devadasi (devadāsī)	lit., servant of god; woman who marries a god; temple dancer
devi-devtaon (devi-devtaon)	lit., gods and goddesses; in Chhattisgarh, phrase used to distinguish Gond deities from puranic deities called bhagvan or devi
devta (devta)	god
dharma (dharma)	code of conduct; social order; religion
dhoti (dhotī)	male lower garment; single piece of unstitched cloth wrapped around waist and between legs
diya (dīyā)	oil lamp
dora (ḍŏra)	ruler; lord; prince
drishti (dṛṣṭi)	evil eye
gadha (gadhā)	donkey
godai; godna (godai; godna)	tattoo; to tattoo
gramadevata (grāmadevata)	village deity, village goddess
harati (hārati)	flame offering to material form of deity
jadu (jādū)	magic; spell
jatara (jātara)	village goddess festival
jati (jāti)	lit., birth; endogamous caste group determined by birth

katha (*kathā*)	story
kavacham (*kavacam*)	lit., armor; metallic anthropomorphic covering over stone image of deity
khamosh (*khamoś*)	quiet, calm
kodistambha (*koḍistambham*)	temple pillar that becomes goddess during *jatara*
kolam (*kolam*)	rice-flour design outside domestic, temple, or commercial doorways
kulam (*kulam*)	caste; lineage
kumkum (*kumkum*)	vermilion powder
lakh (*lākh*)	one hundred thousand
lakshmi nara (*lakṣmī nārā*)	Lakshmi thread
lila (*līlā*)	play; acts of a deity performed for their own pleasure
linga (*liṅga*)	aniconic (phallic) material form of Shiva
mahant (*mahant*)	head priest and administrator of a *matha*
maidan (*maidān*)	open field
mangala (*maṅgala*)	auspicious
mangalsutra (*maṅgalsūtra*)	lit., auspicious thread; in North and Central India, marriage necklace
matam (*matam*)	creed, religion
matamma (*mātamma*)	woman who has exchanged wedding pendant with goddess
matangi (*māṭaṅgi*)	most powerful of Gangamma's *jatara veshams*
matha, Hindi; matham, Telugu (*maṭha; maṭham*)	religious center of learning; monastery
mirasi (*mirāsī*)	hereditary right for particular ritual service

170 / Glossary of Key Terms

mokku (*mŏkku*)	vow
muggu (*muggu*)	auspicious geometric or floral design made of rice flour
murti (*mūrti*)	image; image of deity
murtikar (*mūrtikār*)	image maker
muttaiduva (*muttaiduva*)	auspicious woman; traditionally, married woman
namam (*nāmam*)	lit., name; forehead marking worn by Vaishnavas
namaskaram (*namaskāram*)	salutation (often with hands folded together)
nazar (*nazar*)	evil eye
nityasumangali (*nityasumaṅgalī*)	always auspicious (specifically, a woman with a living husband)
palegadu (*pālĕgāḍu*)	local chieftain
pandit (*paṇḍit*)	learned one, Brahmin priest
pap (*pāp*)	sin
pasupu (*pasupu*)	turmeric
pasupu-kumkum (*pasupu kumkum*)	turmeric-vermilion powders, used together ritually
pelli kuturuni cheyyadam (*pĕḷḷi kūturāni cĕyyaḍam*)	lit., to make a bride; wedding ritual of putting bangles on bride
perantalu (*peraṇṭālu*)	auspicious (married) woman; the last of Gangamma's *jatara veshams*
pongal (*pŏṅgal*)	mixture of cooked rice and lentils
pranam (*praṇām*)	respectful greeting
prasad (*prasād*)	food offered to deity and distributed to worshipers
puja (*pūjā*)	worship; specifically, through offerings to deity
pujari (*pūjāri*)	temple priest who performs *puja*

purana (purāṇa)	old story; legend; myth
putla (putlā)	effigy; doll
rakhi (rākhī)	protective thread
rakshasa (rākṣasa)	anti-god; demon
rasa (rasa)	aesthetic emotion
santosha (santoṣa)	happy; satisfied
santosham (santoṣam)	joy; happiness; satisfaction
saubhagya (saubhāgyā)	of good fortune
shakti (śakti)	power; female power
shaktiswarupini (śaktiswarūpini)	she/he whose form is *shakti* (female noun)
shanta (śānta)	tranquil; pacified
shringar (śṛṅgār); solah shringar (solah śṛṅgār)	ornament, decoration; sixteen ornaments
shubha (śubha)	auspicious
shuddha (śuddha)	pure
sindur (sindūr)	vermilion powder; applied by North Indian married women to the parts in their hair
stri vesham (stri veṣam)	female guise
sumangali (sumaṅgalī)	she who is auspicious; traditionally married woman
sunnapukundalu (sunnapukuṇḍalu)	lime pots; the penultimate Gangamma *jatara vesham*
tali (tāli)	South Indian marriage pendant
tambulam (tāmbūlam)	betel leaf and areca nut; ritual gift of betel and areca nut

tilak (*tilak*)	forehead marking (often with vermilion or ash powders)
ugra (*ugra*)	excessive; ferocious
ugra mukhi (*ugra mukhi*)	lit., fierce face; large clay head of Gangamma on final day of her *jatara*
ugram (*ugram*)	excess; ferocity
uru (*ūru*)	village, home place
utsava murti (*utsava mūrti*)	festival (processional) image of deity
vamsha (*vaṃśa*)	lineage
vastu (*vāstu*)	architecture; traditional science of architecture (like feng shui)
vesham; stri vesham (*veṣam; stri veṣam*)	guise, disguise, clothing; female guise
vidvan (*vidvān*)	learned person; scholar
vishvarupam (*viśvarūpam*)	true form; cosmic form
vodivalu (*voḍivālu*)	lit., lap-rice; rice, coconut, and other ingredients tied to waist of bride
vrat (Hindi); *vratam* (Telugu) (*vrat; vratam*)	ritual vow
vrat katha (*vrat kathā*)	story about the ritual told during *vrat*

References

Aitken, Molly Emma. 2004. *When Gold Blossoms: Jewelry from the Susan L. Beningson Collection*. New York: Asia Society and Philip Wilson Publishers.

Appadurai, Arjun, ed. 1986. *The Social Life of Things: Commodities in Cultural Perspective*. Cambridge, UK: Cambridge University Press.

Austin, J. L. 1975. *How to Do Things with Words*. Cambridge: Harvard University Press. First published 1962.

Babb, Lawrence A. 1981. "Glancing: Visual Interaction in Hinduism." *Journal of Anthropological Research* 37, no. 4: 387–401.

Barron, Lee. 2017. *Tattoo Culture: Theory and Contemporary Contexts*. New York: Rowman and Littlefield.

Bastin, Rohan. 2005. "The Hindu Temple and the Aesthetics of the Imaginary." In *Aesthetics in Performance: Formations of Symbolic Construction and Experience*, ed. Angela Hobart and Bruce Kapferer, 89–108. New York: Berghahn Books.

Bauman, Richard. 1984. *Verbal Art as Performance*. Prospect Heights, IL: Waveland Press.

BBC News. 2018. "India Journalist Threatened over Anti-Rape Cartoon." *BBC News*, April 18, 2018. http://www.bbc.com/news/world-asia-india-43806970. Accessed April 30, 2018.

Bell, Catherine. 1998. "Performance." In *Critical Terms for Religious Studies*, ed. Mark Taylor, 205–24. Chicago: University of Chicago Press.

Bennett, Jane. 2005. "The Agency of Assemblages and the North American Blackout." *Public Culture* 17, no. 3: 445–65.

Bennett, Jane. 2010. *Vibrant Matter: A Political Ecology of Things*. Durham, NC: Duke University Press.

Bhutra, Rahul. 2014. "*Ek Hi Sthal par Sarak Kinare Ram va Ravaṇ ki Pratima*" [In One Place at the Side of a Street, Ram and Ravan Images]. *Haribhoomi*, January 5, 2014: 4.

Brown, Bill. 2003. *A Sense of Things: The Object Matter of American Literature*. Chicago: University of Chicago Press.

Butler, Judith. 1997. *Excitable Speech: A Politics of the Performative.* New York: Routledge.
Butler, Judith. 2008. *Gender Trouble: Feminism and the Subversion of Identity.* New York: Routledge. First published 1990.
Cerulli, Anthony, and Caterina Guenzi. 2016. "Mineral Healing: Gemstone Remedies in Astrological and Medical Traditions." In *Soulless Matter, Seats of Energy: Metals, Gems and Minerals in South Asian Traditions,* ed. Fabrizio M. Ferrari and Thomas W. P. Dahnhardt, 73–93. Bristol, CT: Equinox Publishing.
Cort, John. 2012. "Situating Darśan: Seeing the Digambar Jina Icon in Eighteenth- and Nineteenth-Century North India." *International Journal of Hindu Studies* 16, no. 1: 1–56.
Dabas, Maninder. 2016. "Chennai Group Calls Ravan a Dravidian, Organises 'Ravan Leela' to Protest against Burning Effigies." *India Times,* October 11, 2016. http://www.indiatimes.com/news/chennai-group-calls-ravan-a-dravidian-organises-ravan-leela-to-protest-against-burning-effigies-263290.html. Accessed October 15, 2016.
Daniel, E. Valentine. 1987. *Fluid Signs: Being a Person the Tamil Way.* Berkeley: University of California Press.
Dasgupta, Debarshi. 2014. "Asuras? No, Just Indians: A Common Gondi and a Venerable Ravan Will Hopefully Forge a Gond Cultural Identity." *Outlook* 25. http://www.outlookindia.com/magazine/story/asuras-no-just-indians/291677. Accessed March 19, 2016.
Davis, Richard H. 1997. *Lives of Indian Images.* Princeton, NJ: Princeton University Press.
Dehejia, Vidya. 2009. *The Body Adorned: Dissolving Boundaries between Sacred and Profane in India's Art.* New York: Columbia University Press.
De Koning, Deborah. 2018. "The Ritualizing of the Martial and Benevolent Side of Ravana in Two Annual Rituals at the Sri Devram Maha Viharaya in Pannipitiya, Sri Lanka." *Religions,* no. 9: 250.
Deleuze, Gilles, and Felix Guattari. 1987. *A Thousand Plateaus: Capitalism and Schizophrenia.* Trans. Brian Massumi. Minneapolis: University of Minnesota Press.
Deo, Aditya. 2013. "Spirits, State Effects and Peoples' Politics: Negotiating Sovereignty in 20th Century Kanker, Central India." PhD diss., Emory University.
Doniger O'Flaherty, Wendy. 1980. *Women, Androgynes, and Other Mythical Beasts.* Chicago: University of Chicago Press.
D'Souza, Deborah. 2016. "Top 10 Countries with the Highest Demand for Gold Jewelry." *Investopedia,* October 14, 2016. https://www.investopedia.com/news/top-10-countries-highest-demand-gold-jewelry. Accessed June 8, 2018.
Eck, Diana L. 1998. *Darśan: Seeing the Divine Image in India.* New York: Columbia University Press. First published 1996.
Eicher, Joanne. 2010. "Clothing, Costume, and Dress." In *The Berg Companion to Fashion,* ed. Valerie Steele, 151–52. New York: Berg.

Elias, Jamal J. 2012. *Aisha's Cushion: Religious Art, Perception, and Practice in Islam*. Cambridge: Harvard University Press.
Elison, William. 2018. "Site, Sight, Cite: Wayside Shrines as Stations of Visual Culture." *South Asian Multidisciplinary Academic Journal*, no. 18, https://journals.openedition.org/samaj/4540.
Feld, Steven, and Keith Basso, eds. 1996. *Senses of Place*. Santa Fe, NM: School of American Research Press.
Feldhaus, Anne. 1995. *Water and Womanhood: Religious Meanings of Rivers in Maharastra*. New York: Oxford University Press.
Ferrari, Fabrizio. 2010. Old Rituals for New Threats: Possession and Healing in the Cult of Shitala. In *Ritual Matters: Dynamic Dimensions in Practice*, ed. Ute Husken and Christiane Brosius, 144–72. New Delhi: Routledge.
Ferrari, Fabrizio. 2015. *Religion, Devotion, and Medicine in North India: The Healing Power of Sitala*. New York: Bloomsbury.
Flueckiger, Joyce Burkhalter. 1996. *Gender and Genre in the Folklore of Middle India*. Ithaca, NY: Cornell University Press.
Flueckiger, Joyce Burkhalter. 2006. *In Amma's Healing Room: Gender and Vernacular Islam in South India*. Bloomington: Indiana University Press.
Flueckiger, Joyce Burkhalter. 2013a. *When the World Becomes Female: Guises of a South Indian Goddess*. Bloomington: Indiana University Press.
Flueckiger, Joyce Burkhalter. 2013b. "'He Should Have Worn a Sari': A 'Failed' Performance of a Central Indian Oral Epic." *The Anthropology of Performance: A Reader*, ed. Frank Korom, 124–32. West Sussex, UK: John Wiley and Sons. First published 1988.
Flueckiger, Joyce Burkhalter. 2015. *Everyday Hinduism*. Chichester, West Sussex: Wiley Blackwell.
Gell, Alfred. 1993. *Wrapping in Images: Tattooing in Polynesia*. New York: Oxford University Press.
Gell, Alfred. 1994. "Tattooing in India." Unpublished paper presented to the World Archaeological Congress, Delhi.
Gell, Alfred. 1998. *Art and Agency: An Anthropological Theory*. Oxford: Clarendon Press.
Gentes, J. J. 1992. "Scandalizing the Goddess at Kodungallur." *Asian Folklore Studies*, no. 51: 295–322.
Geslani, Marko. 2018. *Rites of the God-King: Santi and Ritual Change in Early Hinduism*. New York: Oxford University Press.
Ghosh, Srikanta K. 1997. *India Democracy Derailed: Politics and Politicians*. New Delhi: APH Publishing.
Ginzburg, Carlo. 1989. *Clues, Myths, and the Historical Method*. Baltimore: Johns Hopkins University Press.
Gold, Ann Grodzins. 2008. "Deep Beauty: Rajasthani Goddess Shrines Above and Below the Surface." *International Journal of Hindu Studies* 12, no. 2: 153–79.

Gold, Ann Grodzins. 2010. "Damayanti's String: Epic Threads in Women's Ritual Stories." In *Damayanti and Nala: The Many Lives of a Story*, ed. Susan S. Wadley, 109–29. New Delhi: Chronicle Books.

Govindrajan, Radhika. 2018. *Animal Intimacies: Interspecies Relatedness in India's Central Himalayas*. Chicago: University of Chicago Press.

Handelman, Don. 1990. "Christmas Mumming in Newfoundland." In *Models and Mirrors: Towards an Anthropology of Public Events*, 138–59. New York: Cambridge University Press.

Handelman, Don. 1995. "The Guises of the Goddess and the Transformation of the Male: Gangamma's Visit to Tirupati and the Continuum of Gender." In *Syllables of Sky: Studies in South Indian Civilization in Honour of Velcheru Narayana Rao*, ed. David Shulman, 283–337. Delhi: Oxford University Press.

Handelman, Don, M. V. Krishnayya, and David Shulman. 2014. "Growing a Kingdom: The Goddess of Depth in Vizianagaram." In *One God, Two Goddesses, Three Studies of South Indian Cosmology*, ed. Don Handelman, 115–213. Boston: E. J. Brill.

The Hindu. 2012. "A Note on the Charminar Photograph." *The Hindu*, November 21, 2012. http://www.thehindu.com/news/cities/Hyderabad/A-note-on-the-Charminar-photograph/article12515861.ece. Accessed June 6, 2018.

Hindu Janajagruti Samiti. 2015. "Fanatics Ask Governor to Remove Bhagyalakshmi Temple Near Charminar." https://www.hindujagruti.org/news/15074.html. Accessed June 6, 2018.

Hollywood, Amy. 2002. "Performativity, Citationality, Ritualization." *History of Religions* 42, no. 2: 93–115.

Horton, Sarah. 2007. *Living Buddhist Statues in Early Medieval and Modern Japan*. New York: Palgrave Macmillan.

Hoskins, Janet. 1998. *Biographical Objects: How Things Tell the Stories of People's Lives*. New York: Routledge.

Houben, Jan E. M. 2007. "From Material to Deity: Indian Rituals of Consecration." *Journal of the Economic and Social History of the Orient*, no. 50: 77–80.

Houtman, Dick, and Birgit Meyer, eds. 2012. *Things: Religion and the Question of Materiality*. New York: Fordham University Press.

HuffPost Staff. 2016. "This Periyar Group Will Be Celebrating Ravan Leela in Chennai." *Huffington Post*, October 11, 2016. http://www.huffingtonpost.in/2016/10/11/this-periyar-group-will-be-celebrating-ravan-leela-in-chennai. Accessed October 14, 2016.

Ilaiah, Kancha. 2013. "This Diwali, Think Why We Celebrate Death. *Round Table India*. http://roundtableindia.co.in/index.php?option=com_content&view=article&id=7025:this-diwali-think-why-we-celebrate-death&catid=118:thought&Itemid=131. Accessed October 29, 2016.

Jackson, Jason Baird, ed. 2016. *Material Vernaculars: Objects, Images, and Their Social Worlds*. Bloomington: Indiana University Press.

Jain, Kajri. 2007. *Gods in the Bazaar: The Economies of Indian Calendar Art*. Durham, NC: Duke University Press.
Jain, Kajri. 2016. "Post-Reform India's Automotive-Iconic-Cement Assemblages: Uneven Globality, Territorial Spectacle, and Iconic Exhibition Value." *Identities: Global Studies in Culture and Power* 23, no. 2: 327–44.
Kaell, Hillary. 2017. "Seeing the Invisible: Ambient Catholicism on the Side of the Road." *Journal of the American Academy of Religion* 58, no. 1: 136–67.
Kamath, Harshita Mruthinti. 2019. *Impersonations: The Artifice of Brahmin Masculinity in Kuchipudi Dance*. Berkeley: University of California Press.
Keane, Webb. 2006. "Introduction to Part II: 'Subjects and Objects.'" In *Handbook of Material Culture*, ed. Christopher Tilley et al., 197–202. London: Sage Publications.
Kersenboom, Saskia C. 1997. *Nityasumaṅgalī: Devadasi Tradition in South India*. Delhi: Motilal Banarsidass Publishers. First published 1987.
Knuppel, Anandi Silva. 2019. "Beyond Seeing: Darshan as an Embodied Multi-Sensory Practice in Contemporary Transnational Gauḍīya Vaishnavism." PhD diss., Emory University.
Kracauer, Siegfried. 1969. *History: The Last Things before the Last*. New York: Oxford University Press.
Latour, Bruno. 2005. *Reassembling the Social: An Introduction to Actor-Network-Theory*. New York: Oxford University Press.
Lutgendorf, Philip. 1994. "My Hanuman Is Bigger Than Yours." *History of Religions* 33, no. 3: 211–45.
Madan, T. N. 1985. "Concerning the Categories Śubha and Śuddha in Hindu Culture: An Exploratory Essay." In *Purity and Auspiciousness in Indian Society*, ed. John B. Carman and Frederique Apffel Marglin, 11–29. Leiden: E. J. Brill.
Massey, Doreen. 1994. *Space, Place, and Gender*. Cambridge, UK: Polity Press.
McClain, Karline. 2009. *India's Immortal Comic Books: Gods, Kings, and Other Heroes*. Bloomington: Indiana University Press.
McDannel, Coleen. 1998. *Materiality: Religion and Popular Culture in America*. New Haven, CT: Yale University Press.
McGilvray, Dennis B. 1998. *Symbolic Heat: Gender, Health, and Worship among the Tamils of South India and Sri Lanka*. Ahmedabad, Gujarat: Mapin Publishing.
Mifflin, Margot. 2013. *Bodies of Subversion: A Secret History of Women and Tattoo*. New York: PowerHouse Books.
Mitchell, W. J. T. 1995. "The Pictoral Turn." *Picture Theory: Essays on Verbal and Visual Representation*, 9–34. Chicago: University of Chicago Press.
Mitchell, W. J. T. 1996. "What Do Pictures Really Want?" *October*, no. 77: 71–82.
Morgan, David. 2005. *The Sacred Gaze: Religious Visual Culture in Theory and Practice*. Berkeley: University of California Press.
Morgan, David. 2010a. *Religion and Material Culture: The Matter of Belief*. New York: Routledge.

Morgan, David. 2010b. "The Material Culture of Lived Religions." In *Mind and Matter: Selected Papers of Nordic Conference 2009*. Studies in Art History 41. Helsinki: Society of Art History.

Morgan, David. 2018. *Images at Work: The Material Culture of Enchantment*. New York: Oxford University Press.

Morgan, David. 2020. *The Thing about Religion: An Introduction to the Material Study of Religions*. Chapel Hill: University of North Carolina Press.

Nagarajan, Vijaya. 2019. *Feeding a Thousand Souls: Women, Ritual, and Ecology in India*. New York: Oxford University Press.

Napier, David. 1986. *Masks, Transformation, and Paradox*. Berkeley: University of California Press.

Narayanan, Vasudha. 2000. "Diglossic Hinduism: Liberation and Lentils." *Journal of the American Academy of Religion* 68, no. 4: 761–79.

Novetzke, Christian Lee. 2016. *The Quotidian Revolution: Vernacularization, Religion, and the Premodern Public Sphere in India*. New York: Columbia University Press.

Ortegren, Jennifer. Forthcoming. *Middle-Class Dharma: Gender, Aspiration, and the Making of Modern Hinduism*. New York: Oxford University Press.

Packert, Cynthia. 2010. *The Art of Loving Krishna: Ornamentation and Devotion*. Bloomington: Indiana University Press.

Pandey, Geeta. 2017. " 'Don't Brand Me': The Indian Women Saying No to Forced Tattoos." BBC News. http://www.bbc.com/news/world-asia-india-41466751. Accessed April 15, 2018.

Pandian, M. S. S. 1998. "Ravan as Antidote: A Rediscovery of Ravan as a Southern Hero." *Outlook Magazine*, November 2, 1998. http://www.outlookindia.com/magazine/story/ravana-as-antidote/206446. Accessed March 15, 2016.

Patankar, Mayuri. 2016. " 'Gondwana'/'Gondwanaland' as a Homeland of the Gonds: Storytelling in the Paintings of Gond Pilgrims." *Summerhill: IIAS Review* 22, no. 2: 39–48.

Patankar, Mayuri. 2017. "Reconceptualising Ravan through *Ravan Mahotsav* in a Gond Village: A Study of an Epic Character in Folk Imagination." Paper presented at International Seminar on Revisiting Folk Epic Traditions of India, Ambedkar University, Delhi.

Patton, Laurie, trans. 2008. *The Bhagavad Gita*. London: Penguin Books.

Pels, Dick, Kevin Hetherington, and Frédéric Vandenberghe. 2002. "The Status of the Object: Performances, Mediations, and Techniques." *Theory, Culture & Society* 19, nos. 5/6: 1–21.

Pinney, Christopher. 2004. *Photos of the Gods: The Printed Image and Political Struggle in India*. New York: Oxford University Press.

Pinney, Christopher. 2005. "Things Happen: Or, From Which Moment Does That Object Come?" In *Materiality*, ed. Daniel Miller, 256–72. Durham, NC: Duke University Press.

Pinney, Christopher. 2008. *The Coming of Photography in India*. London: British Library.
Pintchman, Tracey. 2005. *Guests at God's Wedding: Celebrating Kartik among the Women of Benares*. Albany: State University of New York Press.
Pintchman, Tracey, and Corinne G. Dempsey, eds. 2015. *Sacred Matters: Material Religion in South Asian Traditions*. Albany: State University of New York Press.
Plate, S. Brent. 2014. *A History of Religion in 5½ Objects: Bringing the Spiritual to Its Senses*. Boston: Beacon Press.
Raj, Selva, and Corinne Dempsey. 2015. "Letting Holy Water and Coconuts Speak for Themselves: Tamil Catholicism and the Work of Selva Raj." In *Sacred Matters: Material Religion*, ed. Tracey Pintchman and Corinne Dempsey, 195–217. Albany: State University of New York Press.
Ramanujan, A. K. 1999. "Is There an Indian Way of Thinking? An Informal Essay." *The Collected Essays of A. K. Ramanujan*, ed. Vinay Dharwadker, 35–51. New Delhi: Oxford University Press. First published 1989.
Rashid, Omar. 2015. "Celebrating Ravan." *The Hindu*, October 25, 2015. http://www.thehindu.com/todayspaper/tp-features/tp-sundaymagazine/celebrating-ravan/article7801083.ece. Accessed March 15, 2016.
Reynolds, Holly. 1991. *The Power of Tamil Women*. Syracuse, NY: Syracuse University Press. First published in 1980.
Richman, Paula, ed. 2001. *Questioning Ramayanas: A South Asia Tradition*. Berkeley: University of California Press.
Robson, James. 2016. "Hidden in Plain View: Concealed Contents, Secluded Statues, and Revealed Religion." In *The Rhetoric of Hiddenness in Traditional Chinese Culture*, ed. Paula M. Varsano, 177–205. Albany: State University of New York Press.
Schildkrout, Enid. 2004. "Inscribing the Body." *Annual Review of Anthropology*, no. 33: 319–44.
Seremetakis, Nadia. 1996. "Memory of the Senses, Part I: Marks of the Transitory." In *The Senses Still*, ed. Nadia Seremetakis, 1–18. Boulder, CO: Westview Press.
Shukla, Pravina. 2008. *The Grace of Four Moons: Dress, Adornment, and the Art of the Body in Modern India*. Bloomington: Indiana University Press.
Shukla, Pravina. 2015. *Costume: Performing Identities through Dress*. Bloomington: Indiana University Press.
Shulman, David. 1993. *The Hungry God: Hindu Tales of Filicide and Devotion*. Chicago: University of Chicago Press.
Shulman, David. 2005. "The Buzz of God and the Click of Delight." In *Aesthetics in Performance: Formations of Symbolic Construction and Experience*, ed. Angela Hobart and Bruce Kapferer, 43–63. New York: Berghahn Books.
Shulman, David, and Katikaneni Vimala. 2008. "The Girl in the Rock: A Telangana Tale and Vasistha's Retelling." *Indian Folklore Research Journal* 5, no. 8: 1–26.

Sivakumar, Deeksha. 2018. "Dolls on Display: A South Indian Festival of Identity and Play." PhD diss., Emory University.

Slouber, Michael. 2017. *Early Tantric Medicine: Snakebite, Mantras, and Healing in the Garuda Tantras*. New York: Oxford University Press.

Sreebitha, P. V. 2013. "'No Gold' Marriages: The Politics of Caste/Class and Gender." *Round Table India*. http://roundtableindia.co.in/index.php?option=com_content&view=article&id=7081%3Acaste-of-gold&catid=119%3Afeature&Itemid=132. Accessed June 12, 2017.

Srinivas, Tulasi. 2018. *The Cow in the Elevator: An Anthropology of Wonder*. Durham, NC: Duke University Press.

Srivathsan, A. 2012. "As Protests Roil Charminar, Hyderabad's Heritage Slowly Vanishes." *The Hindu* (Hyderabad). November 20, 2012. http://www.thehindu.com/news/national/andhra-pradesh/As-protests-roil-Charminar-Hyderabad%E2%80%99s-heritage-slowly-vanishes/article12059217.ece. Accessed June 6, 2018.

Taneja, Anand Vivek. 2013. "Jinnealogy: Everyday Life and Islamic Theology in Post-Partition Delhi." *HAU: Journal of Ethnographic Theory* 3, no. 3: 139–65.

Tarlo, Emma. 1996. *Clothing Matters: Dress and Identity in India*. Chicago: University of Chicago Press.

Taylor, Diana. 2016. *Performance*. Durham, NC: Duke University Press.

Tilley, Christopher. 2006. "Metaphor, Materiality, and Interpretation: Introduction." In *Handbook of Material Culture*, ed. Chris Tilley et al., 23–26. London: Sage Publications.

Times of India. 2012a. "Trust Denies Expansion of Bhagyalakshmi Temple." *Times of India*, November 7, 2012. https://timesofindia.indiatimes.com/city/hyderabad/Trust-denies-expansion-of-Bhagyalakshmi-temple/articleshow/17121490.cms. Accessed June 6, 2018.

Times of India. 2012b. "Temple Older Than Charminar: Rightist." *Times of India*, November 23, 2012. https://timesofindia.indiatimes.com/city/hyderabad/Temple-older-than-Charminar-Rightist/articleshow/17331402.cms. Accessed June 6, 2018.

Tseelon, Efrat. 2001. "Introduction: Masquerade and Identities." In *Masquerade and Identities: Essays on Gender, Sexuality and Marginality*, ed. Efrat Tseelson, 1–17. New York: Routledge.

Vasquez, Manuel A. 2011. *More Than Belief: A Materialist Theory of Religion*. New York: Oxford University Press.

Waghorne, Joanne. 1994. *The Raja's Magic Clothes: Revisioning Kingship and Divinity in England's India*. University Park: Pennsylvania State University.

Waghorne Joanne, Norman Cutler, and Vasudha Narayanan, eds. 1996. *Gods of Flesh/Gods of Stone*. New York: Columbia University Press.

Wharton, Annabel Jane. 2015. *Architectural Agents: The Delusional, Abusive, Addictiveness of Buildings*. Minneapolis: University of Minnesota Press.

Zare, Bonnie, and Afsar Mohammed. 2015. "Burn the Sari or Save the Sari: Dress as a Form of Action in Two Feminist Poems." *Ariel: A Review of International English Literature* 43, no. 2: 69–86.

Index

Page numbers in *italic* refer to illustrations.

abhishekam, 66–67, 88, 113, 162
Adi Para Shakti, 30, 52, 60
adivasis, 146–47, 158. *See also* Gonds
Aitken, Molly, 22n7
alankara, 22, 68
alcohol, 59, 113–14, 115, 119, 141, 146
Allocco, Amy, 28
ambali, 86, 92–93
Ambedkar, B. R., 135
amulets, 5, 22, 28, *28*
animal sacrifice. *See* bali (animal sacrifice)
ankle bracelets, *38*; tattooed, 42
architecture, 8–10, 99–131
Arjuna, 58
Austin, J. L., 10, 15n15, 64, 73, 161

babies, 5, 22, 52
Babri Masjid, 128
Bai, Dilip, 39
Bai, Rupi, 19–22, 37, 38
bali (animal sacrifice), 102n7, 113–14, 115, 116, 119; in Gangamma Jatara, 85, 87, 91–92, 95
bangles, *20*; gold, 23, 43; lacquer, 127; plastic, 21; silver, 19, 20, 107. *See also* glass bangles
basil (tulsi), 36, 81

Bastin, Rohan, 131
beads, 24, *28*, 34
Bennett, Jane, 4n3, 11, 12–13
betel, 105n11; in tambulam, 29, 75
Bhagavad Gita, 58
Bhagya Laxmi temple, Hyderabad, 123–28, *124*, 129
bindis. *See* bottus
body ornamentation. *See* ornaments
Bommai Golu, 76n4
Bonalu, 102, *103*, 105, 116, 118, 120, 123
bottus, 31–32, 69, 107, 108n14, 117
bracelets. *See* ankle bracelets; bangles
Brahma, 60, 152
Brahmins, 79, 82, 84, 130; atonement for killing, 143; bottus, 31n18; buffalo sacrifice, 91–92; Gangamma Jatara and, 61–63, *62*, 88n14, 95; Maisamma-Lakshmi temple and, 121; masculinity, 53n4; Nalla Pochamma temple and, 111–16; Ravana images and, 135, 137, 140, 144–47, *145*, 156, 158, 165; Shiva temples and, 152; talis, 27; thread, 35n23, 135, 144, *145*, 147
building renovation, 9, 107, 111, 113, 116

Burho Dev, 147
burning of effigies. *See* effigies, burning of

caste: bangles and, 20, 43; Gangamma Jatara and, 50n3, 50–52, 57, 61–63, 64, 95; gold and silver and, 44; Pochamma shrine and, 114, 116; Ravana and, 146; talis and, 20, 24, 26, 27, 32; tattoos and, 39, 40, 42, 44; "twice-born" castes, 35n23; Varalakshmi Puja and, 84; Venkateshvara temple and, 1–4
cement images, 1–4, *2*, *3*, 7, 143. *See also* cement Ravanas
cement goddess shrines. *See* gramadevatas
cement pillars and posts, 118n22, 127. *See also* kodistambham
cement Ravanas, Chhattisgarhi, 14, 17, 133–59, 162, 165; Chilhati, 152–54, *153*; Dhamtari, 144–47, *145*; Ghirola, *140*, 155–56; Pirhapal, *150*; Ravan Bhatha, 137–44, *143*; Tari, *136*; Tumgaon, 133, *134*
chains, ornamental. *See* mangalsutras; talis
Chakali veshams, 50–51n3
chakrabandhanam, 87, 95, 97
Charminar, 123–28
Chhattisgarhi Ravanas. *See* cement Ravanas, Chhattisgarhi
child marriage legislation, 27n15
Chilhati, Chhattisgarh, 148n16, 152–54, *153*
classical Indian music, 164
clay heads of Gangamma. *See* ugra mukhis
clay pots: in Bonalu, 102; in Gangamma Jatara, 51, 86, 92, 93; in Ravana story, 145n14; in Varalakshmi Puja, 78

coconuts, 10; decorated, 82, 84, 93n19; in offerings, 34, 47, 88, 141, 147, 152
Coming of Photography in India, The (Pinney), 64
cooking for rituals, 75–76, *77*, 78, 87, 91, 92, 94, 163
Coomaraswamy, Ananda, 22
costume jewelry, 30

dargahs, 33n20, 100
darshan, 7, 8
Dasa Mata Vrat, 35–36
death and tattoos. *See* tattoos: death and
Dehejia, Vidya, 22
Deo, Aditya, 148n16, 149
desecration of shrines. *See* shrine desecration
dharma, 157, 165
disease and illness. *See* illness and disease
disguise. *See* guise
Diwali, 86n12, 124, 128
diyas (oil lamps), 5, 78, 88, 108, 110, 141, 147, 152
Doniger, Wendy, 58–59
donkey iconography, 135, 138–41, *140*, 143, 146, 149n18
doorway paintings, 102–3, *103*, 105
dots: on babies' foreheads and feet, 22; on pots, 90; on stones and pillars, 69, 88; in tattoos, 38, *38*, 41–42; on walls or boards, 92. *See also* bottus
dowry, 43, 141
Dravida Munnetra Kazhagam (DMK), 134
Dravidians, 157n24
drinking. *See* alcohol
drummers and drumming, 51, 86, 90, 95, 118, 119, 152

Dudhadhari Math Ravana. *See* Ravan Bhatha, Raipur
Durga, 42, 102, 105, 109–10, 112, 116, 117, 120, 129
Dussehra, 136–37, 141–43, *143*, 144, 148, 152–54, 156, 159

earrings, 23
effigies, 149, 152; burning of, 141–42, *143*, 144, 146, 154, 157n24, 158
evil eye deflection, 5, 22, 52, 140–41

Feldhaus, Anne, 30–31
female turmeric veshams. *See* turmeric veshams
feminists and feminism, 43, 70n8, 75
Ferrari, Fabrizio, 149
fertility rituals, 28–29, 103n9
festivals, 142, 147. *See also* Bonalu; Diwali; Dussehra; Gangamma Jatara; Navaratri; Paiditalli; Raksha Bandhan
first menstruation rituals, 27–28
flame offering. *See* harati (flame offering)
flowers: in Diwali, 124; in Gangamma Jatara, 47, 51, 53, *54*, 56, *57*, 58, 85; Gangamma Jatara kodistambham and, 88, 89, 90; marigold garlands, 1, *2*, 4, 141; in tattoos, 42; in Varalakshmi Puja, 78, 80, 81; Venkateshvara Maladasari figure and, 1, *2*, 4
Flueckiger, Joyce Burkhalter: *When the World Becomes Female*, 32, 65
foods: in Gangamma Jatara, 61, 86–87, 90, 91, 92–93, 163; in Sudasa Vrat, 34; symbolic offerings, 162; in Varalakshmi Puja, 75–78, *77*, 80, *80*, 83, 163. *See also* milk; rice
forehead markings. *See* bottus; tilaks

"fun" ("for fun only") activities: effigy burning, 142n11; stri vesham, 58, 59, 61, 63, 65

Ganesha, 112, 114, 116
Gangamma, 30, 31, 45–71, 73–74, 84–98
Gangamma Jatara: Tirupati, 16, 30, 45–71, 73, 84–98
Gayatri Mantra, 35n23
gaze. *See* visual gaze
Gell, Alfred, 11, 38n24, 39n25, 40, 41n26
gemstones, 5, 44
Gentes, J. J., 32–33n19
Girhola, Chhattisgarh, *140*, 155–56
glass bangles, 5, 19–20, *20*, 21n2, 23, 43, 107; in Gangamma Jatara, 93; in ritual gifts, 29, 75
goddesses. *See* Gangamma; possession by goddesses; river goddesses
goddess shrines. *See* gramadevata shrines
gold, 29–30; Lakshmi, 74; gramadevatas, 109; rakhis and, 34. *See also* gold ornaments
Gold, Ann, 35–36, 104n10, 108
gold ornaments, 24–25, 36, 37, 43; bangles, 23, 43; caste and, 44; chains, 24, 26, 28; talis, 29, 30; in Varalakshmi Puja, 79, 82
Gonds: Ravana and, 147–54, 158; tattoos, 21, 37–38
gramadevata shrines, 99–131, 162, 165
grave shrines, Muslim. *See* dargahs
guise, 45–71, 78n6. *See also* Kaikala Gangamma veshams; parodic veshams; stri vesham; turmeric vesham

hair, matted. *See* matted hair (in vesham)

Handelman, Don, 78
Hanuman: in Ramlila, 154; in shrines, 158n25; statues, 155, 156; tattoos, 39
harati (flame offering), 47, 67, 90
Hathi Ramji Matham, 61
Hemingson, Vince, 40
Hindutva, 100, 124, 156–57n23, 159
Holliday, Amy, 161n1
Hoskins, Janet, 6
Houtman, Dick, 4n2
Hyderabad: gramadevatas, 99–131. See also Osmania University, Hyderabad

illness and disease, 130–31n29, 149; protection against, 94, 95, 97, 103, 129. See also poxes
Indian classical music. See classical Indian music
infants. See babies
ISKON (International Society for Krishna Consciousness), 155
Islamic monuments and shrines, 123–28

janeu. See threads, Brahmin
jewelry. See ankle bracelets; bangles; costume jewelry; earrings; rings

Kaell, Hillary, 14n13, 139
Kaikala Gangamma veshams, 47–56, 50, 52, 54–55, 71, 86, 90–91
Kali, 102, 103, 105, 109–10, 116, 117, 129
Kamath, Harshita, 53
Karunanidhi, M., 134
Karva Chauth, 81
Katta Maisamma temple, 125n26
kavacham, 125, 126, 126, 128, 129
Keane, Webb, 17
kitchens, 76, 77, 78

Knuppel, Anandi Silva, 7n6
kodistambham, 88, 89, 90, 91, 116
kohl (cosmetics), 5, 22, 78
kolams. See rice-flour designs (kolams and muggus)
Kracauer, Siegfried, 14n14
Krishna, 39, 58
Krishnayya, M. V., 78–79
Kriyakalagunottara, 141n9
Kumar, Uday, 113–15
Kumbhakarna, 142, 152, 153
kumkum. See vermilion powder (kumkum)

lacquer bangles, 127
Lakshmana, 143, 146, 154
Lakshmi, 27, 34–36, 60, 112–13, 73–84, 96–98; eight forms of wealth, 81–82; footprint tattoos, 41, 41; in Pochamma shrine, 112–13. See also Bhagya Laxmi Temple, Hyderabad; Maisamma-Lakshmi temple, Hyderabad
lakshmi nara, 34–36, 35
Latour, Bruno, 11–12, 13, 166

Mahankali, 102n8, 105
Maisamma, 105, 117–23, 125
Maisamma-Lakshmi temple, Hyderabad, 117–23, 122, 129
Majlis-e-Ittehadul Muslimeen (MIM), 128
Maladasari figures, 1–4
Mandavi, Kishan Ravan, 148–49, 151, 157
Mandodari, 152, 153
mangalsutras, 20, 24, 25, 26
marble images, 125–26, 126
Marquesan tattoo culture, 38n24
marriage ornaments, 5, 20, 23, 24, 29–33, 43, 68
matammas, 31, 69–70

matangi vesham, 51, 53–56, *54, 55,* 57, 61, 66, 88n15
matted hair (in vesham), 69, 70
Meghnath (son of Ravana), 138, 139, 142
menstruation, first. *See* first menstruation rituals
Meyer, Birgit, 4n2
milk, 88, 96, 97; in abhishekam, 66, 67
Morgan, David, 6–7
muggus. *See* rice-flour designs (kolams and muggus)
music. *See* classical Indian music; songs and singing
Muslim shrines. *See* dargahs

Nalla Pochamma temple, Hyderabad, *103,* 104–17, *106, 111*
Navaratri, 76n4
Naxalites, 148
necklaces, 36, 39, 112; tattooed, 42. *See also* mangalsutras
neem leaves, 90, 91, 119, 130
neem trees, 88, 116; branches, 97n21, 104n10
Novetzke, Christian, 140

oil lamps. *See* diyas (oil lamps)
open-air shrines, 88n14, 99, 103, 104, 129
ornaments, 13, 19–44; removal and replacement of, *20,* 23, 28–29, 36; resistance to, 43–44. *See also* ankle bracelets; bangles; costume jewelry; earrings; gold ornaments; mangalsutras; silver ornaments; rings; talis; tattoos
Ortegren, Jennifer, 84n10, 165n5
Osmania University, Hyderabad, 9, 113n18

Paiditalli, 78–79, 88n13

paintings around doorways. *See* doorway paintings
Pambalas (drummers), 51, 90
Pandey, Geeta, 44
Panthulu, G. Venkataramana, 119, 120–21
papier-mâché, 48, 82, 90
Parliya Mataji, 108n15
parodic veshams, 59
Parvati, 60, 112, 114
pasupu. *See* turmeric (pasupu)
pasupu guising. *See* turmeric vesham
pasupu-kumkum (turmeric-vermilion powders), 1, 4, 8, 14, 32; in Gangamma Jatara, 47, 56, 68, 69, 85, 90, 91, 93; in gramadevatas, 105, 109; in tambulam, 75, 82; in Varalakshmi Puja, 78, 82
Pels, Dick, 100–101
pendants, marriage. *See* talis
perantalu vesham, 51, 88n15, 94–95
performance analysis, 14–15, 46–47
photography, 63–66, 112
pillars and posts. *See* cement pillars and posts; kodistambham
Pinney, Christopher, 8, 10–11, 14, 64
Pirhapal, Chhattisgarh, 148, *150,* 157
plastic bangles, 21
Plate, S. Brent, 6
Pochamma and Pochamma shrines, 100, 102, *103,* 104–17, *106, 111*
Polynesia tattoo culture, 38n24
pongal, 87, 91, 97
possession by goddesses, 53, 56, 88, 90–91, 95–96, 108, 118–19, 129; in Dussehra rituals, 151, 152
Potu Raju, 102n6; Gangamma and, 53, 69, 90, 91, 102n6; in gramadevatas, 102, *103,* 105, 112, 114, 116, 118, 120
poxes, 103, 130n29, 141n9
Prasad, Leela, 74

precious stones. *See* gemstones
pregnancy rituals, 21n2
prostrate cement figures, 1–4, *2*, *3*
protection against illness and disease. *See* illness and disease: protection against
protective tattoos, 42
protective threads. *See* rakhis
Pujaramma, 31, 70
Pushpagiri Peetham, 121

Raipur Ravana. *See* Ravan Bhatha, Raipur
rakhis, 33–34
Raksha Bandhan, 33–34, 157n23
Rama, 14, 159; festivals, 142; Hanuman and, 158n25; temples, 135n5; in Vadlamudi cartoon, 156–57n23. *See also* Ramayana
Ramanujan, A. K., 164
Ramaswamy, Periyar E. V., 134n2
Ramayana, 139–40, 145, 147. *See also* Ramlilas
Ramcaritmanas (Tulsidas), 141, 145, 146
Ramlilas, 137, 138, 141–42, 144, 146, 150–51, 154, 158, 159; Chilhati, 152–54; Girhola, 155–56; Ravana, 14, 17, 133–59, 162, 165
Ravan Bhatha, Raipur, 137–44, *143*, 157
Reassembling the Social: An Introduction to Actor-Network Theory (Latour), 11–12
removal and replacement of ornaments, *20*, 23, 28–29, 36
renovation of buildings. *See* building renovation
repertoire, 15, 60, 66, 71, 73, 75, 86, 87, 164; vesham and, 56, 59, 64, 66, 71, 162
Reynolds, Holly, 32

rice: in offerings, 87, 88, 90, 91, 93, 102
rice-flour designs (kolams and muggus), 5, 41n26
Richman, Paula: *Questioning Ramayanas*, 137
rings, 5. *See also* toe rings
ritual gifts, 21n2, 23, 82–83. *See also* tambulam
ritual use of threads. *See* threads, ritual use of
river goddesses, 30–31
rocks. *See* stones

sacred threads, Brahmin. *See* threads, Brahmin
sacrifice of animals. *See* bali (animal sacrifice)
Santoshi Mata, 119
Sarasvati, 60, 113
saris, 20–21n1, 23, 27–28, 164; blouse material, 21n1, 29, 75, 78; feminist debate on, 70n8; in Gangamma Jatara, 47, 57, *57*, 59, *62*, 63, 64, 93n19; Gangamma Jatara kodistambham and, 88, *89*; in tambulam, 75, 83; in Varalakshmi Puja, 79, 83
Schildkrout, Enid, 163n3
Seven Sisters shrines. *See* gramadevatas shrines
shantam, 68, 71, 117
Shitala, 141n9, 149–54, 158
Shiva, 27, 30, 58, 60, 70, 112, 141, 156
shrine desecration, 105n11, 128
shrines, goddess. *See* gramadevatas
shrines, grave. *See* grave shrines
shrines, Muslim. *See* dargahs
shrines, open-air. *See* open-air shrines
Shukla, Pravina, 24, 25n13, 46–47
Shulman, David, 66, 78–79

silver, 34; in gramadevatas, 109, 125, *126*, 128, 129; masks and heads, 82, 83, 84
silver ornaments, 39, 43; bangles, 19, 20, 107; caste and, 44
simantam, 21n2
sindur. *See* vermilion powder
Sita, 143, 145n14, 154, 156, 156–57n23
Sivakumar, Deeksha, 76n4
songs and singing, 39, 51–52, 86, 97n21
space, performance ability of, 100–101
Sreebitha, P. V., 43–44
Srinivas, Tulasi, 9, 73n1
Srinivasan (Brahmin man), 61–63, *62*, 64
Srinivasulu, Peta, 1–3
stone images and heads, 66; Gangamma, 66, *67*, 68, 71, 87, 95, 97; in gramadevata shrines, 102, 103, *106*, 110, 112, 118, 121, 125–26; Potu Raju, 69, 102, 112, 118
stones, 7, 108n15; naga, 29; semiprecious, 34. *See also* gemstones
strings, ornamental. *See* mangalsutras; talis
strings, protective. *See* rakhis
strings, ritual use of. *See* threads, ritual use of
stri vesham, 45–49, *46*, 51–66, *62*, 70, 71, 162, 163; lay practice, 56–61, *57*, 86. *See also* matangi vesham; perantalu vesham; sunnapukundalu vesham
Subramanyam, 112, 114, 116
Sudasa Vrat, 34, 35, 36, 76n4
suicide by self-immolation, 119–20
Sundar Mata, 104n10
sunnapukundalu vesham, 51–52, *52*

talis, 20, 21n3, 24–36, *28*, 43, 68, 69–70, 163; in Varalakshmi Puja, 77
Tallapaka temple, Tirupati, 67, 69, 86–87, 90
tambulam, 29, 74–75, 82–83
Tatayyagunta temple, Tirupati, 86–87, 88, 91, 94, 97n21, 104n10
tattoos, *20*, 21, 36–42, *37*, *38*, *41*, 44, 163n3; death and, 21, 38n24, 39n25, 42
Thanthai Periyar Dravida Kazhagam (TPDK), 157n24
threads, Brahmin, 35n23, 135, 144, *145*, 147
threads, ornamental. *See* lakshmi nara; mangalsutras; talis
threads, protective. *See* rakhis
threads, ritual use of, 33–36, 79
tilaks, 144, 149–50, 152
tile images, 105, *106*, 110
Tilley, Christopher, 11
Tirumala, Andhra Pradesh, 1–4, 61
Tirupati. *See* Gangamma Jatara: Tirupati; Tallapaka temple, Tirupati; Tatayyagunta temple, Tirupati
toe rings, 23, 164n4
tottelus, 103n9, 111, *111*
tree trunks, wrapping of, 33n20
tridents, 53, 60, 61, 103, 116, 147
tulsi. *See* basil (tulsi)
Tulsidas: *Ramcaritmanas*, 141, 145, 146
turmeric (pasupu), 78–79; in Bonalu, 102; in first menstruation ritual, 27n14, 28; in Gangamma Jatara, 45, 48, 56, 57, 66–70, *67*, 71, 88; in gramadevatas, 102, 112; in ritual gifts, 29; threads, 24, 25, 27, 28–29, 34, 43; in Varalakshmi Puja, 68, 78, 81, 84. *See also* pasupu-kumkum (turmeric-vermilion powders)
turmeric vesham, 66–70, *67*, 93, 162, 164

"ugram" (word), 85
ugram, 66, 68, 70, 73, 85–86, 87, 91–97; hidden by turmeric mask, 68, 71; vesham and 47, 48, 49, 51, 52, 56, 59, 93
ugra mukhis, 60n5, 69, 85, 87, 94–95, *94*
upanayana, 35n23

Vadlamudi, Swathi, 156–57n23
Vaishno Devi, 105
Varalakshmi Puja, 16, 34n22, 68, 73–84, 85, 96–98
vastu, 8–10
Venkat (Tirupati man), 63, 64, 65
Venkateshvara and Venkateshvara temples, 1–4, 53, 61, 70, 83
Venkateshvarlu (Kaikala man), 47, 49, 51, 56, 67–68, 69, 71, 90–91, 95
vermilion powder (kumkum), 23, 24, 79, 127; in bottus, 31; in Gangamma Jatara, 51, 88; in gramadevatas, 112, 129; in Ravana tilaks, 149–50, 152; in ritual gifts, 29; in Varalakshmi Puja, 83. *See also* pasupu-kumkum (turmeric-vermilion powder)

Veshalamma, 48
vesham. *See* guise
"vesham" (word), 47
veyyikalladuttas ("thousand-eyed pots"), 93
Vibhishana, 144, 152
village goddess shrines. *See* gramadevatas
Vimala, K., 74–75, 84, 117–18, 121
Vishnu, 27, 60, 80, 82
visual gaze, 7, 42; of gods and goddesses, 58, 60n5, 85

wedding pendants. *See* talis
Wharton, Amber Jane, 101
When the World Becomes Female: Guises of a South Indian Goddess (Flueckiger), 32, 65
widows and widowhood, 5, 23, 31

Yama, 39n25
yarn, ritual use of. *See* threads, ritual use of
Yellamma, 105, 117, 119; shrines, 102n7, 113n18